01 TADAO ANDO
安藤忠雄

WORKS
Suntory Museum／Inamori Auditorium／Maxray Headquarters Building／Museum of Gojo Culture／Nariwa Municipal Museum ／Harima Kogen Higashi Primary School

PROJECTS
Oyamazaki Museum／Rokko Housing III／FABRICA／Awajishima Project／Naoshima Contemporary Art Museum II／Annex for Museum of Literature, Himeji／Meditation Space, UNESCO／Tate Gallery of Modern Art／Seaside & Hilltop Housing

168 total pages, 64 in color　　　　　　　¥ 2,903

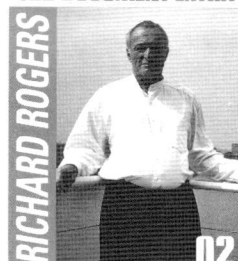

02 RICHARD ROGERS
リチャード・ロジャース

WORKS
Channel 4 Headquarters／European Court of Human Rights

PROJECTS
Terminal 5 Heathrow／Zoofenster Building／Shanghai Lu Jia Zui／Turbine Tower／Bordeaux Cité Judiciare／Daimler Benz Offices and Housing／VR Techno Center／Lloyd's Register of Shipping／Thames Valley University／Saitama Arena／South Bank Redevelopment／Parc BIT／Yokohama Port Terminal

Out of print　絶版

03 ZAHA M. HADID
ザハ・ハディド

WORKS
IBA Housing／Moon Soon Restaurant & Bar／Vitra Fire Station

PROJECTS
Cologne Rheinauhafen Redevelopment／Düsseldorf Art and Media Center／Cardiff Bay Opera House／Spittelau Viaducts／New York City 42nd Street Hotel Project

160 total pages, 64 in color　　　　　　　¥ 2,903

04 CHRISTIAN DE PORTZAMPARC
クリスチャン・ド・ポルザンパルク

WORKS
Cité de la Musique／Rue Nationale, Paris／Apartment in Bercy／Crédit Lyonnais Tower

PROJECTS
Nara International Convention Hall／Law Courts in Grasse／Cultural Center for Bandai Corporation／Extension of the Palais des Congrès／New Cultural Complex, Renne／School of Architecture, Marne la Vallée／Porte Maillot

Out of Print　絶版

05 ARATA ISOZAKI
磯崎新

WORKS
Nagi Museum of Contemporary Art／Toyo-nokuni Libraries for Culture Resources／B-con Plaza／Oita Convention Center／DOMUS: Interactive Museum about Humans／Kyoto Concert Hall

PROJECTS
JR Ueno Railway Station Redevelopment／Nara Convention Hall／Daimler Benz Potsdamer Platz Urban Development／Higashi Shizuoka Plaza Cultural Complex Project／Okayama-Nishi Police Station／etc.

Out of print　絶版

06 STEVEN HOLL
スティーヴン・ホール

WORKS
Storefront for Art and Architecture／Makuhari Housing

PROJECTS
Hypo-Bank Offices and Mixed Use Retail／Museum of Contemporary Art, Helsinki／Chapel of St. Ignatius, Seattle University／Cranbrook Institute of Science／I-Project

160 total pages, 72 in color　　　　　　　¥ 2,903

07 JEAN NOUVEL
ジャン・ヌヴェル

WORKS
Lyon Opera／Tours Congress Center ／Lille-Centre Euralille／Fondation Cartier／Galeries Lafayette

PROJECTS
Court House, Nantes／Swatchmobile Factory／Saitama Arena ／Tenaga Nasional Park／Lucerne Cultural and Congress Center

Out of print　絶版

08 RICHARD MEIER
リチャード・マイヤー

WORKS
Museum of Contemporary Art, Barcelona／Swissair North American HQ／The Hague City Hall／The Gagosian Gallery／Exhibition and Assembly Building, Ulm／Espace Pitôt, Montpellier ／Museum of TV & Radio, Beverly Hills

PROJECTS
US Courthouse & Federal Building, Islip & Phoenix／Euregio Office & Retail Building, Basel／Getty Center, Los Angeles／Rachofsky House, Dallas

192 total pages, 8 in color　　　　　　　¥ 2,903

09 MORPHOSIS
モーフォシス

WORKS
6th Street House／Blades House／Landa House／Sun Tower／Vistor's Center at ASE Design Center

PROJECTS
Diamond Ranch High School／Wagramerstrasse Housing／The Prado Museum Competition／Long Beach International Elementary School／Hypo Alpe Adria Center

144 total pages, 40 in color　　　　　　　¥ 2,848

10 BERNARD TSCHUMI
ベルナール・チュミ

WORKS
Parc de la Villete／Glass Video Gallery／Le Fresnoy National Studio for the Contemporary Arts／Architecture and Event Exhibition, MOMA

PROJECTS
Interface/Bridge-city/Metropont ／CAPC／ZKM Center for Art and Media Technology／National Library of France／School of Architecture／Lerner Student Center／Renault Master Plan／Letzipolis—Department Store

160 total pages, 64 in color　　　　　　　¥ 2,848

11 ALVARO SIZA
アルヴァロ・シザ

WORKS
Santa Maria Church of Marco de Canavezes ／Galician Center for Contemporary Art／Main Library, University of Aveiro／Faculty of Architecture, University of Oporto／Rectory of University of Alicante／Expo'98 Portuguese Pavilion

PROJECTS
Manuel Cargaleiro Foundation／Restaurant of Ocean Swimming Pool／Contemporary Art Museum of Oporto／Faculty of Media Science, Santiago University／Cultural Center of the Precinct of Revellin

160 total pages, 64 in color　　　　　　　¥ 2,848

12 NORMAN FOSTER
ノーマン・フォスター

WORKS
Stansted Airport／Careé d'Art／American Air Museum／University of Cambridge Faculty of Law／Commerzbank Headquarters／Chek Lap Kok Airport

PROJECTS
New German Parliament／Two Bridges: Millau Viaduct and Millennium Bridge／Millennium Tower／Daewoo Electronics Headquarters／Product Design: Nomos Furniture System for Tecno, Door Handle for Fusital, Kitel Chair

160 total pages,

GA HOUSES
Global Architecture

GA HOUSES documents outstanding new residential architecture from all over the world. Included in each issue also are retrospective looks at residential works of the past which are now considered epoch-making. This magazine is essential not only for architects and architectural students but for those who wish to master the art of living.

世界各国の住宅を現地取材により次々に紹介してゆくシリーズ。最近の作品はもちろん、近代住宅や古典の再検討、現代建築家の方法論、世界の村や街のリポートなど、住宅に関わる問題点を広い範囲にわたってとりあげてゆく。

Vols. 1–16, 18–24, 28, 31, 34 are out of print.
1–16, 18–24, 28, 31, 34号は絶版。　　Size: 300 × 228mm

39
連載：巨匠の住宅―ル・コルビュジエ2
作品：マック／ノタ／レゴレッタ／シュヴァイツァー／安藤／ボッタ／他
Essays on Residential Masterpieces–Le Corbusier 2; Ando; Botta; Mack; Schweitzer; and others
160 pages, 64 in color. ￥2,903

40
連載：巨匠の住宅―フランク・ロイド・ライト1
作品：フライ／プレドック／ソットサス／クィグリー／ブルーダー／他
Essays on Residential Masterpieces–F. L. Wright 1; Frey; Predock; Quigley; Sottsass; Bruder; and others
160 pages, 56 in color. ￥2,903

41
特集号：プロジェクト1994
Special Issue: Project 1994
168 pages, 20 in color. ￥2,903

42
連載：巨匠の住宅―フランク・ロイド・ライト2
作品：村上／早川／妹島／飯田／レゴレッタ／ミラージェス／プレドック／他
Essays on Residential Masterpieces–F. L. Wright 2; Murakami; Legorreta; Miralles; Predock; and others
160 pages, 48 in color. ￥2,903

43
連載：巨匠の住宅―フランク・ロイド・ライト3　作品：OMA／クィグリー／グワスミー＆シーゲル／石田／北山／ヌヴェル／他
Essays on Residential Masterpieces–F. L. Wright 3; OMA; Quigley; Ishida; Nouvel; and others
160 pages, 48 in color. ￥2,903

44
連載：巨匠の住宅―ルイス・I・カーン
作品：ブルーダー／プリンス／岸／北川原／ロートナー／他
Essays on Residential Masterpieces–Louis I. Kahn; Lautner Bruder; Waldman; Koenig; Prince; and others
160 pages, 56 in color. ￥2,903

45
特集号：プロジェクト1995
Special Issue: Project 1995
184 pages, 24 in color. ￥2,903

表記価格に消費税は含まれておりません。

46
連載：巨匠の住宅―ジョン・ロートナー
作品：カラチ／ノルテン／イスラエル／近藤／北川原／ミラージェス／他
Essays on Residential Masterpieces–John Lautner; Kalach; Norten; Israel; Niles; Rotondi; and others
160 pages, 64 in color. ￥2,903

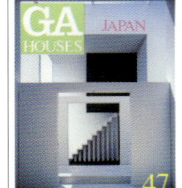
47
特集号：日本の現代住宅　第4集
論文：原広司　エッセイ：石山修武
座談会：山本理顕、岸和郎、妹島和世
Special Issue: Japan Part IV
176 pages, 48 in color. ￥2,903

48
特集号：プロジェクト1996
Special Issue: Project 1996
176 pages, 32 in color. ￥2,903

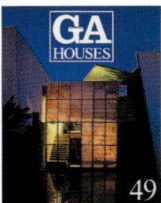
49
作品：ザパタ／フォスター／イスラエル／ビール／ナイルズ／伊東／有馬／ローマックス／塩田／アーリック／窪田
Zapata; Foster; Israel; Beel; Niles; Ito; Arima; Lomax; Shioda; Erhlich; Kubota
160 pages, 72 in color. ￥2,903

50
作品：イスラエル／ノタ／ホルバーグ／クルック＆セクストン／ヴァレリオ／セイトヴィッツ／ベルケル／坂本／他
Israel; Nota; Hallberg; Krueck & Sexton; Valerio; Saitowitz; Berkel; Sakamoto; and others
160 pages, 72 in color. ￥2,903

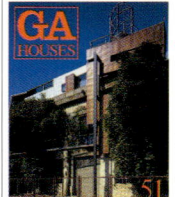
51
作品：ロト・アーキテクツ／マイヤー／ウォルドマン／ヒルドナー／マック／テン・アルキテクトス／ジョイ
Roto Architects; Meier; Waldman; Hildner; Mack; Ten Arquitectos; Joy
160 pages, 72 in color. ￥2,903

52
特集号：プロジェクト1997
Special Issue: Project 1997
176 pages, 32 in color. ￥2,848

53
連載：世界の村と街―西アフリカ・セネガル／巨匠の住宅―R・M・シンドラー
作品：モーフォシス／ナイルズ／他
Villages & Towns–Senegal; Essays on Residential Masterpieces–R. M. Schindler; Morphosis; and others
158 pages, 64 in color. ￥2,848

54
連載：世界の村と街―アラビア・イエメン／作品：コーニッグ／キャピー・アーキテクツ／マック／妹島和世／他
Villages & Towns–Yemen; Koenig; Kappe architects; Mack; Sejima; Saitowitz; Cheng design; and others
160 pages, 72 in color. ￥2,848

55
特集号：プロジェクト1998
Special Issue: Project 1998
144 pages, 32 in color. ￥2,848

56
連載：世界の村と街―西アフリカ／巨匠の住宅―R・M・シンドラー／作品：ブルーダー／アーリック／ナイルズ／他
Villages & Towns–West Africa; Essays on Residential Masterpieces–R. M.Schindler; Bruder; and others
160 pages, 64 in color. ￥2,848

57
連載：世界の村と街―インドネシア／作品：安藤忠雄／コールハース／ペリアン／カラチ＆アルヴァレス／レゴレッタ／他
Villages & Towns–Indonesia; Ando; Koolhaas; Perriand; Kalach & Alvarez; Legorreta; and others
160 pages, 72 in color. ￥2,848

58
作品：レゴレッタ／原広司／スコーギン／イーラム／ブレイ／村上徹／フェーン／岸和郎／中東／マック／イラニ／アーリック
Works; Legorreta ; Hara; Scogin; Elam/bray; Murakami; Fehn; Kishi; Nakahigashi; and others
160 pages, 72 in color. ￥2,848

59
特集号：プロジェクト1999
Special Issue: Project 1999
160 pages, 72 in color. ￥2,848

60
住宅設計のコツ：安藤忠雄／作品：マイヤー／入江経一／ブルーダー／ジョイ／伊東豊雄／ナイルズ／八木敦司／他
Tips on House Design; T. Ando/ Works; Meier; Irie; Bruder; Joy; Ito; Niles; Yagi; and others
160 pages, 72 in color. ￥2,848

61
住宅設計のコツ：スコーギン／イーラム／ブレイ／作品：マイヤーズ／ミラージェス／ソウト・デ・モウラ／レゴレッタ／青木／他
Tips on House Design; Scogin/ Elam/bray; Works; Myers; Miralles; Legorreta; Aoki; and others
160 pages, 72 in color. ￥2,848

GA ARCHITECT 15
ARATA ISOZAKI 磯崎 新 1991-2000

Size: 300×307mm

Forthcoming issue

TEXTS: Arata Isozaki
WORKS: Team Disney Building／B-Con Plaza／Toyonokuni Libraries for Cultural Resources／Kyoto Consert Hall／Nagi Museum of Contemporary Art／Nagi Town Library／Nara Centennial Hall／DOMUS; Interactive Museum La Coruna／Bass Museum of Art／Okayama West Police Station／Shizuoka Perfoming Arts Center/Daendo／Shizuoka Performing Arts Center／Ohio's Center of Science and Industry(COSI)／The Museum of Modern Art, Gunma Cotemporary Art Wing／Gunma Astronomical Observatory／The Akiyoshidai International Art Village／Art Plaza／The Man-made Island Project, "Mirage"／Shenzhen International Trade Plaza／"Art and Fashion"／Yamanaka／Yamaguchi Cultural Complex／The New Exit for the Uffizi, Project for Piazza Castellaniand ／others

論文・作品解説：磯崎新
収録作品：ティーム・ディズニー・ビルディング／ビーコン・プラザ／豊の国ライブラリー／京都コンサートホール／奈義町現代美術館・奈義町立図書館／なら100年会館／ラ・コルーニャ人間科学館／バス・ミュージアム／岡山西警察署／静岡県コンベンション・アーツセンター＜グランシップ＞／静岡県舞台芸術センター／野外劇場＜有度＞，本部棟／オハイオ21世紀科学工業センター／群馬県立近代美術館現代美術棟／県立ぐんま天文台／秋吉台国際芸術村／アートプラザ／海市計画／深圳国際公易広場／アート・アンド・ファッション／フィレンツェ・ビエンナーレ '98／やま中／山口市文化交流プラザ／ウフィツィ美術館新玄関プロジェクト／他

GA JAPAN

42
新 現代建築を考える ○と✕
大社文化プレイス
批評座談会：伊東豊雄・高松伸・二川幸夫

[建築1999/2000] 総括と展望
座談会：小嶋一浩・大西若人・二川幸夫
作品：磯崎新　伊東豊雄　内藤廣　村上徹　竹中工務店　大野美代子
記事：[21世紀の東京を占う超高層プロジェクト]
連載：[世界の現場より]
[世紀末文化欄] 第十参号 石山修武
[建築家登場] ⑧ 内藤廣
「口説・日本建築史」第一回 伊藤ていじ
「建築のエッセンス」プロポーション(2) 齋藤裕

Japanese Text Only
Size: 300×288mm／176 total pages, 72 in color／¥2,333

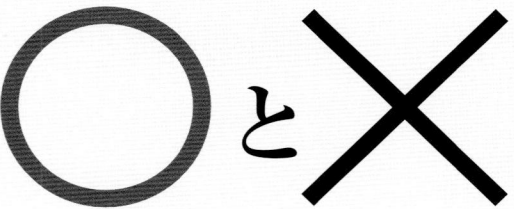

GA JAPAN 別冊①
20世紀の現代建築を検証する ○と✕

近代建築はどのように始まり，どのように展開されたのか？
コルビュジエ，ライト，ミースの影響力は？
技術，政治，戦争など社会の動きに作家の人間性を重ねつつ
20世紀の建築史を一気に縦横断する
建築家・磯崎新と歴史家・鈴木博之の対談集

Japanese Text Only
Size:300mm×228mm／198 total pages, 72 in color／¥2,800

「GA JAPAN」「GA HOUSES」「GA DOCUMENT」「GA DOCUMENT EXTRA」を確実にご購入いただくためには，最寄りの書店に「定期購読」の申込みをして下さい。刊行時に書店にお届けいたします。なお，書店では建築書籍のコーナーでお求めください。

書店での購入が難しい地域の方は，「年間購読」をご利用下さい。（送料弊社負担）
GA JAPAN 14,700円　GA HOUSES 11,960円　GA DOCUMENT 11,960円（消費税込み）
年間購読専用 Tel: 03-3403-7497　Fax: 03-3404-1462

表記価格に消費税は含まれておりません。

隈研吾読本－１９９９

サイバーからリアル，メガからミクロ，アカデミズムからストリート
建築家・隈研吾の境界を越えて横断する思考と重層するアクティビティーを，磯崎新，中沢新一，廣瀬通孝との対談とインタヴューを交えて解明する
初期の作品から代表作「M2」，そして愛知万博会場構成まで収録

第1章　埋蔵：埋めること建築を消すこと
第2章　ルーバー：建築・物質を可能な限りはかなくすること，弱くすること
第3章　サイバースペース：建築（物質）を情報で置換すること
第4章　21世紀の都市：20世紀都市の原理と21世紀都市の原理

対談　磯崎新，廣瀬通孝，中沢新一

Japanese Text Only　Size: 210×148mm／336 total pages, 42 in color／￥2,800

妹島和世読本－１９９８

生い立ち，学校，就職，独立……
建築家の歩んできたバックグラウンドと初期の作品から現在進行中のプロジェクトまでを収めた，インタヴュー形式による＜読む妹島和世＞

収録作品／PLATFORM I, II, III／再春館製薬女子寮／カステルバジャック・スポーツ・ショップ／パチンコパーラー I, II, III／森の別荘／Y-HOUSE／中原中也記念館公開設計競技応募案／せんだいメディアテーク公開設計競技応募案／調布駅北口交番／アパートメントのプロトタイプ／ハウジングスタディ／岐阜県営北方住宅／S-HOUSE／マルチメディア工房／熊野古道なかへち美術館／K本社屋／牛久新駅駅前利便施設／O資料館／世界都市博覧会・警消センター／KAZUYO SEJIMA 12 PROJECTS展／他

Japanese Text Only　Size: 210×148mm／336 total pages, 42 in color／￥2,800

日本の現代建築を考える ○と× I

GA JAPAN 13号より連載を始めた「日本の現代建築を考える○と×」を単行本化。国内外で活躍する11人の作品紹介と共に，建築史家と建築家による分析，作家自身の反論を併せて掲載

収録作品／安藤忠雄：サントリーミュージアム「天保山／マーメイド広場」／磯崎新：豊の国情報ライブラリー／伊東豊雄：八代広域消防本部庁舎／日建設計：JTビル／谷口吉生：豊田市美術館／茶室／高松伸：メテオプラザ／山本理顕：岩出山中学校／ラファエル・ヴィニオリ：東京国際フォーラム／妹島和世＋西沢立衛：マルチメディア工房／横文彦：風の丘葬斎場／原広司：京都駅ビル

評者（五十音順）／石山修武／磯崎新／伊東豊雄／川崎清／隈研吾／鈴木博之／高橋靗一／高松伸／土居義岳／原広司／藤森照信／二川幸夫／六角鬼丈／渡辺豊和

Japanese Text Only　Size: 210×148mm／288 total pages／￥1,900

MODERN ARCHITECTURE

近代建築の名作がいきいきとよみがえる，GA DOCUMENT
特別号「モダン・アーキテクチャー」第2, 3巻の改訂新版。
1851年のクリスタル・パレスより第1次大戦終結までの88作品を収録した第1巻，1920年から第2次世界大戦の終わる1945年までの79作品を収録した第2巻

① **1851-1919** 近代建築の黎明
文：ケネス・フランプトン／企画・撮影：二川幸夫／翻訳：香山壽夫，他

② **1920-1945** 近代建築の開花
文：ケネス・フランプトン／企画・撮影：二川幸夫／翻訳：三宅理一，他

Japanese Text Only　Size: 210×148mm／224①, 256② total pages, 48 in color／￥2,300

表記価格に消費税は含まれておりません。

Key to Abbreviations

ALC	alcove
ARCD	arcade/covered passageway
ART	art room
ATL	atelier
ATR	atrium
ATT	attic
AV	audio-visual room
BAL	balcony
BAR	bar
BK	breakfast room
BR	bedroom
BRG	bridge/catwalk
BTH	bathroom
BVD	belvedere/lookout
CAR	carport/car shelter
CH	children's room
CEL	cellar
CL	closet/walk-in closet
CLK	cloak
CT	court
D	dining room
DEN	den
DK	deck
DN	stairs-down
DRK	darkroom
DRS	dressing room/wardrobe
DRW	drawing room
E	entry
ECT	entrance court
EH	entrance hall
EV	elevator
EXC	exercise room
F	family room
FPL	fireplace
FYR	foyer
GAL	gallery
GDN	garden
GRG	garage
GRN	greenhouse
GST	guest room/guest bedroom
GZBO	gazebo
H	hall
ING	inglenook
K	kitchen
L	living room
LBR	library
LBY	lobby
LDRY	laundry
LFT	loft
LGA	loggia
LGE	lounge
LWL	light well
MAID	maid room
MBR	master bedroom
MECH	mechanical
MLTP	multipurpose room
MSIC	music room
MUD	mud room
OF	office
P	porch/portico
PAN	pantry/larder
PLY	playroom
POOL	swimming pool/pool/pond
PT	patio
RE	rear entry
RT	roof terrace
SHW	shower
SIT	sitting room
SHOP	shop
SKY	skylight
SL	slope/ramp
SLP	sleeping loft
SNA	sauna
STD	studio
STDY	study
ST	staircase/stair hall
STR	storage/storeroom
SUN	sunroom/sun parlor/solarium
SVE	service entry
SVYD	service yard
TAT	tatami room/tea ceremony room
TER	terrace
UP	stairs-up
UTL	utility room
VD	void/open
VRA	veranda
VSTB	vestibule
WC	water closet
WRK	workshop/work room

Cover and title pages: Rifkind Residence by Tod Williams & Billie Tsien
Photos by Yukio Futagawa
pp.8-9: GGG House by Alberto Kalach
Photo by Tomohiro Sakashita

GA HOUSES

《世界の住宅》62
編集・発行人：二川幸夫

2000年1月20日発行
エーディーエー・エディタ・トーキョー
東京都渋谷区千駄ヶ谷3-12-14
電話(03)3403-1581(代)
ファクス(03)3497-0649
E-mail: info@ga-ada.co.jp
http://www.ga-ada.co.jp

ロゴタイプ・デザイン：細谷巖

製本・印刷：凸版印刷株式会社

取次店
トーハン・日販・大阪屋
栗田出版販売・誠光堂
西村書店・中央社・太洋社

禁無断転載

ISBN4-87140-372-6 C1352

GA HOUSES 62
Publisher/Editor: *Yukio Futagawa*

Published in January 2000
© *A.D.A EDITA Tokyo Co., Ltd.*
3-12-14 Sendagaya, Shibuya-ku,
Tokyo, 151-0051 Japan
Tel. 03-3403-1581
Fax.03-3497-0649
E-mail: info@ga-ada.co.jp
http://www.ga-ada.co.jp

Logotype Design: *Gan Hosoya*

Printed in Japan by
Toppan Printing Co., Ltd.

All rights reserved.

Copyright of Photographs:
© *GA photographers*

目次	Contents
住宅設計のコツ トッド・ウィリアムズ ビリー・ツィン	10 TIPS ON HOUSE DESIGN Tod Williams Billie Tsien
トッド・ウィリアムズ ビリー・ツィン リフキンド邸	18 TOD WILLIAMS BILLIE TSIEN Rifkind Residence
アルベルト・カラチ GGGハウス	42 ALBERTO KALACH GGG House
テン・アルキテクトス ハウスR.R.	64 TEN ARQUITECTOS House R.R.
丸山洋志 スラント・グランス/ハウス/スロープ・グラウンド	78 HIROSHI MARUYAMA Slant Grance/House/Slope Ground
ディーン・ノタ レイナ邸	90 DEAN NOTA Reyna Residence
布施茂 幕張西の家	104 SHIGERU FUSE House in Makuhari-nishi
マーク・マック トーマス邸	112 MARK MACK Thomas House
塩田能也/インターデザインアソシエイツ HOUSE MUR	122 YOSHINARI SHIODA/INTERDESIGN ASSOCIATES House MUR
石黒浩一郎 畑中邸	134 KOICHIRO ISHIGURO White Woods
スティーブン・アーリック キャニオンの家	140 STEVEN EHRLICH Canyon Residence
ファーナウ&ハートマン アンダーソン/エイヤース邸	150 FERNAU & HARTMAN Anderson/Ayers Residence

English translation: Lisa Tani / Copyediting(pp.11-17): Takashi Yanai
和訳：菊池泰子

Tips on House Design
住宅設計のコツ
③ Tod Williams Billie Tsien

Interview: Yoshio Futagawa　聞き手：二川由夫

Freeman-Silverman Residence, 1996

GA: House projects are a way many architects begin their careers. This is especially true, it seems, in the United States and in Japan. In this way, residential design is also a way critics can trace the roots of an architects design philosophy. But this isn't necessarily the case for you. How many houses have you designed in your career?

Tod Williams: Not that many, and you're right in that it is not really how I began. So much of New York City has already been built and so most of the early work was in interiors. I think the very first work that I got when I went on my own in 1973 after working for Richard Meier was a commercial project. New York is such a big banking center and that still is the case, there were securities traders that wanted securities offices and so on. There were a lot of commercial interiors as I just mentioned, and rarely, but almost never, there were storefront projects. I also had a number of very small apartments or parts of apartments like a kitchen renovation or a child's loft. Eventually we got more complex work. So the residential work started at that smallest scale and grew into a complete apartment and then the complete apartment eventually became a house. Similarly the work we did for commercial interiors grew. At one time we were doing work the size of this room, and that eventually grew into 2000s.f. or more. It was a slow process. If I were a young architect working in any other city than New York, particularly out West, I would have had the chance to build more houses. So I really see that as being a consequence of being in New York. Now in Los Angeles, you can do a quite inexpensive house on an inexpensive piece of land. You can experiment with architecture outside because the weather is milder and also the clientele is younger. Here in New York it's been a slow process of maturing. But I don't regret that kind of work at all. I'm perfectly happy because those smaller apartment projects gave me a sense of how to be concerned with small details and the intimate texture of a person's life. Although I don't only want to work at that level I think that very intimate detail and texture is something that you want to have in any work, whether it's a house or an institutional project or a commercial project. So it's a very good thing to be working always in the house, it gets you back into the moment where it means something to a particular person; it's of utmost importance to one person or two people or a family. That scale is wonderful to work on although sometimes it can be quite frustrating and is always very time consuming. There's always a lot of emotional commitment to it.

GA: I'd like to know more about your process. How do you and Billie work together? When you get a project how do you begin together and how does the staff work into a project?

TW: Billie and I believe that if we take on a project we should both be interested in it. We both interview for a project. And I think that for us it's very important that the chemistry be right between us and the client. We want to respect the client and we want them to respect and like us. That's the most important thing. Architecture is very personal, so if it's someone we can't like and respect then we shouldn't take on the project and similarly they shouldn't take us on if they don't feel comfortable with us. That issue of chemistry is first and foremost. The other thing that's important is that the project be inspirational to us. Like I've said, we don't do many houses. In my life I've done fewer than ten houses. I'm not in the house business and honestly I'd rather do fewer houses and use each one as a point to explore something new. They should be important moments for me and that's why I think it's important that we're very interested in the project. Of course it has to make financial sense, but it also has to make emotional sense. The connection to the client and the connection to the project and the site is very important. And one of the things that I'm most interested in is not becoming a house expert. I always want to be able to find some wonderment, something new to be learned through the project, it's site, or its location in America. For example, we're about to take on a new house, for a single man who is younger than we are. He had a house facing the ocean on a high bluff which burned down. There are some remaining pieces of the old structure there, a column or two, and I kind of sensed that something should come back. The client is very open to the possibility of that and that's very exciting to me. That kind of enthusiasm and excitement are very important issues to me. Once we get a house project, Billie and I try to get an understanding of the program after get-

Tod Williams & Billie Tsien

GA 住宅作品は，多くの建築家にとって，そのキャリアをスタートさせる契機になっています。アメリカと日本は，特にそうであるようにみえます。この意味で，批評家は住宅デザインから建築家の設計思想の根をたどることもできます。けれど，これはあなたの場合には必ずしもあてはまりません。今までに，何軒くらいの住宅を設計していますか？

トッド・ウィリアムズ（以下TW）それほど多くありません。住宅から出発していないというのはその通りなのです。ニューヨーク市のほとんどが既に建ってしまっているわけですから，最初のころの作品は大部分がインテリアの仕事です。一番最初の仕事，1973年にリチャード・マイヤーのところを離れ，独立したときに受けたのは商業関係のものだったと思います。ニューヨークは大金融センターですから，証券業務のオフィスなどを必要とするトレーダーが大勢いたのです。こういった商業施設のインテリアをたくさん手がけましたし，そして希に，店舗のファサードをデザインすることもありました。そのうちに，非常に小さなアパートや，台所の改造や子供のためのロフトのようなアパートの一部を設計する仕事がいくつかきました。ようやく複雑な建物の仕事を手にしたのです。つまり住宅作品の仕事はごく小さなスケールに始まり，アパート一戸全部に広がり，一戸のアパートから，やっと一軒の住宅をやるようになったのです。商業施設のインテリアの仕事も同じでした。最初はこの部屋くらいの大きさの仕事をし，それがついには2000平方フィートやそれ以上の広さのものになっていったのです。ゆっくりとしたプロセスでした。ニューヨーク以外の，それも西部の街で仕事をする若い建築家だったとしたら，もっと多くの住宅を設計する機会に恵まれていたでしょう。ですからこうした状況は，まったくニューヨークにいることの結果であると思っています。今，ロサンジェルスでは，安い土地に非常に安い価格で建てられますし，気候もずっと穏やかで，依頼人も若いですから，戸外に開いた建築を実験できます。ニューヨークではゆっくりと成熟して行くのです。でも，こうした仕事の在り方を残念だとは思っていません。完全に満足しています。小さなアパートの仕事は，細かいディテールや個人の生活に密接した表情を考えるための感覚を与えてくれたからです。また，そのレベルでの仕事だけでなく，そうした居心地よいディテールや表情は，住宅であろうと公共建築であろうと，商業施設であろうと，どのような作品にも望まれるものだと思います。ですから，住宅の仕事を常にしているのはとても良いことです。特定の個人，あるいは家族にとって最も大切な何かを意味する場所へと立ち返らせてくれます。こうした規模の仕事をしていくのは素晴らしいことです。しかしときには，とてもフラストレーションがたまりますし，常に膨大な時間が費やされてしまいます。そこには感情が入ってくるからです。

GA プロセスについて知りたいのです。ビリーさんと，どんなふうに一緒に仕事を進めて行かれるのか。仕事がきたとき，二人でどのように始め，所員はどのように加わって行くのですか？

TW ビリーと私は，仕事がきたらそれに対し両方が関心をもつべきであると信じています。そのプロジェクトのためのインタヴューを二人ともやります。私たちにとって，施主との相性が合うかどうかが非常に重要であると思っています。施主を尊敬したいと思いますし，施主の側も私たちを尊敬し，好きになってもらいたいと思います。それが最も大切です。建築はとてもパーソナルなものです。ですから，好きになることも敬意をもつこともできなかったら，仕事を引き受けるべきではないですし，同様に，施主の側も，私たちと気持ちが合わないと感じたら，頼むべきではないのです。相性が一番の問題です。他に重要なことは，その仕事にインスピレーションを感じられるかどうかです。前に言ったように，住宅の仕事を多くはしていません。今までに設計したのは，10軒に足りません。住宅ビジネスには関わっていませんし，正直いって，もっと少ない数の住宅を受け，それぞれで何か新しいことを探求してみたいのです。それらは私にとって重要な瞬間になるはずですし，だからこそ，そのプロジェクトに非常な興味をもつことが重要だと思うのです。もちろん，経済感覚も必要ですが，情緒的感覚もまた必要なのです。施主とのつながり，プロジェクトと敷地とのつながりはとても大切です。なかでも最も意識していることは，エキスパートにならないこと，何らかの驚きや，プロジェクトやその敷地や，アメリカのなかでの敷地の位置から学べる新しい何かを常に発見することです。たとえば，今，新しい仕事にとりかかるところなのです。私たちより若い独身

ting to know the client and the site. Then we will have a first intuition, which may come in the form of a very rough sketch.

GA: Do you both do early sketches for a design?
TW: Well I might be the first one to make a mark, and then Billie and I will talk about that mark or thought. That first thought may have been a bad one and dry up in a day or two or maybe a week. But if the thought is good, then it begins to have it's own life, independent of Billie or me. It's a little bit maybe like giving life to a child. There's something there that has to be a nourished. It's a seed that slowly turns into something else. That life allows the project it's own momentum. Billie and I both need to have our understanding of what this house is before it can go anywhere. Then, right at the beginning of a project, we also assign it to a project architect. In the case of the Rifkind house it was a person named Peter Arnold. That person becomes another piece of the equation. He or she helps nourish the idea of the house too. Then at some point we share our early ideas with the client. We ask if it feels right to them. We ask if the relationship between the spaces we're proposing makes sense to them. So the client also helps let this project grow on its own terms. We believe that each project has its own terms. Truthfully, when I leave a house, I want it to be only mine, as if I'm the only author but, really, I recognize that I'm not the only author. Billie is also the author and I'm sure she must feel just as I do, that it's all hers. And at the same time we want the client to feel that it's all theirs, and the project architect to feel that it's all his or hers. It's a very interesting problem. If that can work, then it means that the idea of the house, this seed, can actually live on its own, and that somehow it can exist outside of us. This is the way I think about a house. It doesn't have to do with a preconception of how I think about space, but how I think about space and use, and the house in this place on the earth at this moment.

GA: Is your approach to residential design different than your approach to institutional building?
TW: I don't really think so. I suppose the process of designing a public building isn't that different. The one difference is that I think that its rare that the public client believes that the building is an extension of themselves in the same way the house is the extension of an owner. If we're fortunate, there is someone involved with a public project that feels that the building is a piece of their life, that the building has that kind of personal importance to them. For example, when we were working on the Neuroscience Institute in La Jolla, Dr. Gerald Edelman took the project on as his own in a way. It was his baby. And he felt so passionately about it, that he had to believe we were doing work for him. In a way we were making his own house. I like that very much and that kind of intense interest always makes a project better. It's much better than having to deal only through bureaucrats or a committee who is more concerned with rules and doesn't really see the importance of what we could do together. I like houses because it's the reverse, it would be very rare that a client isn't passionate about the project. This might be true in some cases where the client just wants a very large extravagant house to impress his friends or colleagues. Obviously different things are important to them, but for most residential clients there is a critical interest in the process of design.

GA: I'd like to ask about your influences. You're early work is obviously influenced by Richard Meier. What other architects have influenced your career?
TW: For me, the development of my approach to architecture and its creation has been a patient search. When I first left Richard's office I very much wanted to explore materials. So when I first started working with Billie I was interested in material and in color and texture. Billie helped bring that on board. I think increasingly we both begin to feel that making a house and making architecture in a world that is ever more fast-paced and more energetic should be about creating a place of quiet and serenity. For me, one of the requirements of a house is that it be able to hold dreams and possibilities. It should have a certain gentle quality to it, rather than an aggressive quality. We're working towards that. I also think that increasingly I don't look to other people for ideas. I can look to the outside world, the museum of natural history, or to artists, and very often to our own work. I'm learning as I go along, so I react and make this next house relate to a previous work. Now what people do I admire? Of course I can't help but come out of Richard Meier, and the work of other early teachers. In recent years, I've gone back to appreciate Frank Lloyd Wright. I was taught as a student that his work was bad and I shouldn't look at it. I was also taught that late Le Corbusier was very bad. I never really believed that they were bad, but at the same time I never made the conscious effort to look for myself. In recent years I've come to enjoy looking at this work. Louis Kahn is important to me. Alvar Aalto is important to me. There are also a number of architects that are living and working today that I look to. Will Bruder in Phoenix is a

Barn in Sagaponack, 1978

longtime friend and even a mentor in certain ways. I admire the work of our friend Elias Torres. I have a tremendous admiration for Glen Murcutt as a singular soul practitioner who very much believes that each project has to do with the client and the site. I like the work of Peter Zumthor who has a kind of heat in this work that makes each project seem like it was a piece of coal that was pressed together into a diamond. In a lot of cases I'm influenced by the work of architects who are our friends and whose work I naturally come across.

GA: Architectural design can be a difficult thing to explain in the abstract. Perhaps you could make an example of one of your residential projects to illustrate some of your thoughts on spatial design and the application of materials.

TW: We could use the Rifkind house a little bit. In this particular site, everywhere you looked you had an attractive view. There was something of interest in each direction. We felt that there was no reason to have a formal front to the house. There is a courtyard that is slightly more opaque, a little bit more solid, and I suppose that sense of a courtyard gives a kind of sense of frontality. But we wanted to extend the threshold of the house. I felt strongly about this very early on. The site is a kind of series of layers, not only layers of trees, the pitch pines on the site, but also layers that extend out to where you can see water in the distance in one direction, and water in the distance in another. There is no sense that there are any neighbors coming close to you. We also very much wanted to leave the car behind. You walk to the house and I think this sense of walking through the land to the house will become an even stronger feature of the design in time. And then beside the house we felt strongly that there should be many paths that go out into the land, so every single private room has a door that goes out into the land. The house has a great deal of perimeter and this came mostly from the program. We originally thought of it as several buildings in the land. We wanted the master bedroom and study to be an autonomous unit and we wanted the living/dining/kitchen to have it's own autonomy to some extent. And then we wanted the guest bedroom wing which is for the children or guests to have it's own autonomy. Both the master and the guestroom wings would be able to use the central rooms independently or together.

GA: I've noticed that the separation program is something evident in a lot in your work.

TW: Yes that's true. I do use that a lot. You will also notice that I feel that it's very important that every person who engages in our work can find many different paths through it. I don't want there to be a single set way of experiencing the house. I want every person who visits our houses to find their own way through it. Some people have suggested that this has to do with a fear of

Tarlo House, 1979

being trapped. But I actually believe that it's more in tune with this idea that everyone should have the opportunity to find their own house within a house, so your house can be very different from my house. Our experiences may be very similar but they don't have to be the same. In a Richard Meier work, every single interpretation has to be Richard's interpretation. In our work we don't want that to be the case, and that's why they're multiple routes. It's all about how you experience the spaces as you find your own ways to move through them. Sometimes being inside and sometimes being outside.

GA: Tell me about how you came to this particular material palette.

TW: Very early on, the owners indicated to us that they wanted the house to be warm, and we knew very early on that the most economical and practical way of building a house out there on Long Island would be to build with wood. We thought, first the structure, then maybe the siding should be wood. The introduction of stone came as counterpoint to the wood, and these two along with glass became the principal materials. If you look at the house, the most important thing is the site, and the materials allow the house to relate to these surroundings. So it's a wood-stud house with wood siding, and the wood windows. Another thing we wanted to do was to use wood on the inside of the house as well. And that was an idea that I felt very strongly about. I wanted it to feel as if the whole house was principally a wooden house. I wanted to use wood on the interior of the perimeter walls. Perhaps I would have liked to use wood even more than we did, but the clients were concerned that the house would be too dark. They didn't want the wood to be too oppressive. That

かに，他と違っていることが彼らには大切なのです。けれど，住宅を依頼してくる人のほとんどは設計プロセスに大きな関心をもっています。

GA 影響についてうかがいたいと思います。初期の作品がリチャード・マイヤーの影響下にあることは明らかです。他にはどのような建築家の影響を仕事の上で受けていますか？

TW 私にとって，建築に対する方法を発展させ，建築を創造することは粘り強い探求をつづけて行くことでした。リチャードの事務所を離れたばかりのとき，材料について研究してみたいと強く思いました。ですから，ビリーと仕事を始めたときは，材料や色彩やテクスチャーに関心があったのです。ビリーがそれを仕事に取り込むのを助けてくれました。だんだんに私たちは，ある世界のなかに家をつくること，建築をつくること，つまり，静かで清澄な場所を創造することに，これまで以上の速度とエネルギーをかけるべきであると感じはじめていたのだと思います。私にとって，住宅に求めることの一つは，夢と可能性を保ち続けられることです。アグレッシヴな性格よりむしろある優しい性格をもたせるべきです。私たちはその方向で仕事をしています。また，アイディアを求めて他の作品を見ることが少なくなっています。外の世界，自然史博物館や芸術家の作品を見，そして自分たちの作品を見直すことも多いのです。仕事を進めながら学んでいます。そうすれば，次の作品をその前の作品と対応させ，そのつながりのなかでつくることができます。さて，誰を敬愛しているかということです。もちろん，リチャード・マイヤーや最初に学んだ人たちの作品から受けたものを挙げないわけにいきません。ここ数年は，

Tarlo House, 1979

フランク・ロイド・ライトを評価しなおしています。学生のとき，彼の作品は良くないから見るべきではないと教えられました。ル・コルビュジエの晩年の作品も非常に悪いものだとも教えられました。それを心底信じたわけではありませんが，同時に，自分の目で見る努力もまったくしなかったのです。最近はこうした作品を見るのを楽しんでいます。ルイス・カーンは私にとって大切ですし，アルヴァ・アアルトも大切です。また，注目する，現役で仕事をしている建築家も何人かいます。フェニックスのウィル・ブルーダーは長い友人ですが，ある意味では師匠でもあります。友人のエリアス・トーレスの作品も素晴らしいと思います。一つ一つのプロジェクトが住み人と敷地と結ばれていなくてはならないと固く信じている，希にみる魂の実践者として，グレン・マーカットに対しては非常な敬意を抱いています。ピーター・ズントーの作品も好きです。ひとまとめに圧縮されてダイアモンドになった石炭のかけらかのように，それぞれの作品をつくる彼の仕事には一種の熱があります。多くの場合，友人の作品や日常出会う作品から影響されています。

GA 建築デザインを抽象的に説明するのは難しいことであるかもしれません。たぶん，あなたの住宅プロジェクトの一つについて，空間デザインと材料の適用に対する考えのいくつかを説明することで，その一つの模範をつくれませんか？

TW リフキンド邸で少しやってみましょう。この特徴のある敷地には，どこを見ても魅力的な眺望が広がっています。すべての方向に何かしらの魅力があるのです。この家にフォーマルな正面をつくる理由は何もないと感じました。やや不透明で，少しソリッドなコートヤードがあり，その雰囲気は，一種の正面性を家に与えるのではないかと思いました。しかし私たちはこの家の入り口を広げたかったのです。このことはごく早くからずっと強く感じていました。この敷地は一種のレイヤーで構成されています。敷地にあるヤニマツのつくる木立のレイヤーばかりでなく，一方に遠く見える水面まで，また別の方にも遠く見える水面まで広がって行くレイヤーがあるのです。近くまで隣家が迫ってくるという感じはありません。車を背後で乗り捨てるようにしたいとも強く思いました。家まで歩いて行く，そしてこ

in turn led to the decision to use douglas fir since it is a little lighter in color. In the end, we used four different kinds of wood in the house. We used douglas fir for the flooring and on the inside, mahogany windows, cedar siding, and cherry and mahogany furniture.

GA: And what about the stone?

TW: It's not a very expensive stone. It's not from Long Island but is relatively local. We used this stone in two finishes: honed, which is sanded smooth, and split-face or natural face. We wanted to use this rich palette where the materials really meant something. But at the same time we wanted the palette to be somewhat controlled.

GA: You mentioned that color was a reason you chose douglas fir for the floors. What are some other reasons for using these particular materials.

TW: Why did we use the cedar siding on the outside? Well, first it's a traditional material for exterior siding and it's not very expensive, after all the house did have a budget. The mahogany windows are the most durable windows we could get, except teak, which is more durable but much more expensive. We used cherry as a hard wood on the interior although it's rather soft. The douglas fir we used really because it's also somewhere between a soft and a hardwood, and it's readily available and comes in large pieces. We knew we could make it into plywood and we could make it into boards for the floor. The palette of materials was very important in this house. In every house that I want to do in the future, you will see that materials will be very important. And there won't be a single material. I don't believe that's really what I want to explore, I think that if we did use a singular material we would try to explore different aspects and application for that material. So for instance, if it were poured-in-place concrete I would want it to be polished concrete in some places and sand-blasted in other places and bush-hammered in others, whatever, because I think not everything should be of the same temperature, the same texture, the same feel. In the end I would want the houses to have a variety of qualities to it.

GA: What do you think about the kinds of more industrial materials being used by younger-generation designers. You tend to use a more traditional palette.

TW: I use modern materials too.

GA: Yes, but the treatment is a little bit different from that of the younger designers.

TW: We're not very interested in straight-off-the-shelf. No, whatever material I look at I will always want to love the material. I want to find something in it that is sensual for me. I want to find something that is remarkable about the material. I don't think there are any forbidden materials, and actually I'm interested in all materials in a certain way. I don't have a desire to use only traditional materials or only modern or synthetic materials. I want to explore the possibilities of all materials because I believe every material has value, and the issue and challenge is how we can revalue it, how can we appreciate it. I never want to take things without thinking about them. I don't like to take things casually. I have nothing against any single material. I'm not strictly a green architect. I mean this may sound blasphemous but I have nothing inherently against a material which seems to be wrong for the earth, because I don't think materials themselves are good or evil. It's what we do with them that makes them good or evil, or positive or negative. My concern is when designers use materials arbitrarily. What one sees out there is essentially arbitrary but what you do with it is not. For me, the possibilities are infinite.

GA: What about your approach to details?

TW: Well you can see that details are very important to me. Relative to the entire design process this is actually a very important point. I'm sure this is the case for a lot of architects but it is especially true for me. If I could keep on designing I would keep on designing. It's very difficult for me to stop. Part of this is because I don't pre-imagine a design. It evolves and working out details is a way of working out an idea. It is part of the evolution of a design. Richard Meier probably pre-imagines what he wants to do. Maybe this is true of Tadao Ando, I don't know, I'm not sure. But I know I don't do this and it depends on the situation so I always want to keep the project moving forward. I always believe that a project will always get better as we go forward. It's not best in my head and gets worse as you build it. It actually starts out and gets better as you build it. So if I had a patient, very patient client who had a lot of money, who didn't care about time and didn't care about money, I would probably keep on designing and slowly let the building evolve. But I'm also practical and my clients are practical and I'm happy for that and we put restrictions on the process. You may know that we're going to be doing some more work on the Rifkind house. I knew when they built the house they would not be happy with this library. They felt in order to have this house in the country they needed to work in it and they needed to feel in a way like they were working in New York. We used plastic laminate, and made it cold and feel like an office in New York a little bit, because they wanted it that way. We did it the way they

の土地を家まで歩き抜けて行くその感覚が，やがてこのデザインのさらに強力な特徴になるだろうと考えました。次に，家のそばで，この土地のなかに入って行くたくさんの道がなくてはならないと強く感じたのです。そこで，すべての個室にこの土地に出て行けるドアをつけました。この家の周縁はとても長いもので，これはほとんどプログラムから出てきたものです。もともとはこれを敷地のなかに建ついくつかの棟として考えていました。主寝室と書斎は自立したユニットにしたいし，リビング／ダイニング／キッチンもある程度まで自立性をもたせたかったのです。次に，客や子供たちのためのゲスト用寝室ウィングにも自立性がほしかったのです。主寝室翼もゲスト翼も，中央の部屋を個別にも共有してもつかえるでしょう。

GA 分離させるプログラム構成は，あなたの作品の多くに見られます。

TW よく使っています。私たちの設計した建物に来るすべての人が，いくつもの違った道筋を発見することがとても大切であると私が感じていることにも気づくと思います。その家をたった一つの方法で経験してほしくないのです。訪れる一人一人が自分の道筋を見つけてほしい。これには罠に捕らえられる恐怖を感じると言う人もいます。けれど私は，これはむしろ，誰もが家の内に自分の家を見つける機会をもつべきだという考えにかなっていると信じています。つまり，あなたの家は私の家とはまったく違うものにできる。私たちの経験は非常に似ているかもしれないが，同じであってはならないのです。リチャード・マイヤーの作品では，一つ一つの解釈はすべてリチャードの解釈でなければならない。私たちはそうしたくないのです。それが多様な道筋のある理由です。自分の進む道を見つけながらどのように空間を経験するかがすべてです。あるときは内であり，あるときは外なのです。

GA ここで使われている材料はどんな理由で選択されたのですか？

TW ごく最初から，オーナーが暖かな雰囲気の家にしてほしいと言っていましたし，私もごく早くから，ロングアイランドで住宅を最も経済的に実際的に建てる方法は木造にすることだと知っていました。まず構造を，次に外壁も木にすべきだろうと思いました。木の対旋律として石を導入し，この2つにガラスが加わって主要材料を構成しています。ここで一番重要なものは敷地であり，材料はその周囲の環境にこの家を結びつけていることが分かります。ということで，木の壁をもつ木構造の家，そして窓枠も木なのです。もう一つやりたかったことは，内部にも同じように木を使うことでした。これはやってみたいと，とても強く感じていたアイディアでした。家全体の主題が木造の家なのだと感じられるものにしたかったのです。外壁の内側にも木を使いたかった。たぶん私は，実際より，もっとたくさん木を使いたかったのだと思いますが，施主はそれでは家があまりに暗い感じになるのではないかと考えたのです。木が過剰になることを嫌いました。そこで，ダグラス樅を使うことにしたのです。色が少し明るいからです。結局，4種類の木を使っています。フローリングと内壁にダグラス樅，窓はマホガニー，外壁はシーダー，家具はサクラとマホガニーです。

GA 石についてはどうですか？

TW それほど高価なものではありません。ロングアイランドのものではないけれど，比較的ローカルなものです。この石を2種類の仕上げ方で使っています。サンドブラスト仕上げと，割肌です。材料が何かを意味するところに，この多彩な材料を使いたかったのです。しかし同時に，ある程度，使い方をコントロールしたいとも思っていました。

GA 床にダグラス樅を選んだ理由は色調のためだと言われました。これらの特定の材料を選んだその他の理由には何がありますか？

TW なぜ，外側をシーダーの下見にしたかといったことですか？ まず，最初にそれは外壁の下見に使われる伝統的な材料であるからであり，それほど高価なものでもないからです。やはり住宅は予算あってのものですから。マホガニーの窓はチークを除いて――これは一番強いのですが，ずっと高価です――入手できた最も耐久性のあるものでした。サクラは内部に使う硬木として使っています。しかも比較的柔らかな感じをもっています。ダグラス樅は，柔らかさと硬木のどこか中間にあるところから選んだのですが，すぐに大量に購入可能だったこともあります。合板にすることも，床板にすることもできることを知っていました。この家では材料構成はとても重要でした。これから建てたいと思っているどの住宅でも，こうした材料がとても重要になるだろうと思います。そこでは材料が一種類ということはないでしょう。それは私がほんとうに追求したいことではないと思っています。仮に一つの材料だけを使ったとしたら，その材料の違った局面や扱い方を探そうとするでしょう。たとえば現場打ちのコンクリートだとしたら，ある箇所は磨き仕上げに，ある箇所はサンドブラストで仕上げ，またある箇所はび

wanted even though we disagreed with it. I said we can build it this way but we know you won't be happy with that, and we were right. And so there are things that continue to evolve and get better. It may be frustrating for the office but I feel quite happy that the Rifkind come back to us to say, "now we're ready to change the study and make it right." And I feel fortunate to think about how their programs can translate and how we can make this room work for them better. That's exactly the way I like to proceed with building. I always want to be in the position where when I see the choice even as we're under construction to make a better decision. And it frustrates me when I find myself as we did in the library, for whatever reason, maybe because of my inadequacy or the inadequacy of the client, or the budget, or something that's not possible on the site that we don't get it right. I never know ahead of time what will be perfect so that sense of evolution and constantly designing is an important aspect of working for me.

GA: There is one particular think I'm curious about and that is the sense of proportion in your work. I'm curious since I found that the ceiling heights in the Rifkind house were quite high. Frank Lloyd Wright used low ceilings to achieve certain experiences such as horizontal extension, but it also had to do with his own personal sense of proportions. Can I ask about proportion issue. When you design, how do you decide proportion. What drives your decisions?

TW: Well I don't know if I feel that the ceiling heights are that high. And as you say, this may be just my personal sense of it. There are three heights in the Rifkind house. One is, the low height, which I actually would have made lower—strangely enough the Rifkind are quite small but they wanted everything to be tall. I am tall and I like things that are small.

GA: Well what about not just the height of ceilings but proportions of space?

TW: What I believe is important is that there is not a preconceived proportion that is right in my head. I need to study it, and look at models and I need to look at what goes on inside the space. A square or a golden section doesn't necessarily mean anything to me. I believe that they have value in and of themselves but that's a kind of starting point from which we make the right decision, and that right decision is not something that can be preconceived. One thing you will find is that I believe very strongly in the change of scale. In that case I think I do share something with Frank Lloyd Wright who uses a very compressed space to release to a taller space. In almost all of the work you will see some place where you can feel the dimensions of the whole space. For example there are three places in the Rifkind house where you can feel the whole dimension of the room. In the living room you can

Eisenberg Residence, 1985

look from one end of the room to the other end of the dining room. If you're in the hallway of the bedroom wing and you open the two doors you can look from one end to the next. And the same thing is true of the bedroom. So at some point on that house I wanted to feel a very extended long dimension. And I also wanted to experience the full height of the living room as a high volume. At other points I want to compress it so that I can both deal with the proportions of the smaller space which are necessary but also feel the change from small to middle to large, or from small to large. I think the range of scales is quite successful in this house. That's why I say it's a layered house, because the approach there actually has to do with three basic heights. One is 7 feet plus a little bit, the other one is at the level of 9 feet and the other one is at 11 feet. So there are a series of steps in scale. And that gives a kind of layering effect that extends the eye from bottom to top and extends the eye the length of the space but stops it in certain points and allows your eye to go out to the sides. I don't know that every house needs to be this way, but there is something about this house and this piece of property that needed that layering. Once again I don't believe at all that there is a perfect proportion that means anything.

GA: But you have your own proportional system, I think. Anyone would recognize it as your work.

TW: Well there is a sense of proportion, agreed. There is a strong sense of proportion and proportions are important to me, but it's not something I can quantify. In most architectural situations buildings are made up of a horizontal dimension and a vertical dimension. They are related to one another but the horizontal needs to find it's horizontal line and the vertical needs to find it's ver-

しゃん仕上げに，その他なんでもやってみると思います。すべてが同じ強度，同じテクスチャー，同じ感じであるべきだとは思わないからです。結局，私は，住宅が多彩な質をもってほしいのです。

GA 若い世代のデザイナーが使っている工業的な材料についてはどう思いますか？ あなたはむしろ伝統的な材料を使う方向に行っていると思います。

TW 現代的な材料も使います。

GA ええ，でもその扱い方が若いデザイナーとは少し違っています。

TW 在庫棚から取り寄せることにはあまり興味がないのです。目にした材料にはどんなものであろうと，常に，愛情を注ぎたいと思うでしょう。そのなかに，私の感覚に訴えるものを見つけたいのです。その材料のもつ非凡な何かを見つけたい。禁じられた材料があるとは思っていませんし，事実，ある意味ですべての材料に興味があります。伝統的な材料だけ，現代的あるいは合成的な材料だけを使うことを望んではいません。あらゆる材料の可能性を探したいのです。すべての材料が価値をもっていると信じるからです。課題であり挑戦は，それをいかに再評価し，いかに味わうことができるかです。これらのことを考えずに取り上げたくないのです。ものを気楽に取り上げるのは好きではない。どんな材料も拒否しません。厳格なグリーン・アーキテクトではないのです。これは冒涜的に響くかもしれませんが，地球によくないようにみえる材料に対する否定を生来的にもってはいないという意味です。なぜなら，材料そのものが善か悪かであるとは考えないからです。私たちがどう扱うかがその善悪や是非をつくりだすのです。心配なのはデザイナーが材料を恣意的

Eisenberg Residence, 1985

に使うときです。外面的なものは本質的に恣意的ですが，材料と共につくりだすことはそうではありません。私には可能性は無限に思えます。

GA ディテールについてはどうですか？

TW 私にとってディテールがとても大切なことははっきりしています。全体のデザイン・プロセスに関連してこれは実際にとても重要な点なのです。多くの建築家にとってもそうであると思いますが，私の場合は特にそうなのです。もし許されるなら，いつまでもデザインし続けるでしょう。私にはそれを止めるのがとても難しいのです。これはひとつにはデザインをあらかじめ思い描かないからです。ディテールを展開させ，描くことが，アイディアを考えだす方法なのです。それはデザインの展開の一部なのです。リチャード・マイヤーはたぶんやりたいことをあらかじめ想定しています。安藤忠雄もそうでしょう，知っているわけではありませんし，確かではありません。しかし，自分はそうしないことが分かっていますし，アイディアは状況に依存してい

るわけですから，仕事を常に先に進めていたいのです。先に進めるほど，作品は良くなって行くだろうといつも信じているのです。頭のなかではそれは最善のものにはならず，組み立てるにつれて悪くなって行きます。実際に始めると，建てるに連れて良くなって行く。ですから，金をたくさんもち，時間も金も問題にしない，非常に忍耐強い施主がいれば，たぶん，デザインし続け，ゆっくりと建物を展開させます。しかし私は実践的でもあり，私の施主も現実的ですから，私は喜んで受け入れ，プロセスに制限をおきます。知っているかもしれませんが，私たちはリフキンド邸にいくつか手を加えることになっています。あの家が完成したとき，図書室を気に入っていないことは知っていました。施主は，この家が田舎にあるため，そこで仕事をする必要があり，どこかニューヨークで仕事をしているように感じられることが必要でした。プラスティックの集成材を使い，ニューヨークのオフィスのような，少し冷たい感じにしました。施主がそう望んだからです。私たちは賛成しませんでしたが，望み通りにしたのです。この方法でつくることはできますが，居心地よくないと思いますよと説明したのです。結局私たちは正しかったわけです。展開しつづけることで，良くなっていくものがあるのです。事務所にとっては困ったことかもしれませんが，私は，リフキンド夫妻が私たちのところに戻ってきて，「よろしい，書斎を変えて，正しくする準備ができた」と言われてとても幸せでした。そして，どのように彼らのプログラムを翻案できるか，この部屋が彼らにとって良くなるようにどうやってできるか考えることを幸運だと感じてます。これこそ，私が建物を進めて行き

tical line. And these two things are almost independent in some point and then they come together at other points. It is this interrelationship that can be interesting. And what you'll never see is that I have a square. I mean there's never a fixed square, it's almost always sliding, even the way we stack stone is always sliding. So the eye slides, moves, and is not fixed in a single position. When you come in a space there should be a moment where you see it but I don't think it should be fixed and static.

GA: This kind of movement is very different from your early work. Do you ever look back to it?

TW: I don't really deny it, but there was a point when I was very interested in the defined object, the defined facade. What a threshold was, what a window was, and that was something that was generally in the air. It was a point in time when post-modernism was very strong. I wasn't a very strong post-modernist but I was very much influenced by it and was trying to find that static sense, the fixed sense of what architecture could be. I was searching for something that you could fix in time, fix in space, and fix in history. There was a historical idea of what a window was in my head. That was a short period that I think was very important for my development so I accept that I was there, I don't deny it. But I'm happier not to be there because I don't think perfection, or the ideal, is something you can preconceive.

GA: Today there is a fascination with light architecture. What is your take on this?

TW: I believe that architecture is basically heavy. It has mass. Ando probably believes that it has to have more mass than we do, but I believe that architecture is basically heavy. I think light exists in contrast to mass. And I think the basic act of building is one of mass and what is light can be released by understanding mass. The wooden house is not essentially a heavy house type but I would say that this house is heavy in the sense that it is bound to the earth. The extensive use of wood in the house tends to make it a little bit more weighty. It connects it more to the earth. The stone fireplace of course makes it even more connected to the earth. And some of the vertical mullions of the windows help to ground it, and the horizontal lines connect it to the earth in the sense that it extends into the horizon. All these things help to bind the house to the earth, although not all of them are about weight.

GA: Do you have any opinion about American residential design, how it's going to change in the future as lifestyles change? I often get the sense that people are less interested in space as long as they have the modern comforts, a couch and a television.

TW: Well, in that respect I'm very traditional. I believe that because life is ever faster in the way in which it changes and the way in which we posses all the surface of the earth and none of it at the same time. Because of the speed with which society is moving I think that's all the more reason why we need to locate ourselves on the surface of the earth. I would say that it's up to the architect to find the appropriate anchors or ties. That's why I believe that this house should be a house for that particular place in Long Island and not anyplace else. I'm looking for ways to connect us to this earth and I think this is very important. I don't think it's the same everywhere because I think it's different because of the climate and so on. I think that increasingly you will see that America and other countries will be open to different ways of solving problems. If we look back a hundred years, a Japanese house was rather well defined, but today, a Japanese house is defined in many different ways. And in another hundred years, when Japan is really open and maybe many other people are living in Japan and the Japanese are living elsewhere on the earth, we will find that it will be even less singular. I think it will be very plural and in America particularly because we're made of so many different kinds of people and America itself has many different kinds of climates and topographies. I think there are many opportunities for us to find different ways we can make an appropriate house on this earth. Will that be confusing? Probably. The idea of isolated societies which was possible to some extent 1000 years ago, 500 years ago, even 50 years ago in some very special places, will not be possible in the near future. I hope there will be conflict, and then we then can begin to resolve what the earth is about, what we are about as a society that inhabits this earth. I think there are a lot of possibilities for us in our lifetime, and I think that it's an interesting time because of these possibilities, but I don't think we can pretend to know any answers. The house is a chance to explore our relationship to place. Our place here in New York, for example. That's why I like the house as a problem. It's particularly complicated, but I don't ever want to be a house expert. I'm happy because this is a way of coming back to a kind of touchstone for us as architects.

(at office of TWBT, New York, November, 1999)

たいと思う方法なのです。ある選択肢がみえたとき，工事中であっても，より良い決定ができるところに常にいたいのです。そして，理由が何であれ——私の不備あるいは施主の不備，あるいは予算，またはわれわれが正しく理解していない，敷地には不可能な何かがあったにせよ，図書室でやったことを見るとがっかりします。何が完璧になりうるか，前もって知ることはないのです。ですから，発展させて行く感覚，常にデザインしていることは，私には大切な仕事の側面なのです。

GA 知りたいことが一つあります。あなたの作品におけるプロポーション感覚です。なぜ興味があるかというと，リフキンド邸の天井はとても高いことに気づいたからです。フランク・ロイド・ライトは，水平な広がりといった特定の経験をつくりだすために天井を低くしていますが，それはまたライトの個人的な寸法感覚と関係しています。プロポーションの問題についておたずねしたいのですが。デザインするとき，プロポーションをどのように決めているのか。また何がその決定に働いているのか。

TW 天井がそんなに高いと感じるか自分でも分からないのですが。あなたの言うように，これは単に私の個人的感覚であるのかもしれない。リフキンド邸には3種類の高さがあります。一つは低いもので，意識的に低くしたものだったと思います——不思議なことにリフキンド夫妻はかなり背が低いのに，すべて背の高いものにすることを望んでいました。私は背が高いのに，低いものが好きなんです。

GA 天井の高さだけでなく，空間のプロポーションはどうですか？

TW 私が重要だと信じているのは，頭のなかに正しい，予測されたプロポーションなどないということです。それをスタディすることが必要で，模型で検証し，空間内部ではどうなるかを見ることが必要です。正方形や黄金分割は私には必ずしも何も意味しません。そのなかにあるものや，それ自身に価値があると信じていますが，それは正しい決定をするための一種の出発点であり，この正しい決定は予測できるようなものではないのです。一つ発見できるとすれば，私がスケールの変化を強く信じていることです。この点ではフランク・ロイド・ライトと共有しているものがあると思います。ライトは非常に圧縮された空間を背の高い空間へと解き放つ方法を使っています。私の作品のほとんどには，空間全体のディメンションを知覚できる場所があります。たとえば，リフキンド邸には，部屋全体のディメンションを感じとれる場所が3つある。リビングルームでは，一方の端から，食堂の一方の端まで見通せます。寝室ウィングの廊下に立てば，2つのドアを開けて，一方の端から次の端まで見えるのです。それは寝室でも同じことです。つまり，あの家のいくつかの地点で，非常に長く引き延ばされたディメンションを感じてほしかったのです。またリビングルームの床から天井までの高さ全体を，背の高いヴォリュームとして経験してほしいとも思いました。他のところでは圧縮させたいですから，必要な小さな空間のプロポーションとも関われます。しかしまた，小さなものから，中間のもの，大きなもの，あるいは小さなものから大きなものへの変化も感じられます。スケールの幅はこの住宅ではとても成功していると思います。これが層構成の家（レイヤード・ハウス）と呼ぶ理由でもあるのです。現実に，アプローチは3種類の基本的な高さと関わっています。一つは7フィートに少しプラス，もう一つは9フィートレベル，さらに一つは11フィートレベルです。つまりスケールによる一連の段差があるのです。それが一種レイヤーによる効果を与えます。視線は底から頂部へと広がり，視線を空間の長さに沿って広げますが，ある地点でそれは止められ，視線は側面へそれてゆく。すべての住宅にこの方法が必要かどうかは分かりませんが，この住宅，この敷地には，このレイヤーを必要とする何かがあるのです。やはり，何かを意味する完璧なプロポーションがあるとは全く信じません。

GA しかし，自分のプロポーション・システムをもっていると思います。あなたの作品のなかに誰でもそれを認めるはずです。

TW プロポーションに対する感覚があることは認めます。それは私にとって重要なものですが，定量化できるようなものではないのです。ほとんどの建築的状況のなかでは，建物は水平と垂直のディメンションからつくられます。それらはお互いに関係しているわけですが，水平はその水平線を見つける必要があり，垂直はその垂直線を見つける必要があります。そしてこれら2つのことは，ある地点ではほとんど独立しており，また別の地点でひとつになります。面白いのはこの相互関係なのです。私が正方形を使っているのを見ることはまず不可能でしょう。固定した正方形は絶対に存在させないという意味ですが。それはほとんど常にスライドしており，石を積む方法でさえ常にそうなので，目は滑り，動き，一つの位置に固定されることはありません。ある空間に入るとき，それを見る瞬間があるはずです。しかしそれが固定し，静止すべきであるとは思いま

Grodd Residence, 1996

せん。
GA このやり方は初期の作品とはかなり違います。その点を振り返ってみたことがありますか？
TW そのことをまったく否定はしませんが，はっきりと規定された物体，はっきりと規定されたファサードにとても興味をもった時期がありました。敷居とは何か，窓とは何か，そしてそのほとんどが未解決のままでした。ポスト・モダニズムが盛んなときでした。熱心なポスト・モダニストというわけではありませんでしたが，それにかなりの影響を受け，建築がそうあるはずの，あの静止的な感覚，固定的な感覚を見つけようとしていました。時間のなかに，空間のなかに，歴史のなかに固定できる何かを探していました。頭のなかには，窓とは何かという歴史に基づいた考えがつまっていました。私の成長過程のなかで非常に重要な短い時期だったと思いますから，そこにいたことを受け入れますし，それを否定しません。しかし，そこにとどまらないほうが幸せです。完璧性や理想は，予測可能なものであるとは思わないからです。
GA 今，軽い建築に対する一種の熱狂があります。これをどう受け取っていますか？
TW 建築は基本的には重いものだと信じています。マッスをもっています。安藤はたぶん，私たちがしているよりもっとマッスをもたせなければならないと思っているかもしれませんが，軽さはマッスとの対比において存在すると思います。そして，建物の基本的行為はマッスのひとつであり，軽さというものはマッスを理解することで解放されるのです。木造の家は本質的には重いタイプの家ではありませんが，大地につながっているという意味において重い

と，私なら言うでしょう。この住宅では木を広範に使っていますから，少し重すぎる傾きがあります。それは土地に建物を結びつけます。石の暖炉は，もちろん，建物をさらに土地に結びつけています。窓の垂直なマリオンのいくつかも建物を地に据える助けをしていますし，水平な線も，水平線に広がって行くという意味で建物を土地に結んでいます。これらのことすべてが——そのすべてが重さに関わっているものでないにもかかわらず——この家を地につなげることを助けています。
GA アメリカの住宅デザインをどう思いますか。ライフスタイルの変化に伴って，将来それはどんなふうに変わって行くのでしょうか？ 現代的な安逸，カウチ，テレビを手にした長い間に，空間に対する関心が薄れているとよく感じるのですが。
TW その点については，私はとても伝統的な考え方をしています。生活の変化は絶えまなく速くなり，あらゆる地表を埋め尽くしながら，それでいて何もないからこそ，私はそのことを信じているのです。社会の動きの速さに，大地の上に自身を落ち着かせることが必要だという理由のすべてがあるのだと思います。つまり適切な碇やきずなを見つけることが建築家にかかっていると言いたいのです。それが，リフキンド邸が，他のどこでもなく，ロングアイランドの特定の場所のためのものであるべきだと信じる理由です。私たちをこの土地に結びつける方法を探しているのであり，これがとても大切だと思います。それはどこでも同じだとは思いません。違っているのです。気候などが違いますから。アメリカや他の国々が，問題を解く方法に対してますます開かれるだろうと思います。100年前を振り返れば，日

本の住宅は明確に定義されていましたが，今は多様な定義が可能です。また，100年が過ぎ，日本がほんとうに開かれたとき，他の国の人が多く住むようになり，日本人も地球上の至る所に住むようになるとき，特異性はさらに希薄になっているでしょう。高度な複合社会になっているでしょうし，アメリカは特にそうだと思います。多民族で構成され，アメリカの土地そのものも多彩な気候と地形をもっているからです。この地球上に適切な家をつくることのできる異なった方法を見つける機会がたくさんあるのだと思います。それは困惑することでしょうか？ たぶん，そうかもしれない。千年前，五百年前に，五十年前でさえ特定の場所のいくつかでは可能であった，孤立した社会という考えは，近い将来，不可能になるでしょう。それについて論争があってほしいと思います。そこから，地球について，この地球に根を下ろす社会について答えを見つけ始めることができますから。一生のあいだに，私たちには多くの可能性があると思いますし，これらの可能性ゆえに興味深い時代だと思いますが，どのような答えも知っているふりはできません。住宅は場所との関係を探求する機会なのです。たとえば，私たちの場所はここニューヨークにあります。課題としての住宅が好きな理由はこのためなのです。とても複雑ですが，住宅のエキスパートになりたいと思ったことはありません。私は幸福です。なぜなら，建築家としての私たちにとって，住宅設計は，一種の試金石へと立ち返る方法なのですから。

（1999年11月，ニューヨーク，ＴＷＢＴ事務所にて）

TOD WILLIAMS
BILLIE TSIEN

RIFKIND RESIDENCE
Georgica Pond, Long Island,
N.Y., U.S.A.
Design: 1996–97
Construction: 1997–98

Photos: Y. Futagawa

Overall view from east

The clients, a busy professional couple with grown children asked us to design a house that would be marked by quiet serenity, an openness to the landscape and a sense of spaciousness without monumentality. They wanted a house that would provide a civilized, relaxed setting, sympathetic to needs for privacy and for sociability, that would serve as a weekend retreat, a "place apart"; an antidote to the intensity of New York and the compression of apartment life.

The house is sited on three acres at the edge of a large pond, with distant views of the ocean. Beautiful mature pitch pines surround the site, and woods and thicket separate it from its neighbors. The parking area is kept at a distance from the buildings and screened by bushes. The house has been kept low, 11 feet four inches exterior height primarily, with 17 feet elevation and clerestory only in the living room. The living space is all on one level, except for a small reading loft and outdoor balcony intended to afford a varient inward and outward point of view.

The house is comprised of four volumes: the public spaces, a master bedroom wing, a guest wing and a planting and storage shed. The first three volumes are connected by glass passageways. So as to preserve maximum openness to the outdoors the house has not been air-conditioned and takes advantages of cross breezes by the careful placement of operable windows.

The central pavilion contains the kitchen at its center, with living room on one side and dining room on the other and small reading loft above.

The master bedroom wing includes dressing area, a large bathroom with indoor and outdoor showers, and a study. The guest wing contains three bedrooms, each with its own bathroom. To make the house as inviting as possible to the children and other visitors, each of the guest rooms frames a distinctive view of the land and has its own door to the outside. One of the guest bedrooms includes a sitting room area to serve the wing.

The house is wood frame with cedar exterior siding. Douglas fir panels are used or the inside of the exterior walls. The interior and exterior window frames are mahogany. Floors are Douglas fir and New York bluestone in honed and split face, The fireplace chimney which is the dominant element in the living room, is also faced in splitface bluestone. Built-in bookshelves, beds, dressers and custom furniture are American cherry.

We tried to design a house whose own aesthetic order would compliment the surroundings and provide a variety of new ways to see and appreciate the beauty of the land. The articulation of the volumes was meant to be at once serene and stimulating, simple and complex. The house does not present itself all at once but unfolds as one walks through or around it. Its immediate relationship to the landscape results in changing qualities of light and shadow throughout the day and seasons. We hope that it connects the rhythm of lives and nature in a new way.

Architects: Tod Williams Billie Tsien and Associates—Tod Williams, Billie Tsien, principals-in-charge; Peter Arnold, project architect
Clients: Robert and Aileen Rifkind
Consultants: Severud Associates, structural; Steven Iino, cabinetmaker (various tables, credenza, furniture)
General contractor: Andreassen and Bulgin
Structural system: Wood frame supporting glue lam continuous roof beam
Major materials: Cedar siding, Mahogany (Duratherm) windows, Doug. fir floors + Wood paneling, Honed + split face New York blue stone for floors + chimney
Custom built-in woodwork: American cherry, Lead coated copper fascia

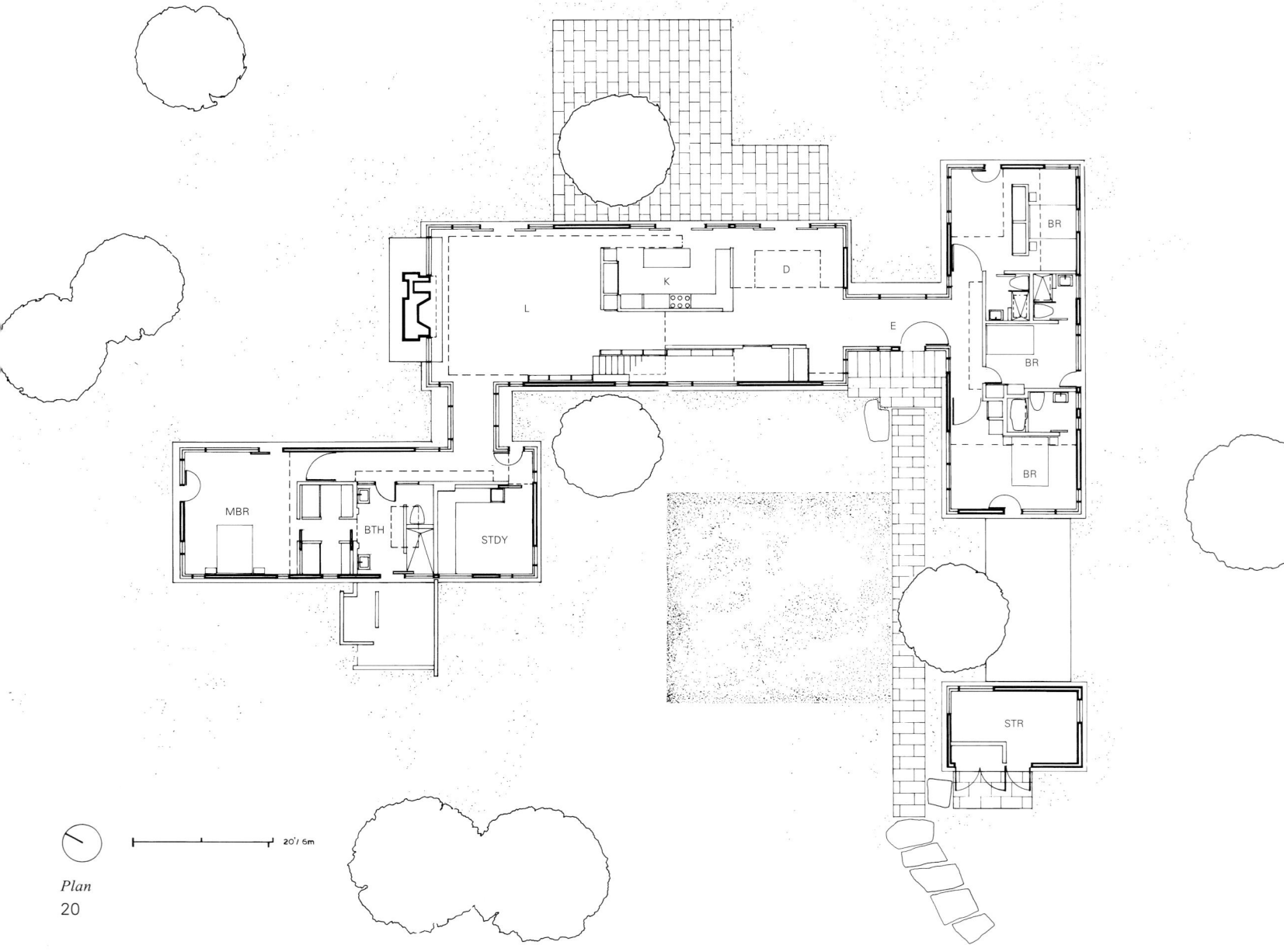

Plan

Model ©TWBT

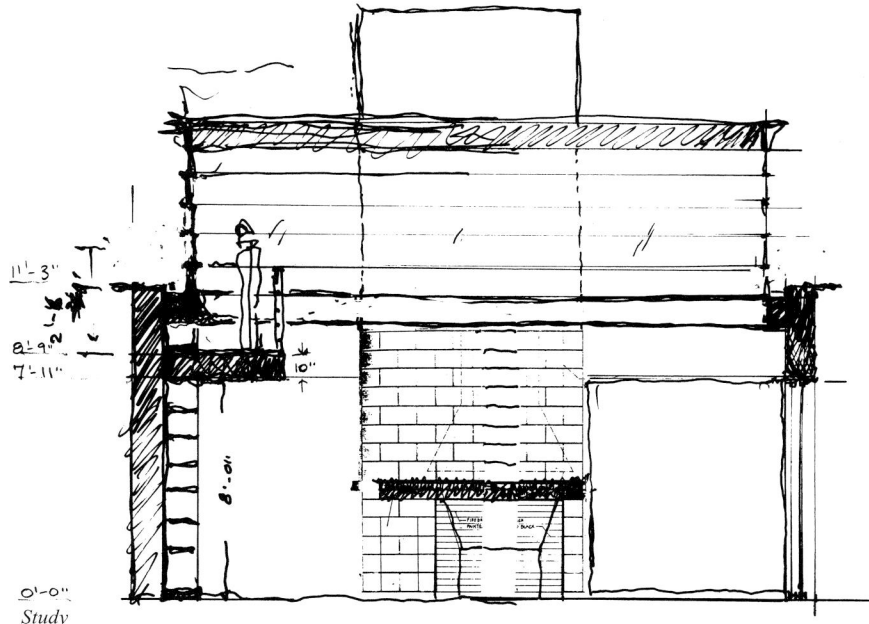

Study

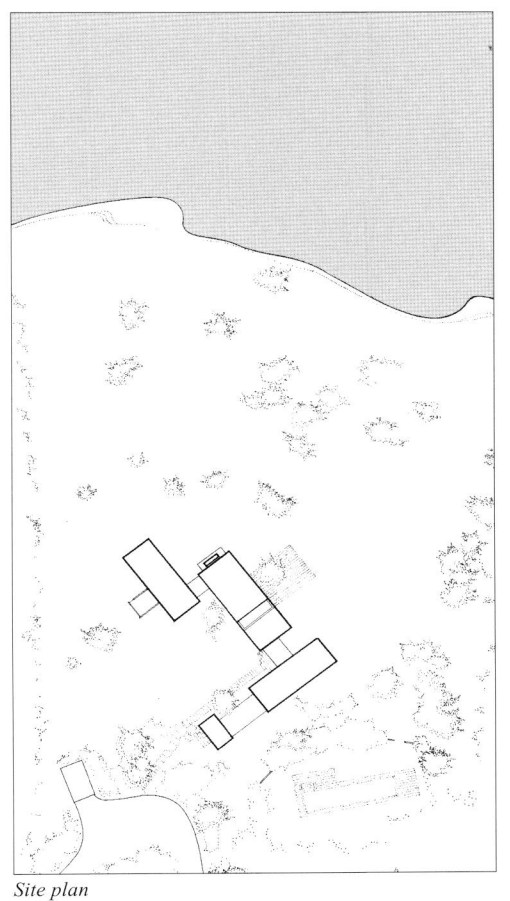

Site plan

　すでに子供も大きくなっている，専門職をもつ多忙な夫妻から，静けさに満ち，風景に開き，大袈裟ではないが広々とした空間を備えた住宅の設計を依頼された。ニューヨークでの厳しい仕事とアパート生活の圧迫感から解放してくれる週末の隠れ家つまり"離れるための場所"，洗練されていながらくつろいだ構成をもち，私的生活にも公的生活にも気持ちよく対応できる家が夫妻の要望である。

　大きな池のほとりに広がる3エーカーの敷地で，海が遠くに見える。大きく成熟した美しいヤニマツの木立に囲まれ，林と灌木の茂みが隣家との境界をつくっている。パーキング・エリアは建物から離され，藪で目隠しされている。家は低く抑えられ，外壁の高さは大体が11フィート4インチ，リビングルームだけが17フィートあり，高窓が付いている。内外に向けてさまざまな眺めが楽しめる場所とすることを考えた小さな読書用ロフトと屋外バルコニーを除いて，すべて1層である。

　4つの棟が全体を構成している。パブリック・スペース，主寝室ウイング，ゲスト・ウイング，園芸／収納小屋。最初の3棟は互いにガラス張りの通路でつながっている。戸外への開放性を最大限保つために，エアコンは設置せずに，開閉可能な窓を慎重に配置することで，自然換気を活用する。

　中央の棟は，真ん中に台所があり，その片側にリビングルーム，反対側にダイニングルーム，上に小さな読書用ロフトがある。主寝室ウイングには，ドレッシング・エリアと屋外屋内両方にシャワーの付いた広い浴室，書斎が付いている。ゲスト・ウイングは3寝室で構成され，それぞれに浴室が付いている。子供たちやその他の泊まり客が，できるだけ気持ちよく滞在できるように，各部屋には美しい眺めが見える開口がとられ，外に直接出られる専用のドアがある。寝室の一つには，ゲスト・ウイング共有の居間が配置されている。

　建物は木造枠組に外壁はシーダーの下見。外壁の内張りにはダグラス樅のパネルが使われている。窓の内枠と外枠はマホガニー。床はダグラス樅と面を研ぎ出して割ったニューヨーク産のブルーストーン。リビングルームの中心的存在である暖炉の煙突にもブルーストーンの割石が使われている。造り付けの書棚，ベッド，ドレッサー，特注の家具はアメリカン・チェリー。

　建物を構成する独自の美的形式が，周辺風景を補足し，この土地の美しさを観賞し味わうのに，以前にはなかった多彩な方法を与えるようにデザインしようとつとめた。ヴォリュームの分節は，静かでありながら刺激的，単純でありながら複雑なものとなるように意識した。この家はその姿を一度にみせることはない，その内部や周囲を歩いて行くうちに徐々に開かれてくるのである。風景と直接つながっていることが，一日のなかで，季節のなかで，光や影の変化をつくりだす。それが生命のリズムと自然を新しい方法で結びつけてほしいと思う。

View from north

Public space wing

Master bedroom wing on left

Guest wing ▷

View towards entrance

Guest wing (left) and public space wing (right)

Entrance

Dining area on left

Dining area on right

Kitchen

View toward living room from kitchen ▷

Living room

Study on mezzanin level

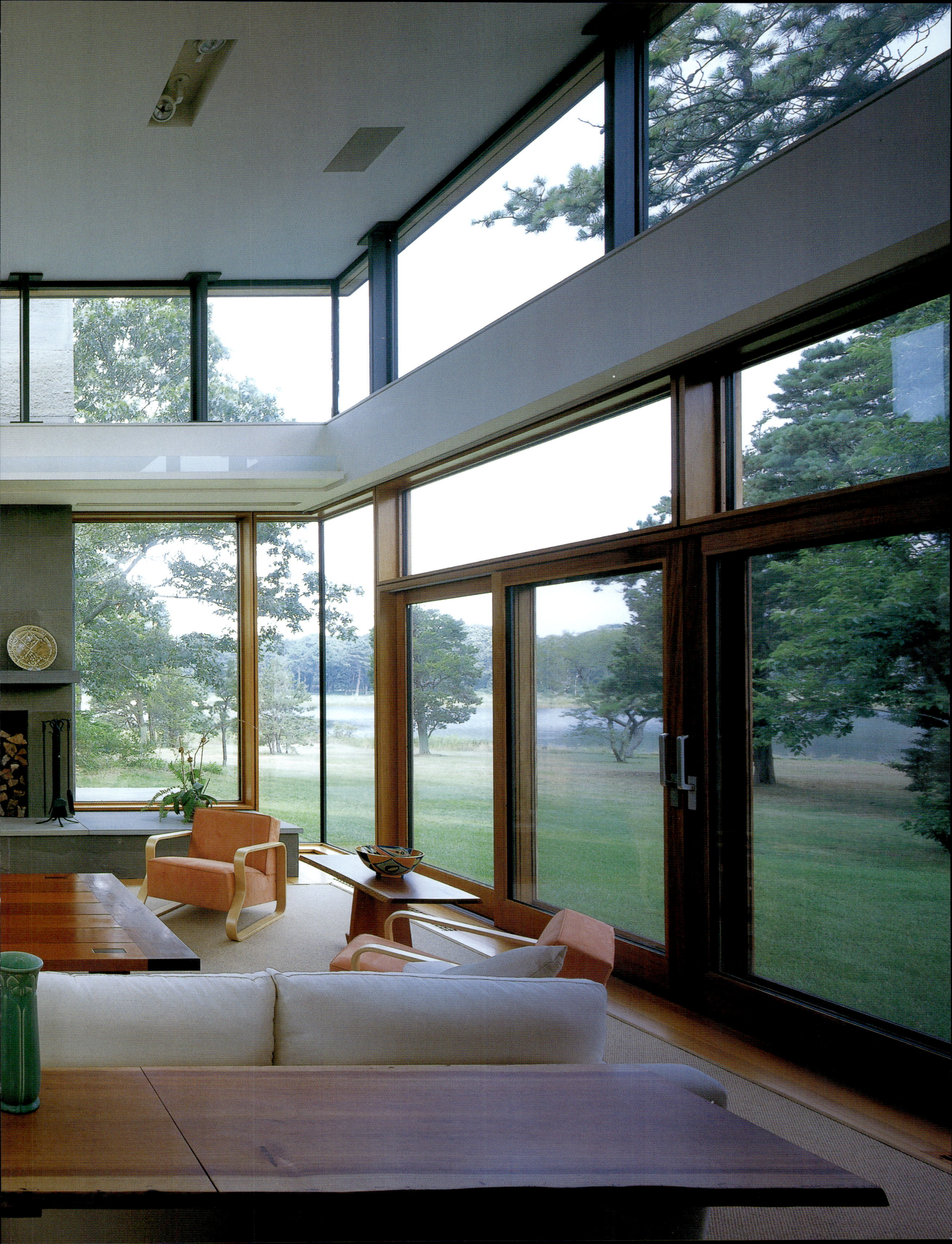

Master bedroom

Guest room

Guest room

Study

Terrace

Detail

Bathroom

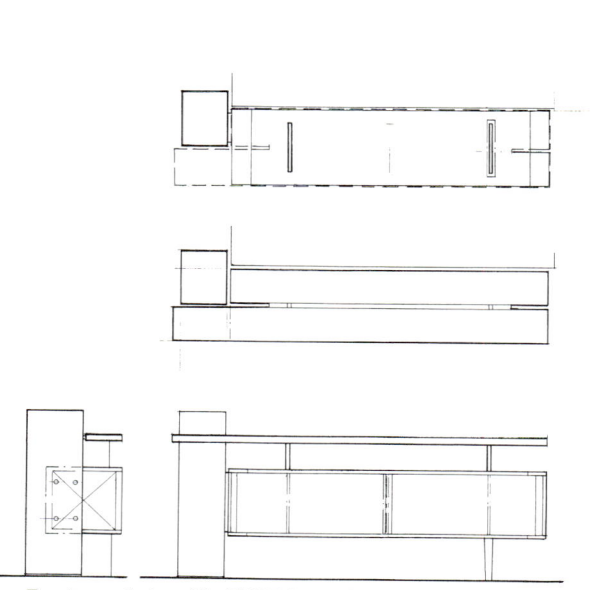

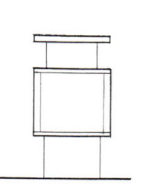

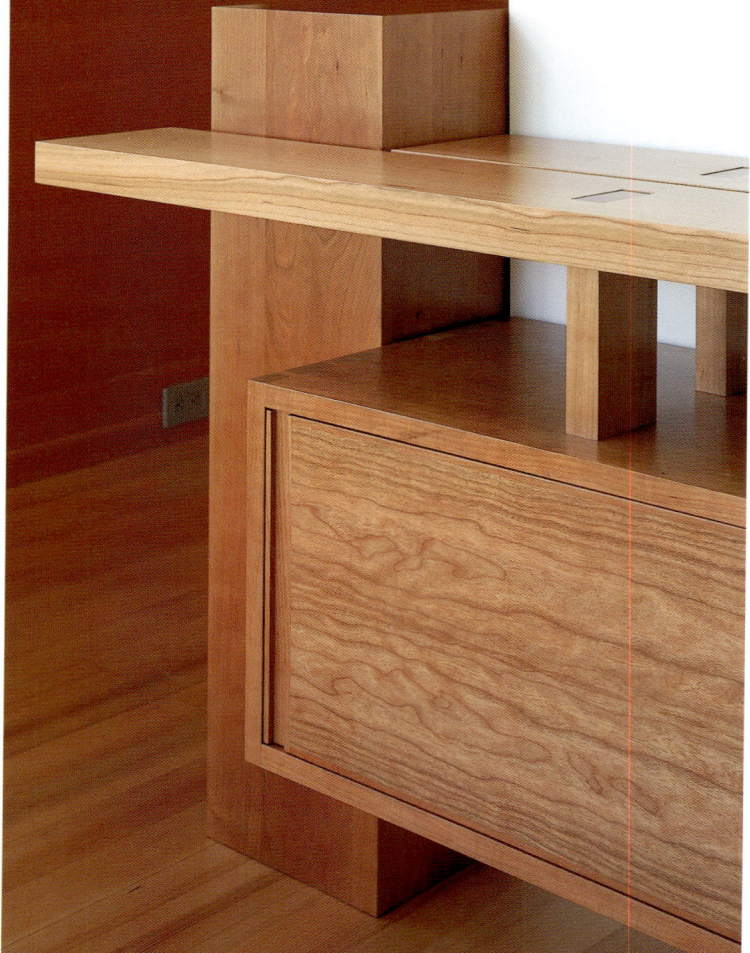

Furniture: designed by TWBT / manufactured by Steven Iino

41

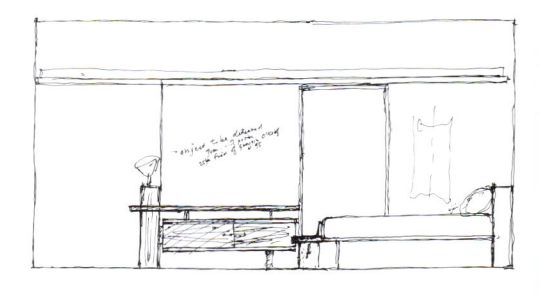

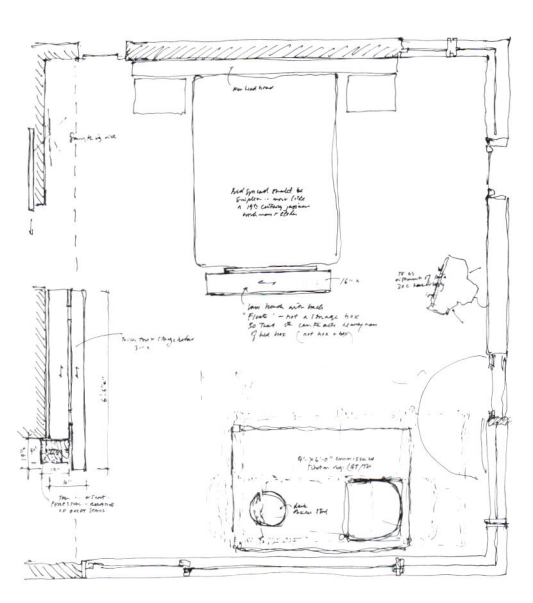

ALBERTO KALACH

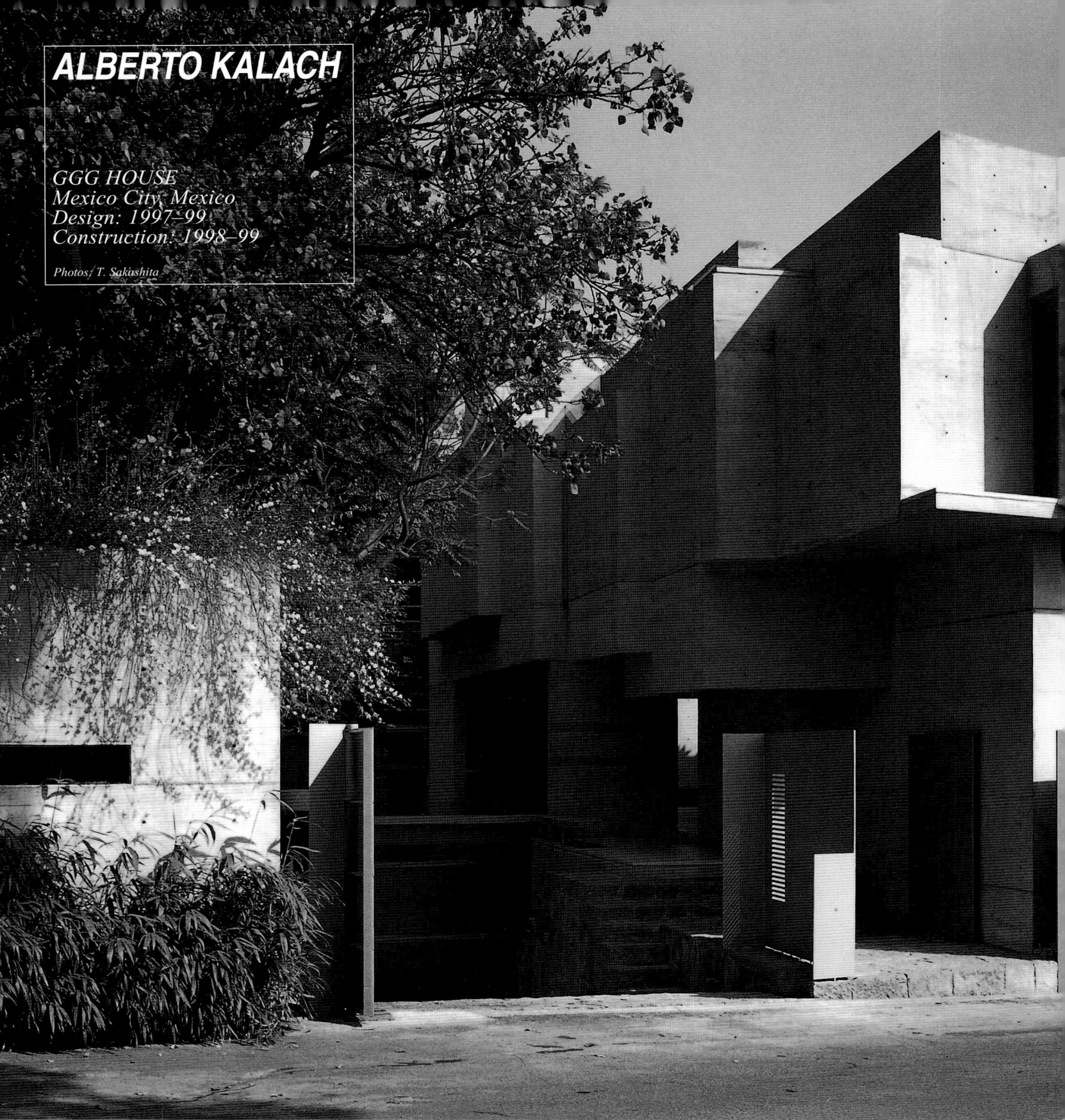

GGG HOUSE
Mexico City, Mexico
Design: 1997–99
Construction: 1998–99

Photos: T. Sakashita

Entrance

The house could be seen as the most simple and yet the most complex and exiting architectural theme. I understand it as a passage that transport their inhabitants from the every day life, the street, to an inner world of intimacy. The succession of spaces that are discovered always indirectly, diagonally or at a turn without being seen until you enter to each of them, are the scenario to compel the human act, but also they conform a plot in itself.

Its spatial idea, inspired in the work of the sculptor Jorge Yazpik, starts with a basic accommodation of the program, that allow afterwards, with more freedom, the exploration of spatial relations through clay models. Each indentation or cut in the mass suggest the next one, in a progressive work where the space is discovered rather than invented, until reaching the final volume.

The house is imagined as a great concrete monolith that is fragmented geometrically and progressively within a spatial network defined by the successive inscription of sphere within cube, and this within a sphere.

The light filters through the cracks as rays, but at times light explodes softly flooding the spaces. The shadows, the brightness and the penumbra, enliven the passages through the house and contrasts the spaces marking the time flow. Gardens, pools, patios, pavilions and alcoves, are linked by the cracks that break the monolith.

The general volumes of the house respond to

Second floor

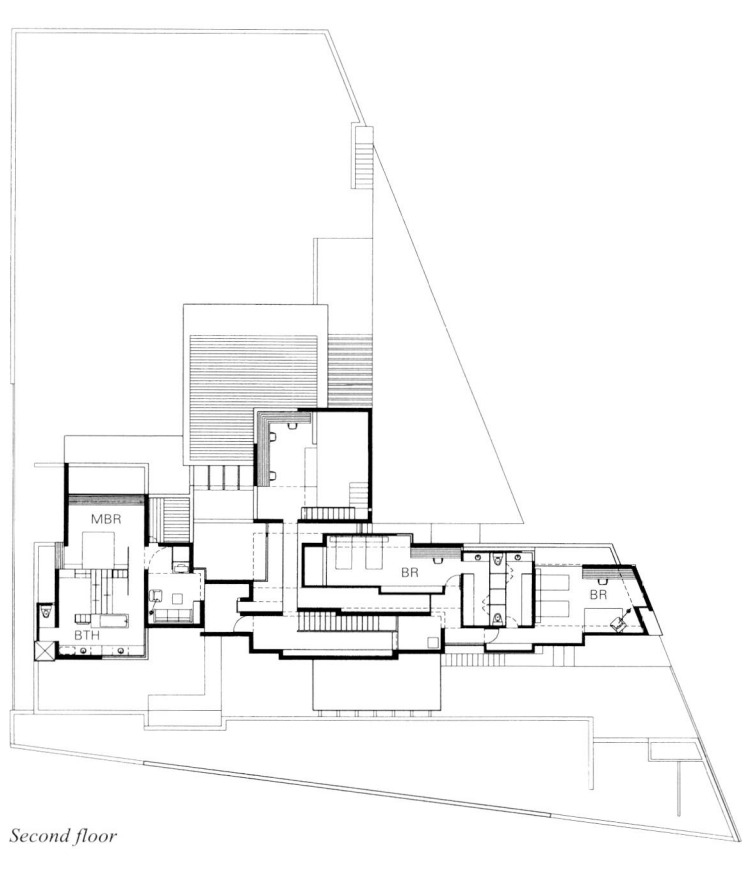

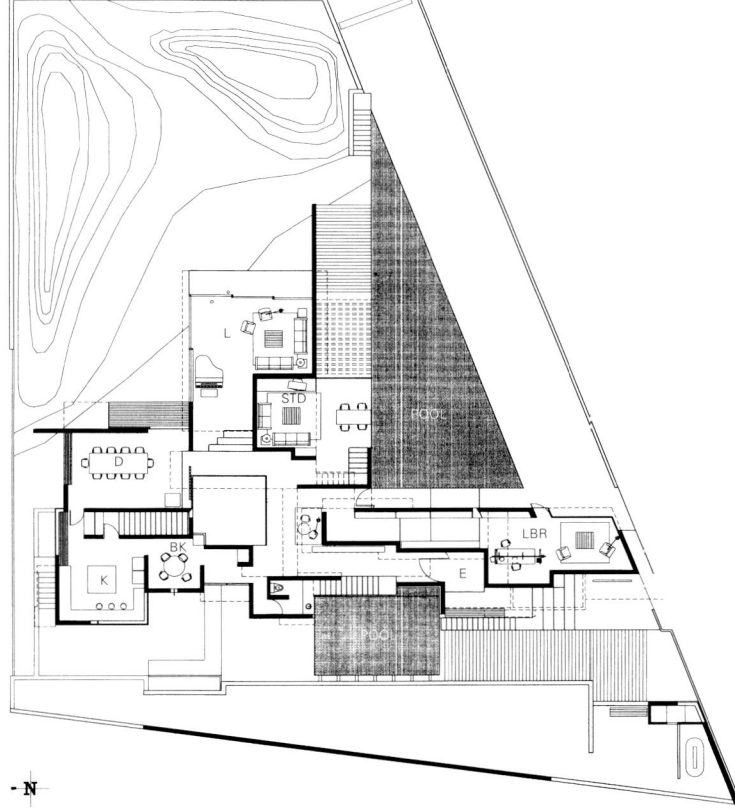

Ground floor

the compelling location of the site, wedged between a beautiful golf course, a warehouse and a five story apartment building.

Architects: Alberto Kalach—Alberto Kalach-Guilermo Gonzalez, principals-in-charge; Félix Madrazo, project team
Client: GGG
Consultants: Javier Juárez, Jesus Bravo, supervisor; Enrique Martinez Romero, structural; Rafael Lopez, mechanical; Jorge Segura, José Chavez, steel work; Abelardo Palma, carpenter; Tonatiuh Martínez, landscape; Fausto Serrano, scaffolding
General contractor: Miguel Cornejo
Structural system: Continuos concrete carcass, reinforced concrete
Major materials: Concrete, travertine, "Nogal" wood
Site area: 1500 m^2
Total floor area: 770 m^2
Cost of construction: $1,000,000

East view from garden

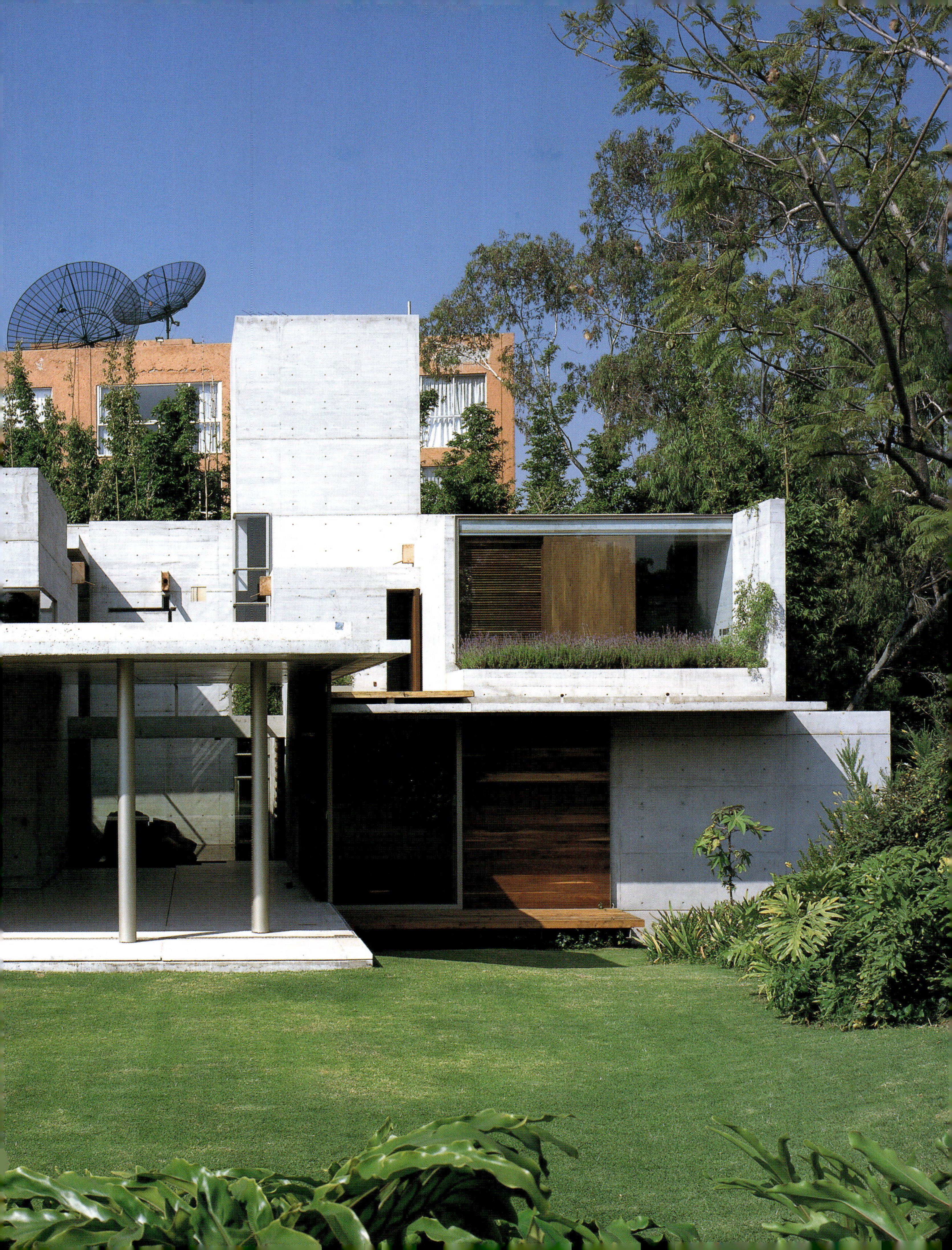

この住宅は，極めて単純でありながら，極めて複雑で刺激的な建築テーマを表現していると言い得るだろう。わたしはこの家を，住む人を日常性や街路から，心地よい内部世界へ運ぶ通路であると理解している。連続して行く内部空間は——その一つ一つに入るまで空間は知覚されず，常に間接的に，対角方向に，屈折点に発見される——人の動きを強要するためのシナリオであるが，また空間自身のもつプロットに従ってもいる。

こうした空間に対する考え方は，彫刻家ホルヘ・ヤズピクの作品に啓発されたもので，まずプログラムに対応する基本的な枠組みをつくってから，粘土模型によって，空間関係をさらに自由に，探求して行くことができる。マッスに刻みや切り込みを入れて行くたびに次の切り込みへ導かれる。それは，最終的なヴォリューム構成に至るまで，空間を創造するというよりむしろ発見して行く作業である。

この家は，幾何学形態によって次々に断片化されてゆく巨大なコンクリート・モノリスとして構想されている。そこでは，キューブのなかに球，キューブは球のなかにと，継続的に刻みこむことで構成された空間のネットワークが生まれている。

光は細い亀裂から光線の束となって浸透するが，ときどき，柔らかに広がって空間をあふれるように満たす。明と暗，そしてその境界域が家全体にわたって通路を生き生きさせ，時の流れを刻印しながら空間を対比させる。

庭園，プール，パティオ，東屋，アルコーヴはモノリスを破る亀裂によってつながれている。

この家の全体的なヴォリュームは，美しいゴルフコース，納屋そして5階建てのアパートのあいだに楔のように割り込んだ，制約の多い敷地のロケーションに対する解答である。

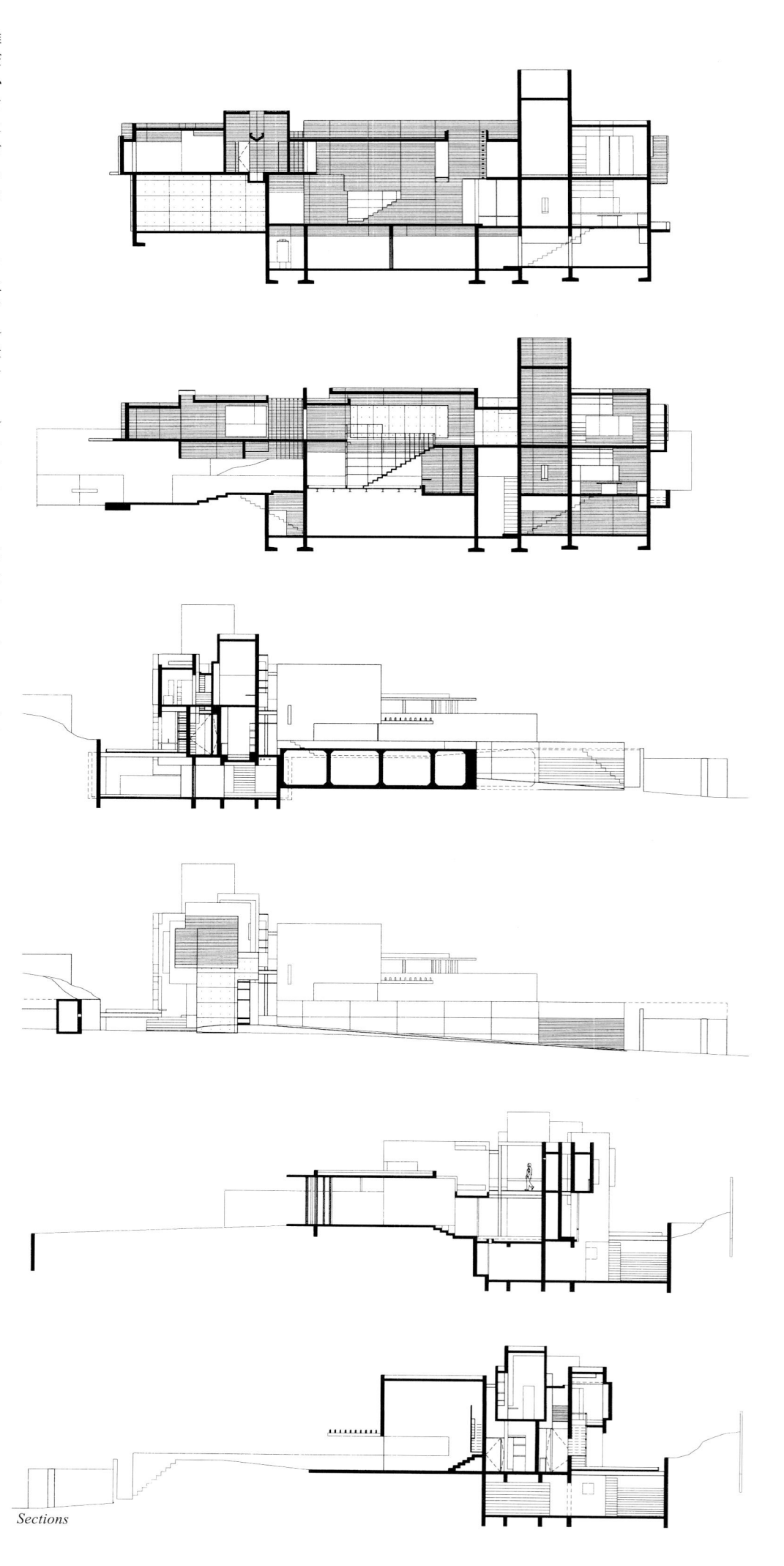

Sections

View from northeast

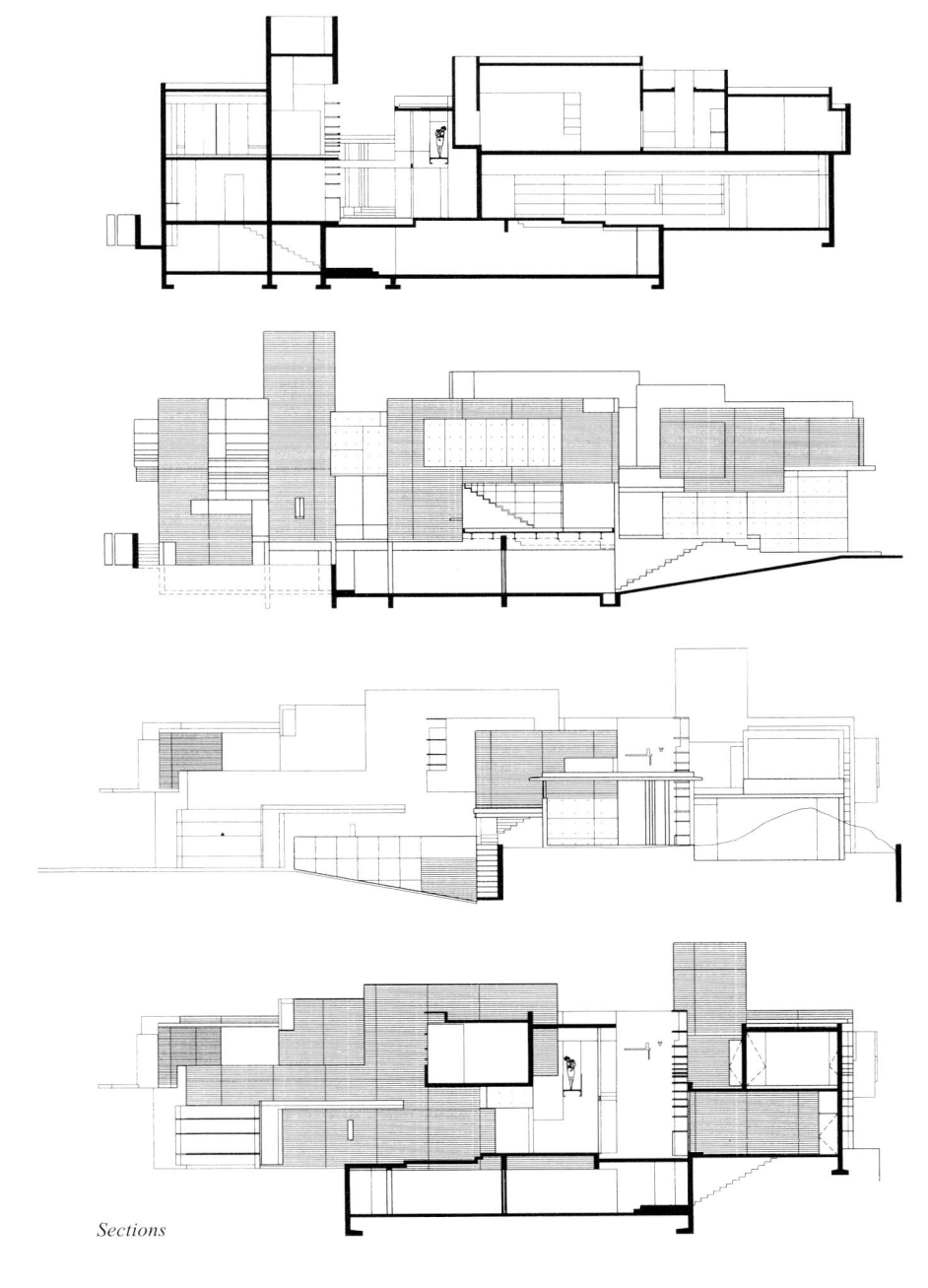

Sections

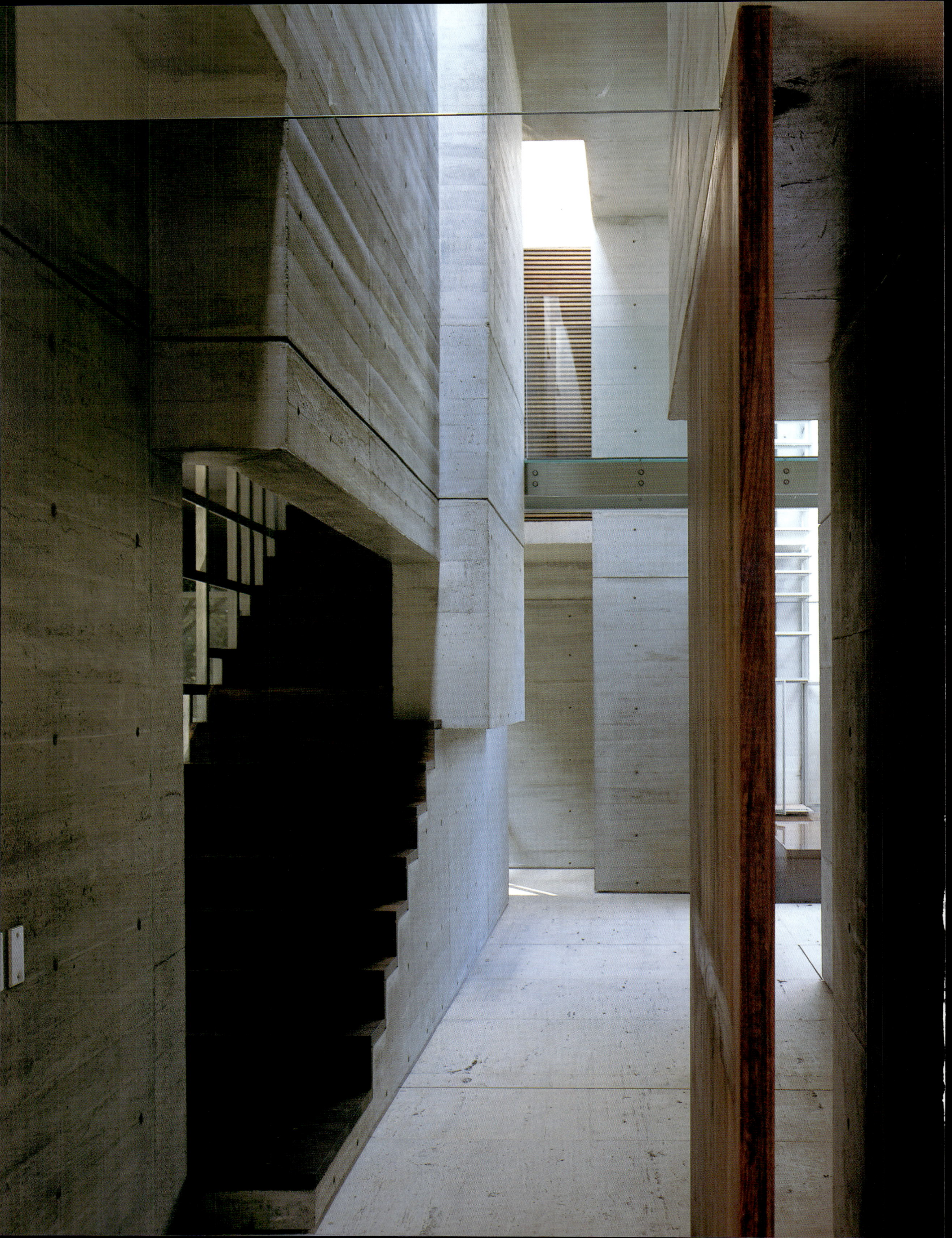

View toward entrance on west

Entrance

◁ *Hall: view from entrance*

Hall: view toward entrance

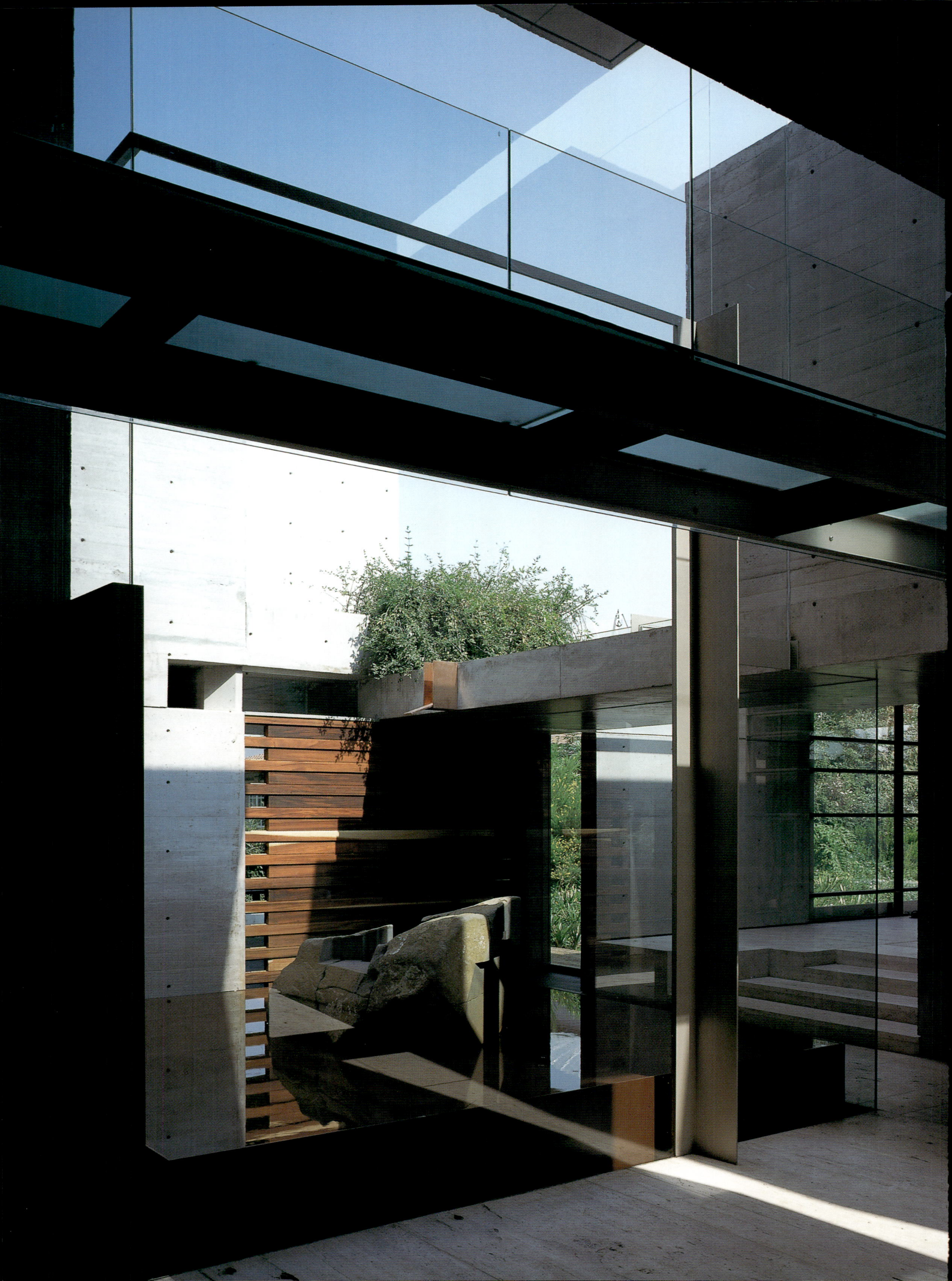

▽ Patio △ View toward living room

Patio

Patio: view from second floor

Living room

Patio of studio

Pool on southeast

View from south

Studio

View toward patio from studio

Roof terrace

Dining room

Kitchen

56

▽ Living room   △ Glass bridge

Window detail

Roof terrace

Hall on second floor

Skylight *Skylight*

Bedroom

Skylit corridor on second floor ▷

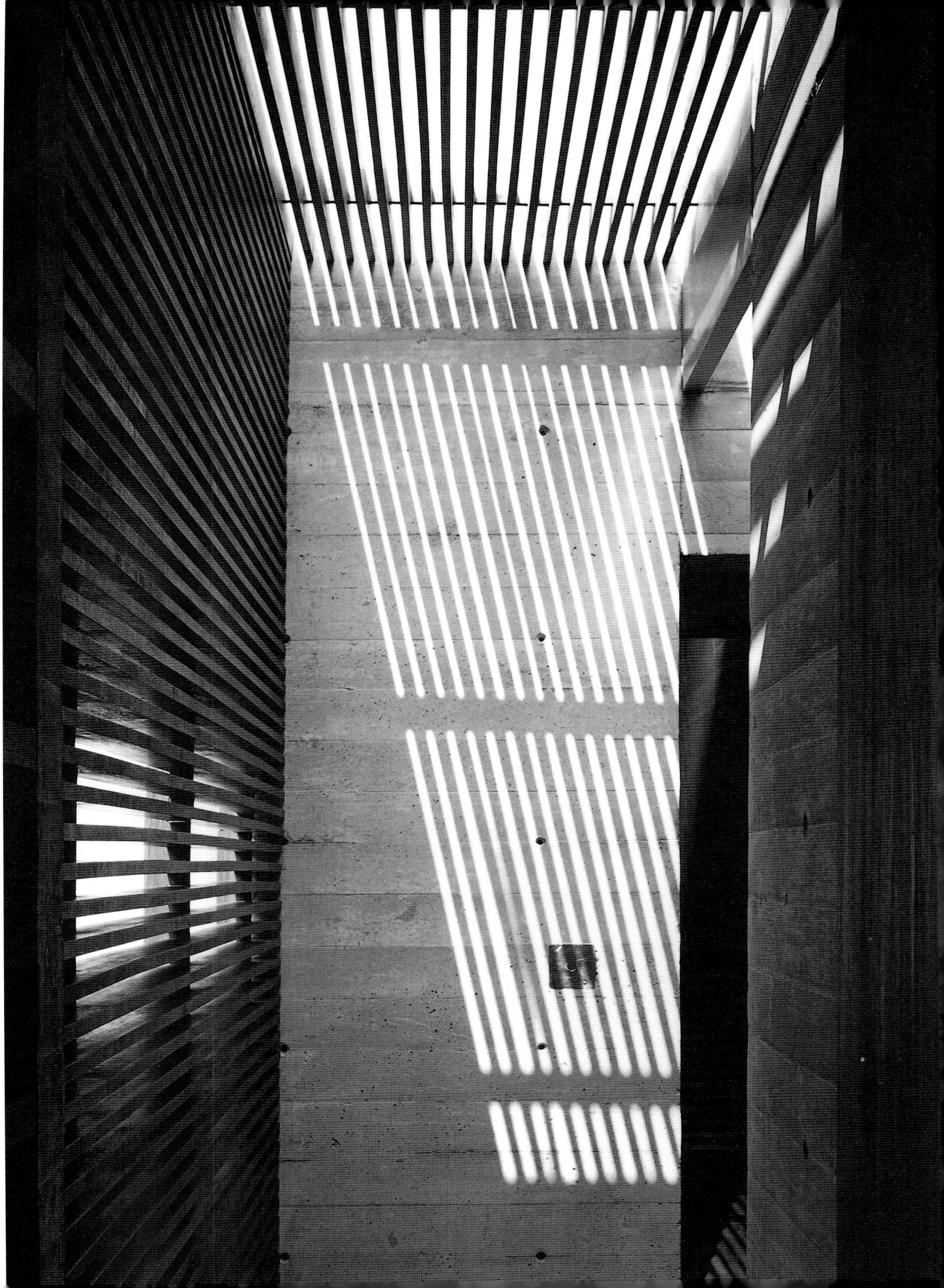

Master bedroom

Master bedroom

Bathroom  *Window detail*

TEN ARQUITECTOS

HOUSE R.R.
Mexico City, Mexico
Design: 1996
Construction: 1997

Photos: T. Sakashita

A single family house located in a residential area of townhouses in the southern suburbs of Mexico City. The site is a 17 × 21 meter slot of space sharing party walls with its neighbors, and the short end of one of the continuous facades create the defined street wall typical of this townhouse neighborhood type.

The site is divided in two along its longitudinal axis as a consequence to its pronounced level variation and orientation. It has in the lowest part a three floor structure, which creates an intimate outdoor patio; providing southern exposure to the house as well as privacy from the street and neighboring houses. The disposition of the patio along with the rest of the house creates a "L" shape plan solution.

The program and budget called for a rational, straightforward organization. The spaces of the house are defined by the superimposition of parallel layers in both directions (north-south, west-east). Each layer expresses itself by its own materiality and tectonic solution, creating a virtual transparency.

Following the "L" shape plan: on the short side and in the middle level, are located the access and the principal living with a double height; perpendicular to it, dining, kitchen, breakfast room, service room and the lower part of the studio, facing the patio and the lap pool which runs along the lot in the same axis of the stairs which are contained in a transparent-glass volume. The portico is the transition between indoors and outdoors. In the upper floor are located the family room, followed by a crystal bridge to the bedrooms and the upper part of the studio, as part as the master bedroom. The southern sun is blocked by a system of louvers in another plane parallel to the glass facade, providing privacy to the bedrooms. The ground floor contains the garage, service entry and laundry.

Architects: Taller de Enrique Norten Arquitectos S.C. (TEN Arquitectos)—Enrique Norten, Bernardo Gomez-Pimienta, principals; Francisco Pardo, Aarón Hernández, project team; Julio Amezcua, model
Client: Lorenzo Reyes Retana
Consultant: Ing. Vicente Robles, structural
Program: Single family house
Major material: walls of exposed concrete or concrete block with plaster, patio facade of glazing, louvers of red cider, floors of lava stone and oak wood, exposed steel structure supporting roof
Area (approx.): 224m^2

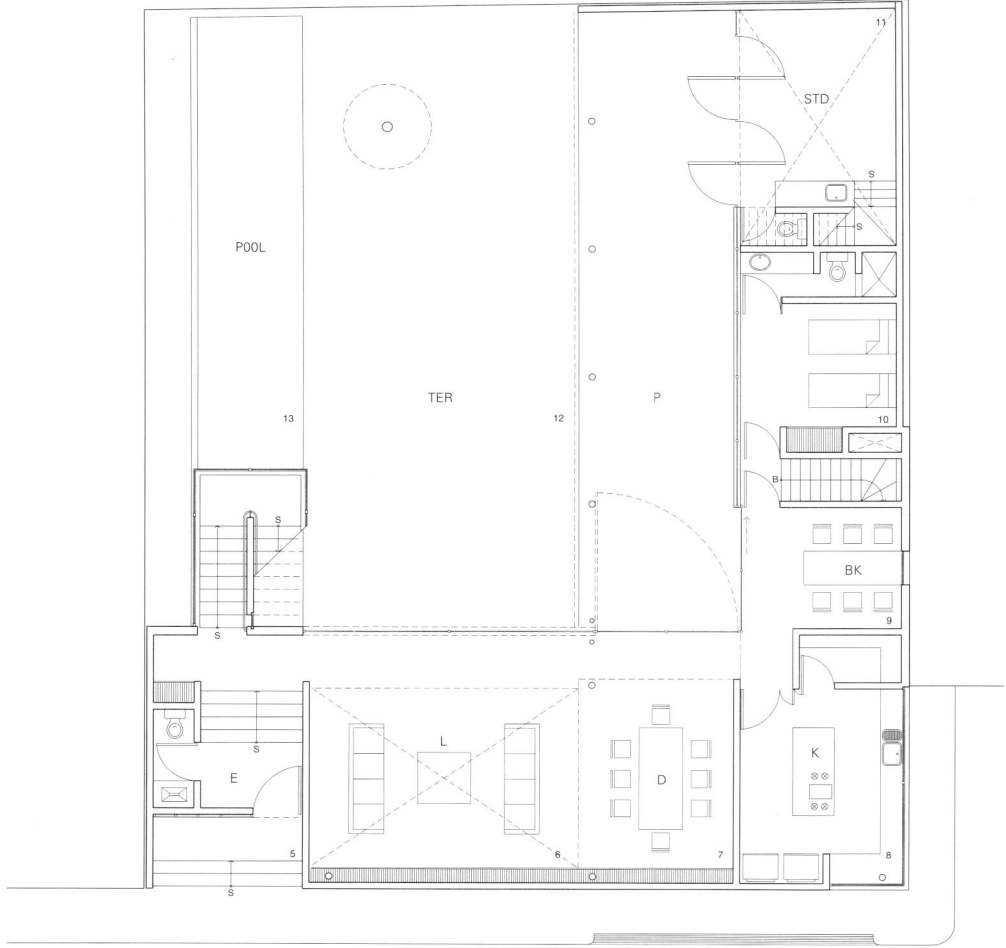

Access level

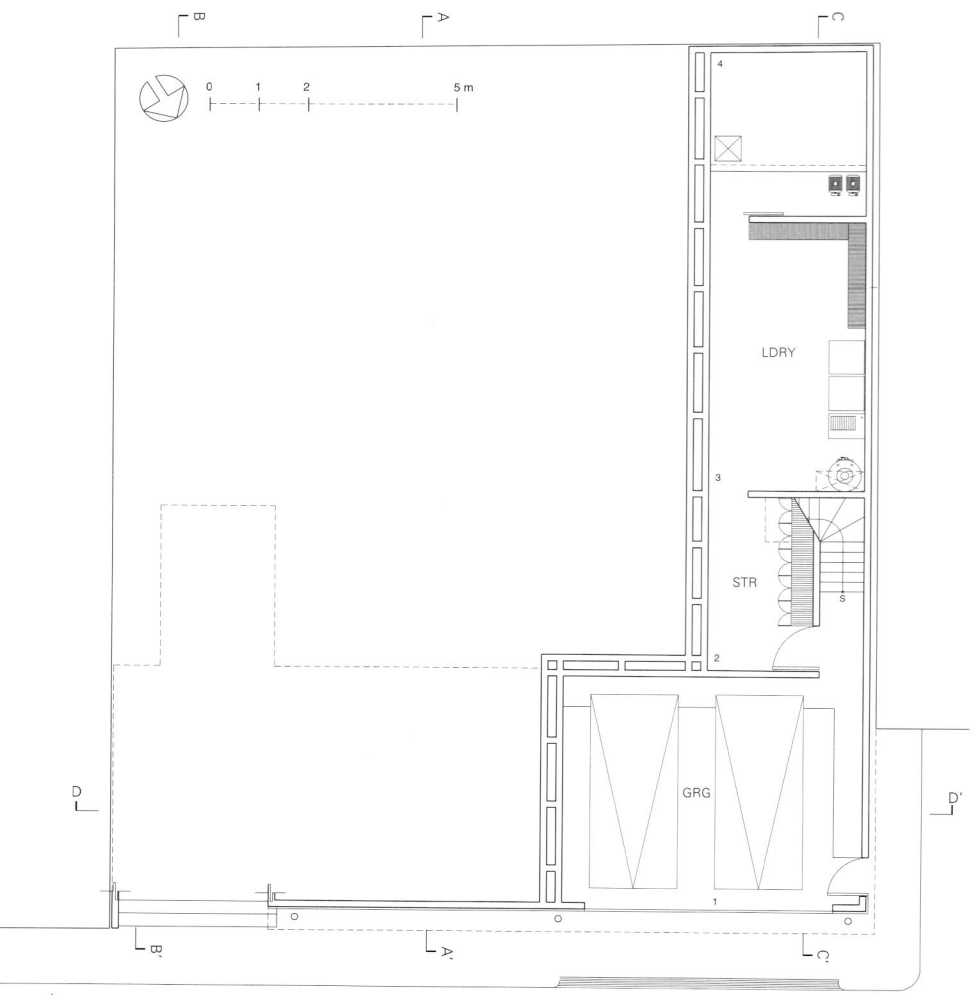

Basement

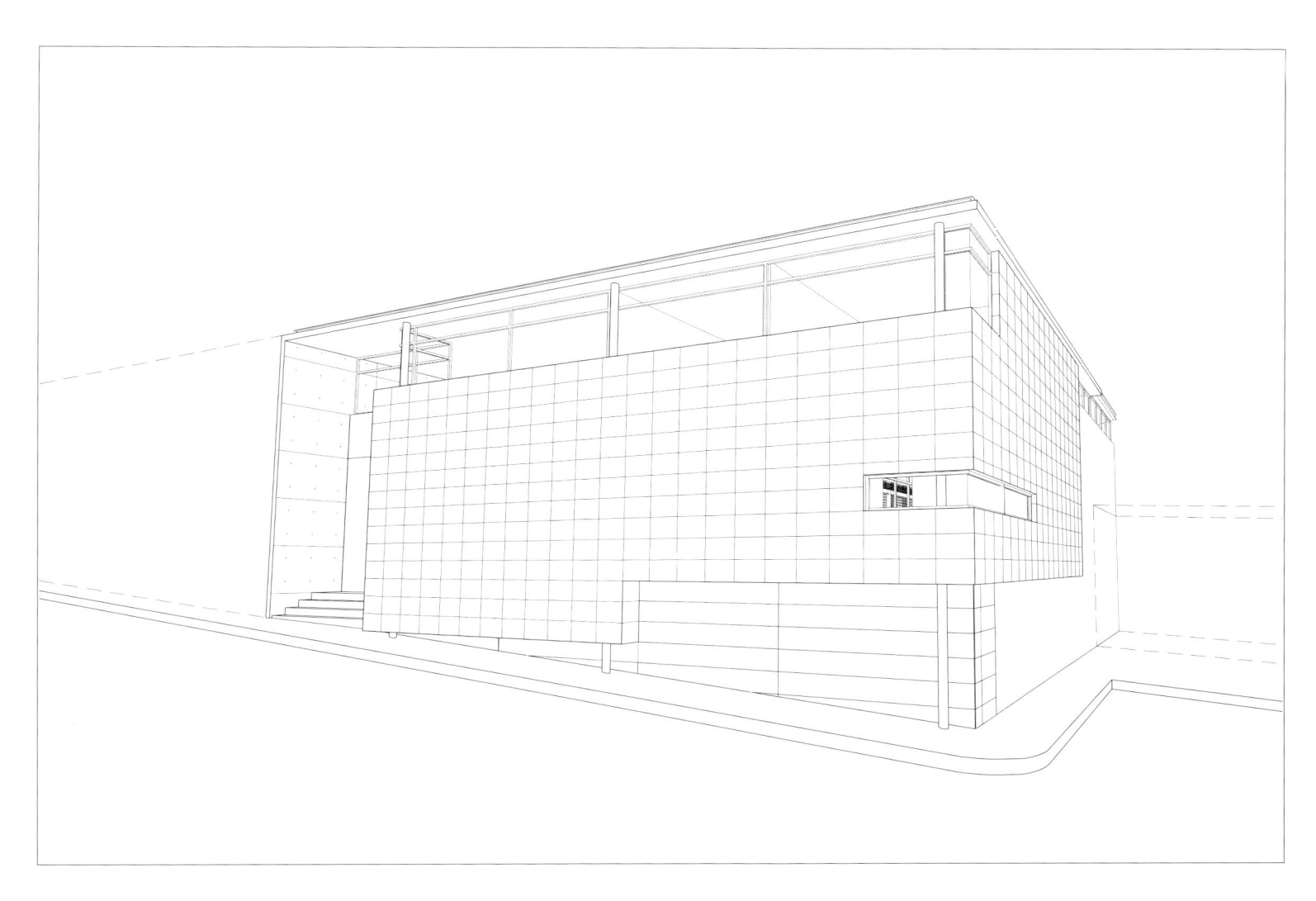

この一戸建ての住宅は，メキシコ市の南郊に位置する，タウンハウスの並ぶ住宅地区にある。間口17m，奥行21mの細長い敷地は，両隣と境界壁を共有し，切れ目なく続く短手側の壁は，周辺のタウンハウスに典型的に見られる，壁を立てたような特徴のある街路側ファサードを構成している。

明快なレベル差があることや方位を考え，敷地を長手軸に沿って二分した。敷地の一番低い部分に3層の棟を置き，前面に小さな屋外パティオをつくる。パティオは家の南面を開放し，道路や隣家からのプライバシーを守ってくれる。パティオと3層棟に鍵の字につながる棟からL型プランが生まれる。

プログラムと予算は，合理的で簡単な構成を必要としていた。住空間は，両方向（北－南，西－東）に沿って平行に重なる層によって規定されている。各層はヴァーチャルな透明性をつくりながら，それぞれの物質性と構造によって自らを表現する。

L型プランに従って，道路側に面して下層階にはアクセスと2層吹抜の主リビングがあり，これに直角に食堂，台所，朝食室，サービス，2層吹抜のスタジオが並び，パティオとラッププールに面している。プールは，透明なガラスの箱の中に収まった階段と同軸線上を敷地に沿って延びる。ポルチコは屋内と屋外の転換域である。上層階には家族用の居間があり，そこからクリスタル・ブリッジを経て寝室，主寝室，主寝室の一部であるスタジオ上層部へつながる。南の日差しは，ガラス面に平行して設置されたルーヴァーによって遮られ，ルーヴァーはまた寝室のプライバシーを守る。地上階にはガレージ，サービス・エントリー，ランドリーが置かれている。

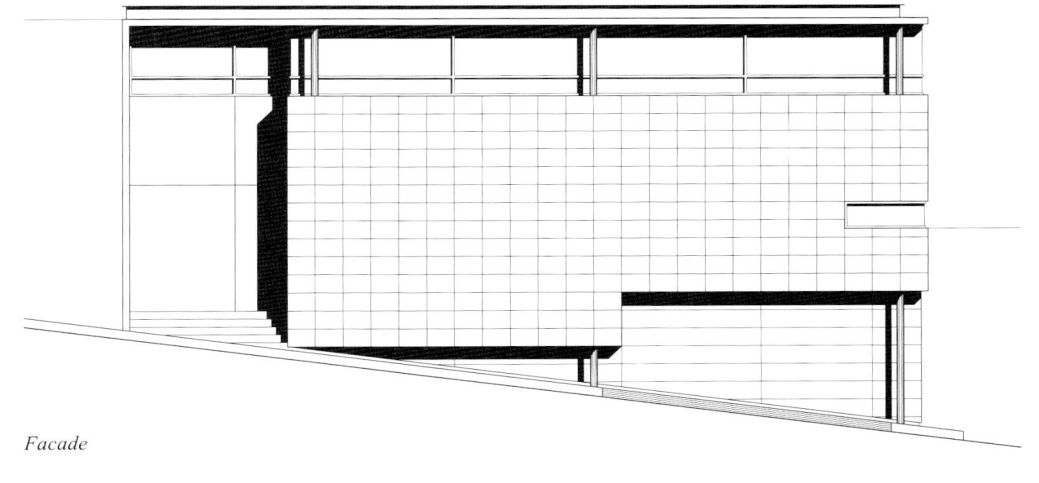

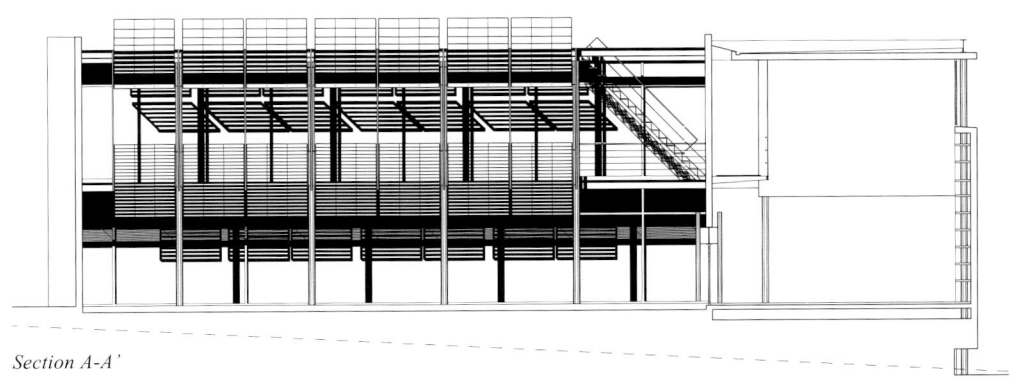

Facade

Section A-A'

East view

Facade

View of north-south wing

Section B-B'

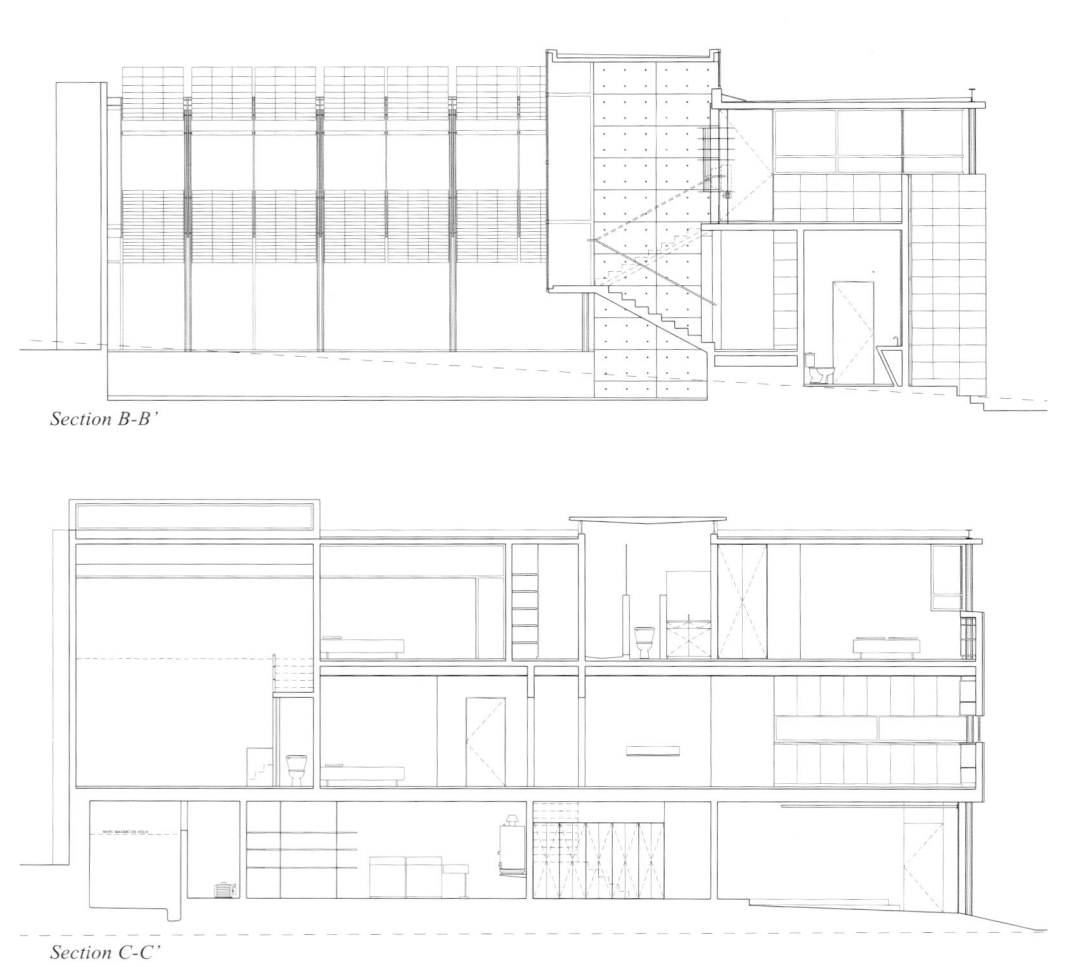

Section C-C'

Section D-D'

Entrance

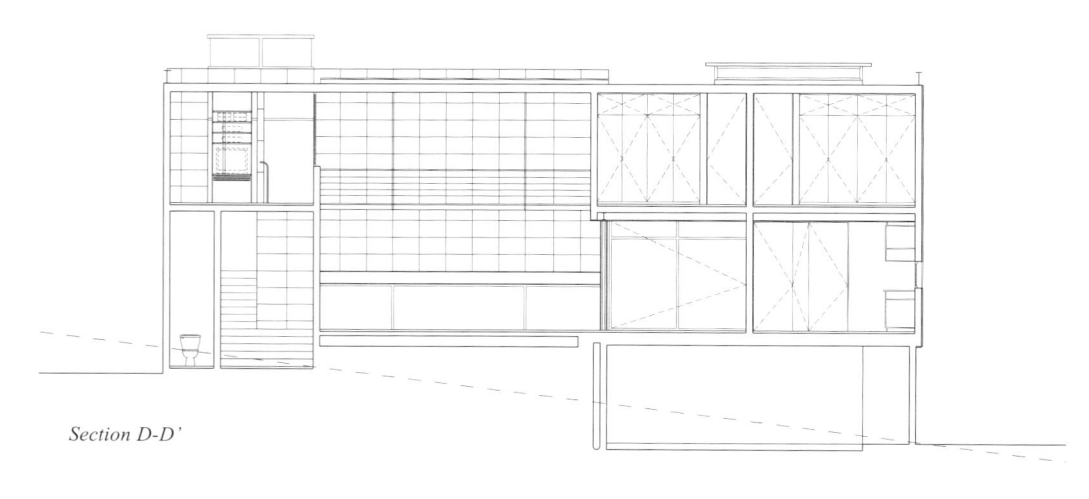

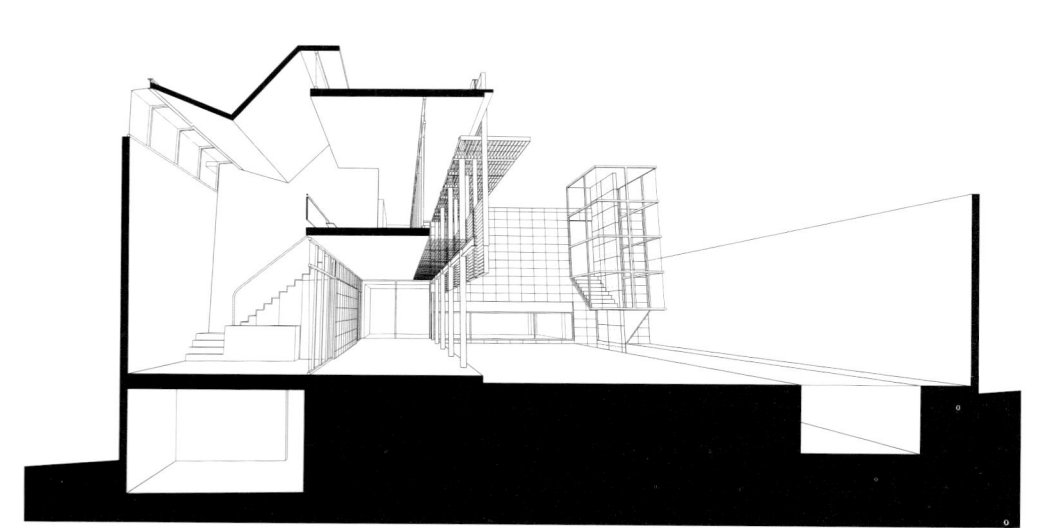

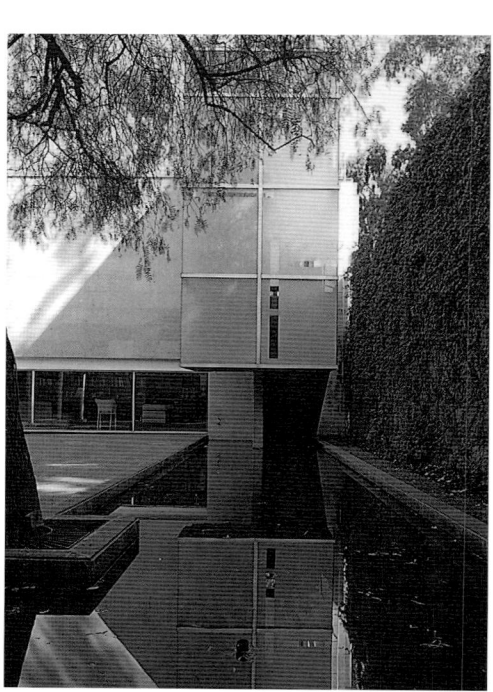

Pool *View of "L" corner from terrace* ▷

68

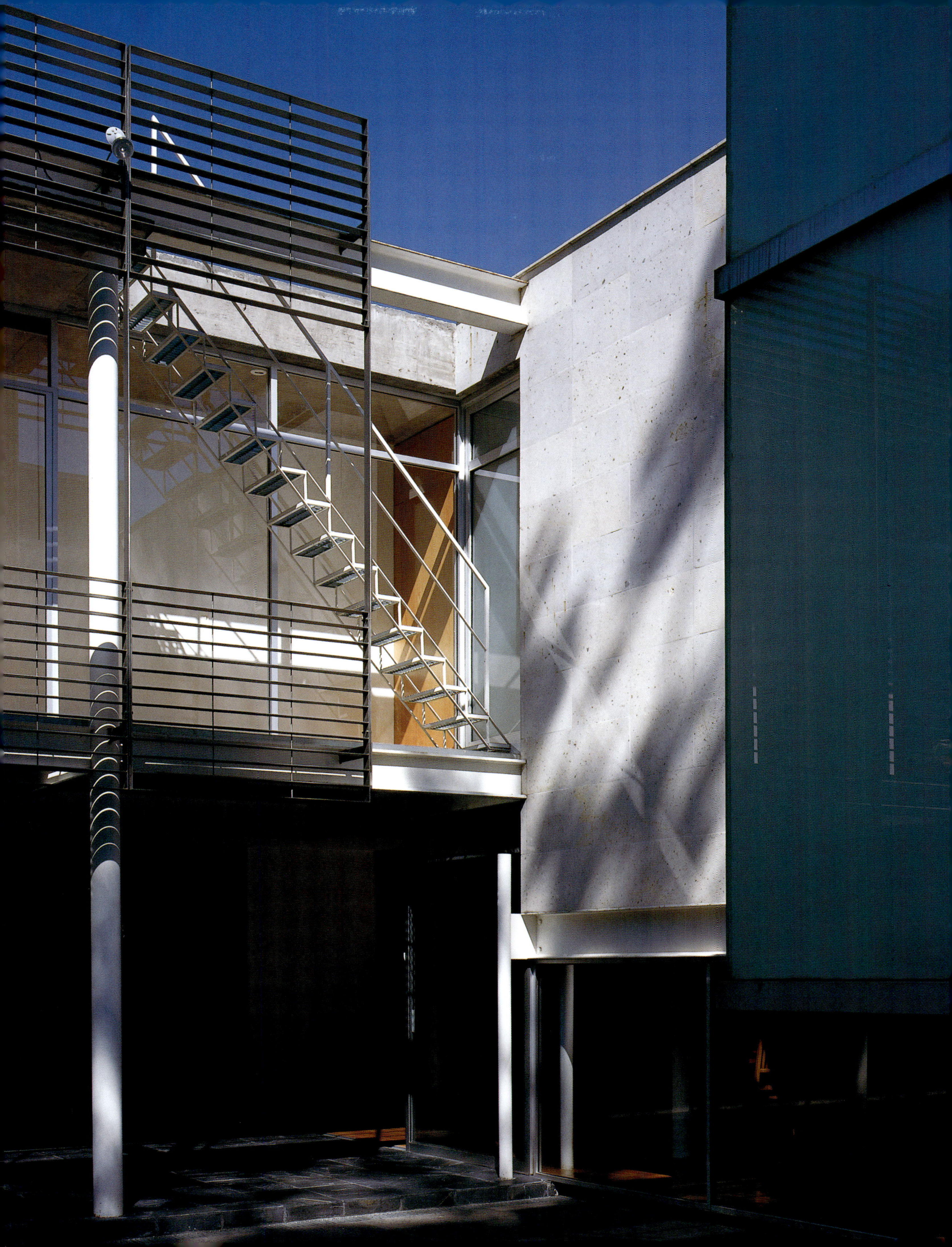

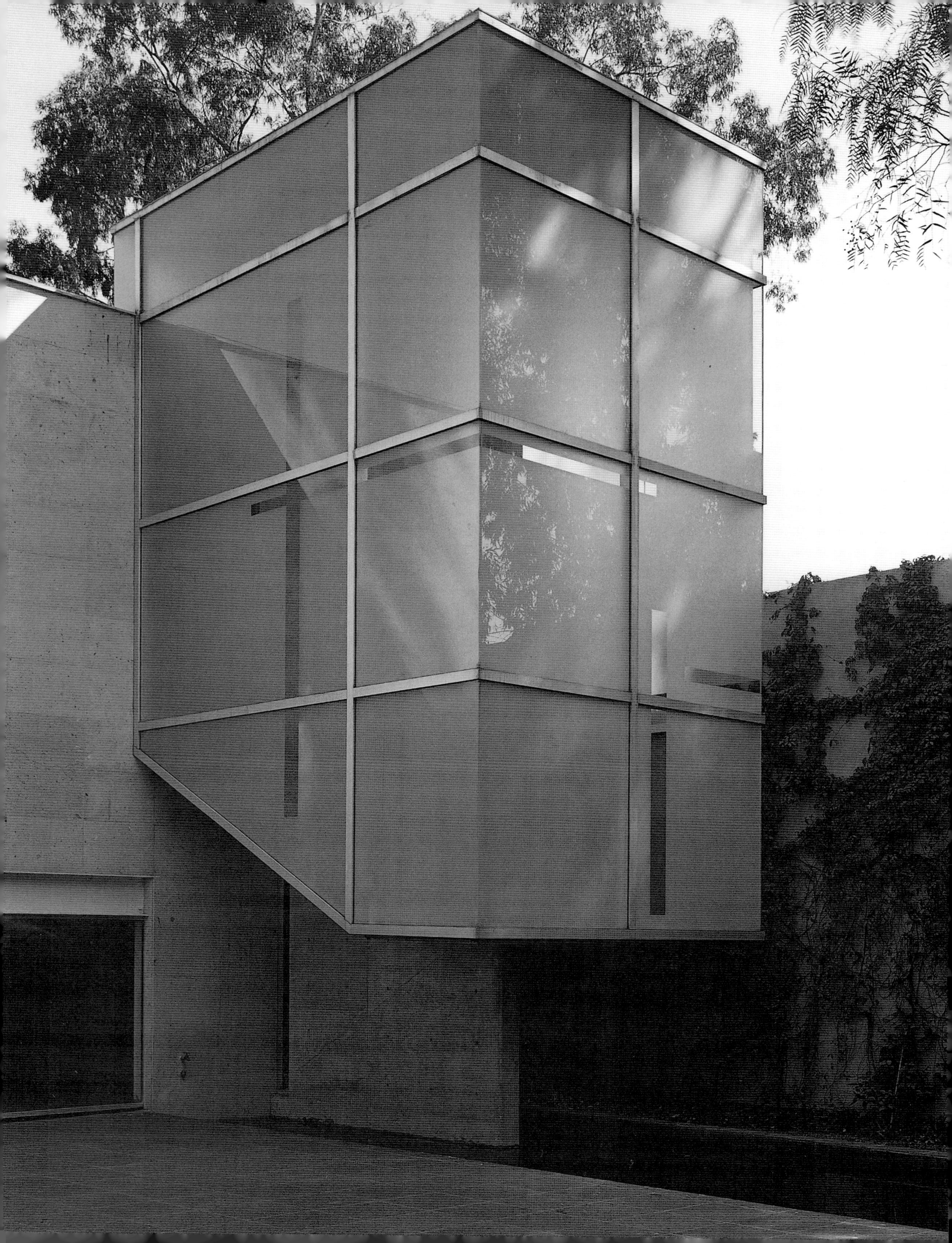

Terrace

◁ *Glazed staircase*

Portico

Living room

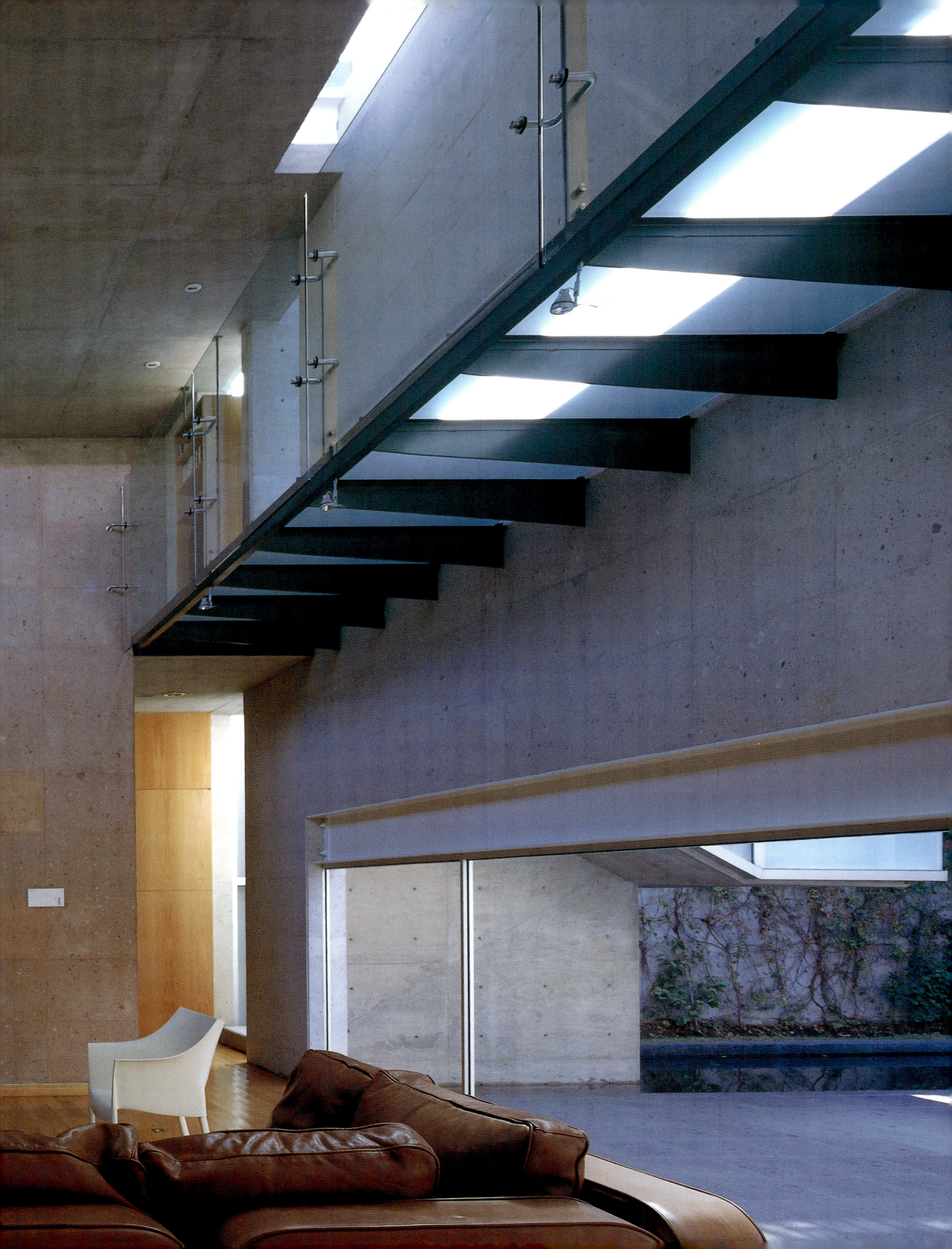

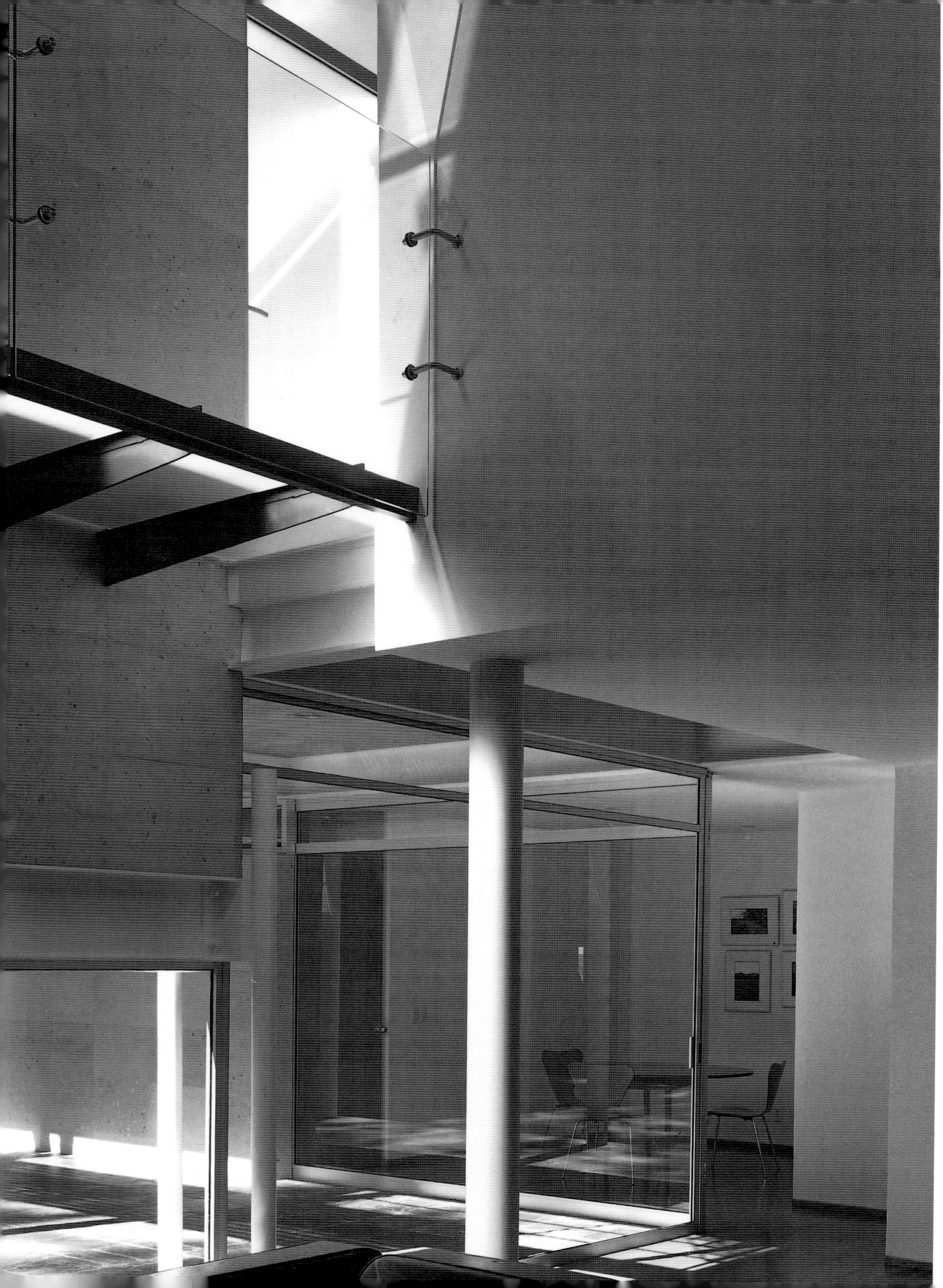

◁ *Living room: corner detail*

Portico: view from dining room

Master bedroom on second level

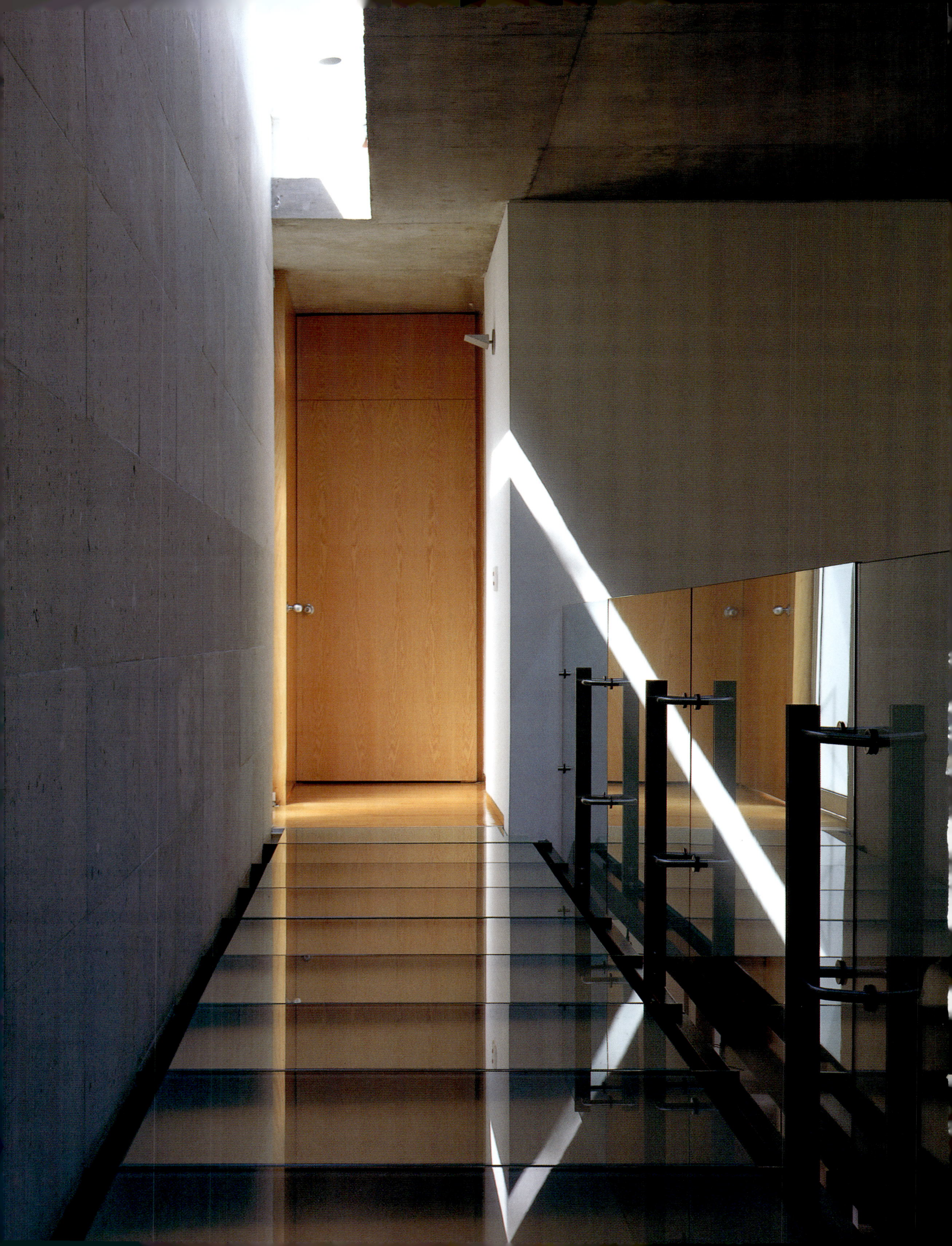

Upper level of studio

Family room

Cristal bridge

Studio

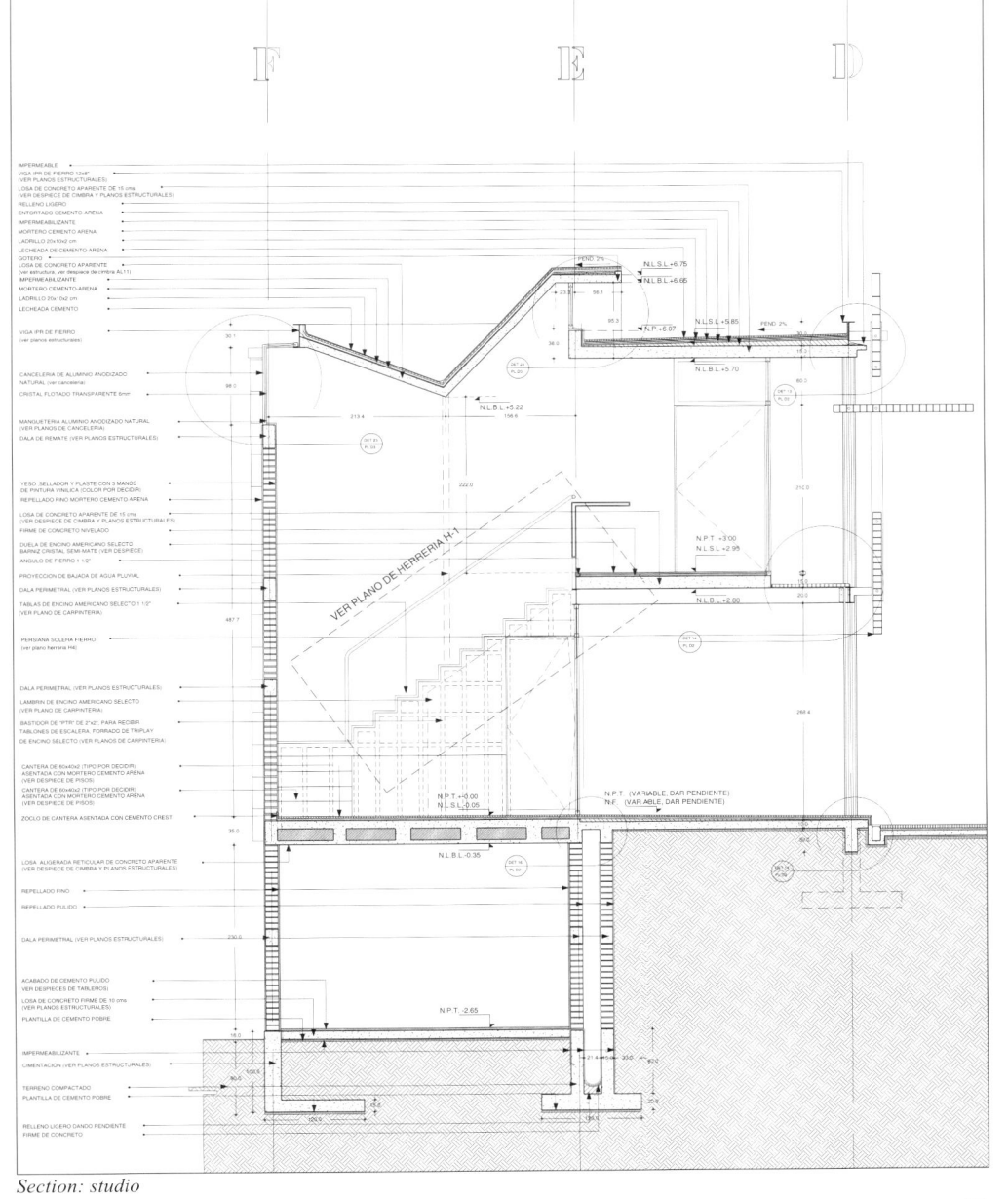

Section: studio

HIROSHI MARUYAMA

SLANT GLANCE/
HOUSE/SLOPE GROUND
Yokohama, Japan
Design: 1996–98
Construction: 1998–99

Photos: Y. Takase

A traditional architectural space, whether it may be Western or Japanese, attributes its value to the extent of how, at the end, the space "looks natural" (despite the obvious fact that the process and quality of the nature are extensively different). In other words, the framework that is architecture, has always existed as something constantly restraining the vision from its "just seeing" it. However, providing frameworks to make it "look unnatural" or coating the whole architecture with "unnatural-looking" images would only result in the disclosure of an architectural space that "looks natural". This is what current projects taught us, where virtual images have been applied.

The project [SH/H/SG] is an attempt to overcome architecture's traditional harmful effects on vision. Yet it is not an exercise of deformation of architecture as a visual framework through some kind of scientific/abstract spatial principle, nor a search in the dark for a coincidence between architecture as the object and a new image. The fundamental idea lying beneath this project's visual process is, and at the same time, what is targeted by this project's direct criticism is, the act itself to perceive an architectural space as a phenomenon, based upon human understanding and inner intuition (as well as space/time as formality).

An extremely simplified version of depicting this project would read as follows: individual objects featured in [SH/H/SG] do not stand as factors to be acknowledged objectively as law-abiding architectural factors, but that they exist as the media for "sensory realization" of inner intuition within an architectural environment - the media for creation of images by touch and feel. It may be assumed as being similar to a new 'diagram' that goes beyond Kant-esque 'consception force', which is a result of choosing 'immanence' and a sort of partnership (not subjective nor objective) as media, different from a diagram based on human understanding (Kant).

In this manner, objectivity as legal architectural factors nor architectural space that "looks natural" are in no way denied but only withdrawn to a distance, making way to new possibilities for architectural space. Space as the image itself, endowed with visibility, touch and variability.
Hiroshi Maruyama

East view

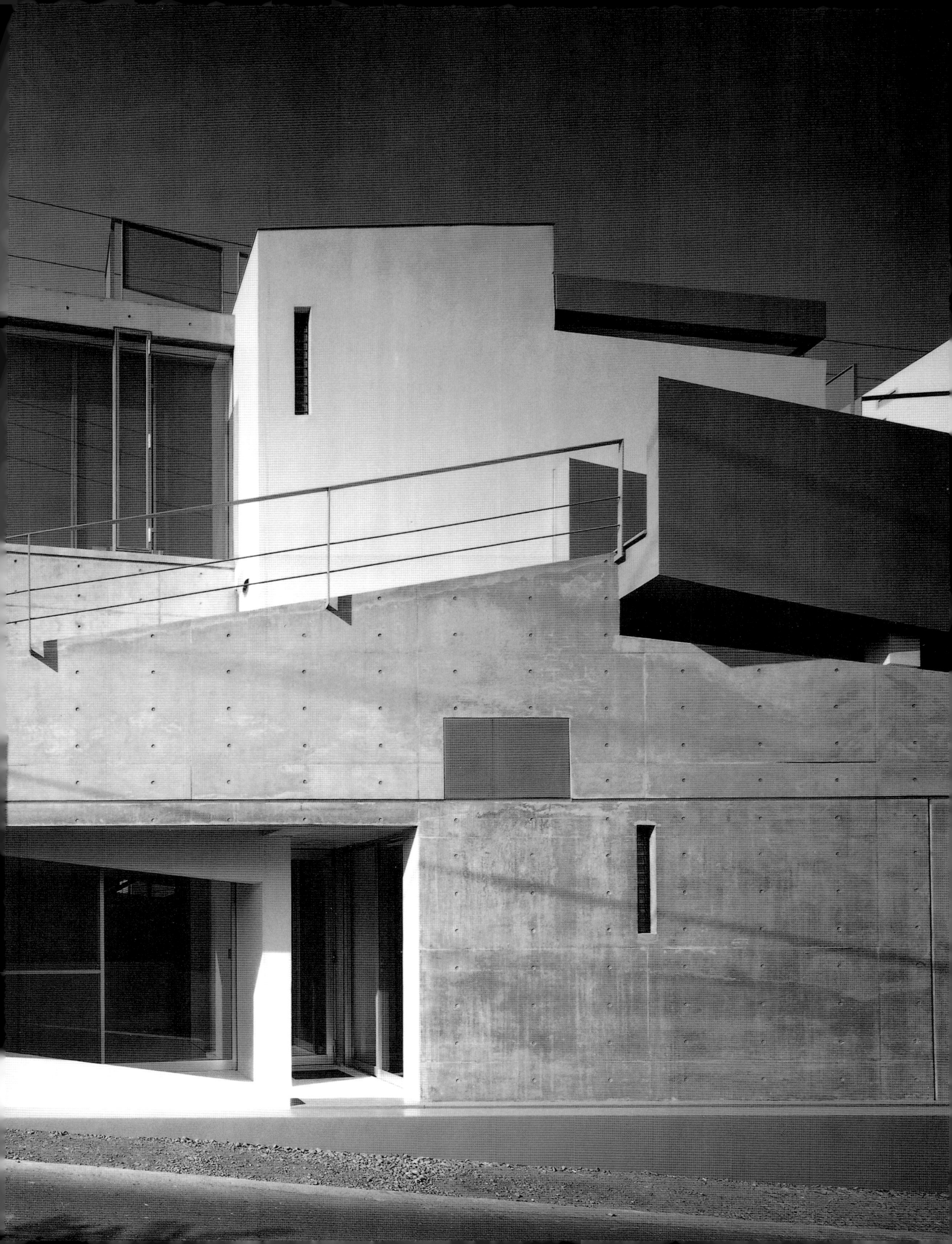

伝統的な建築空間は、西洋であろうが日本であろうが、最終的にその空間が「自然に見える」ことを価値としている（もちろん、自然の質やプロセスは大きく異なるが）。別な言い方をするならば、建築という枠組みは、視覚にとって、「単に見ること」を常に抑圧する存在としてあったのである。しかし、「自然に見えない」ための枠組みを用意したり、「自然に見えない」イメージによって建築全体を被覆したところで、結局のところ、「自然に見える」建築空間が露呈してしまうことを昨今のヴァーチャル・イメージを応用したプロジェクトは教えている。

プロジェクト［SH／H／SG］は、建築の視覚における伝統的な弊害を克服しようとする試みであるが、何らかの科学的・抽象的空間理念によって建築という視覚的枠組みのデフォルマシオンを試みたものでもなければ、客体としての建築と新たなイメージの偶然的一致を当てどもなく模索したものではない。このプロジェクトの視覚的なプロセスの基本となっているのは、そして同時に、直接的批判の対象となっているのは、人間の内的直感（そして、形式として時間・空間）と悟性に基づきながら、建築空間を現象として捉えること、そのものである。

極めて単純化して言うと、［SH／H／SG］における個別的なオブジェクトは合法的な建築要素として客体的に認知される要素（建築空間なるものを媒体として認知される）としてあるのではなく、建築環境における内的直感を「感覚的に実現」するため、すなわち触知的イメージの想像するための媒体としてある。悟性に基づいた図式（カント）ではなく、「内在」と、客観的ではないけれど主観的でもないある種の共同性を媒介にしながら、そのことによって、カント的「構想力」を越える新たな「図式」のごとくに想定されたものと言えるかもしれない。

それゆえに、合法的な建築要素としての客体性や、「自然に見える」建築空間は否定されているわけではなく、ただ遠方に退けられ、その前に新たな建築の可能空間が生まれているだけなのである。可視性、触知性、可変性を携えたイメージそのものとしての空間が。　　　　　　　　　　　（丸山洋志）

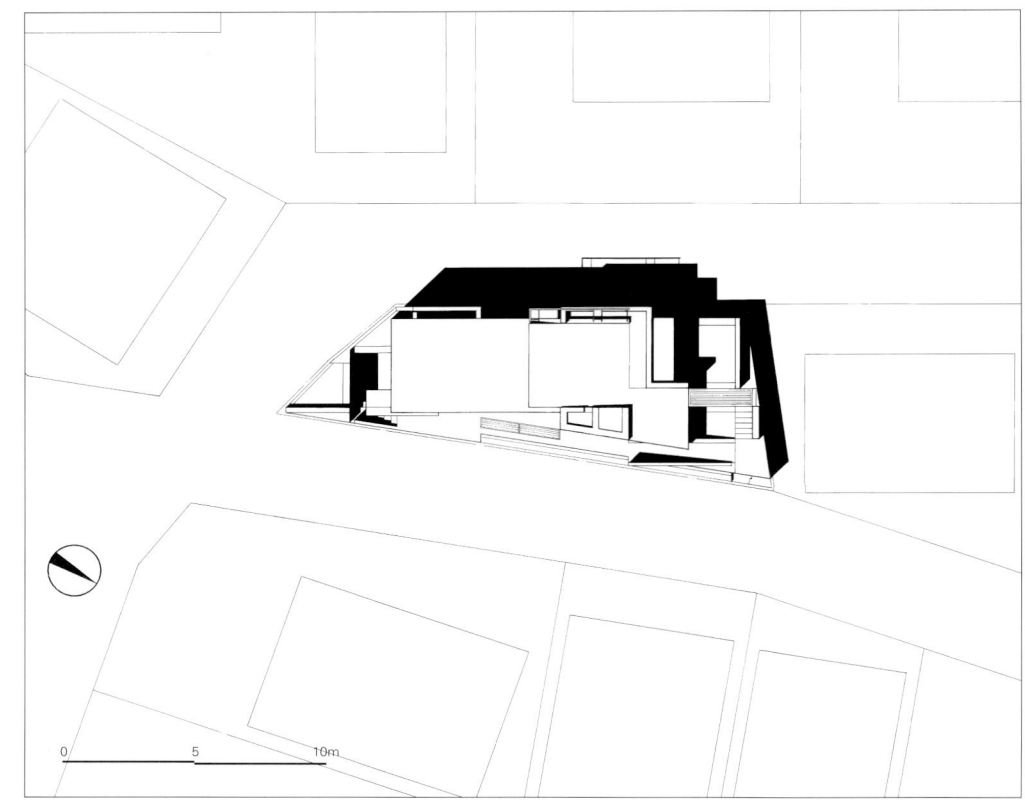

Site plan

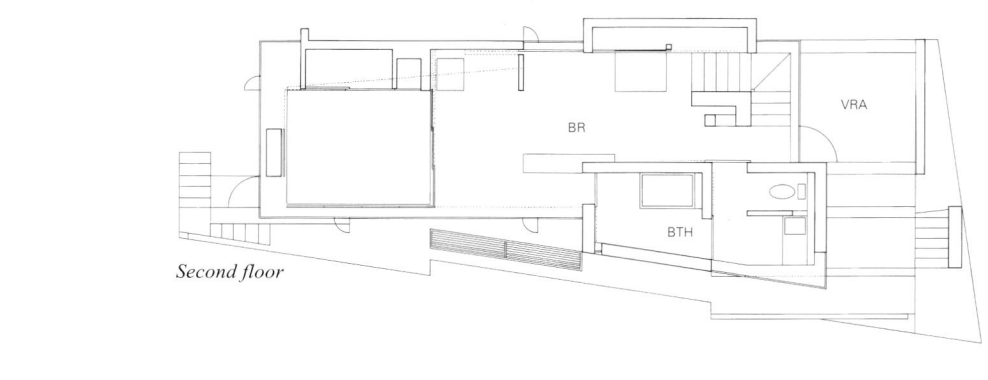

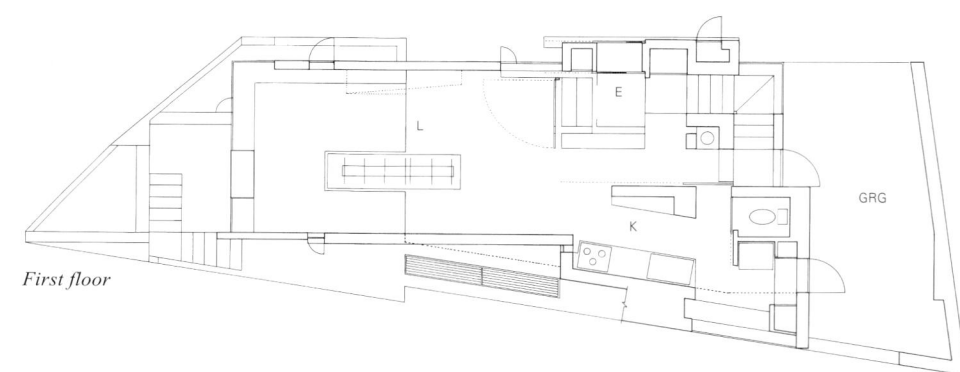

Second floor

First floor

Basement S=1:150

Architects: Maruyama Atelier/Kenchiku Produce—Hiroshi Maruyama, principal-in-charge; Ran Nagahama, Takayuki Koga, project team
Clients: Hisae Kikuchi
Consultants: Junichi Igarashi/Keishosha, structural
General contractor: Nakamuraya Construction
Structural system: reinforced concrete
Major materials: exposed concrete and wateroof, exterior wall; plaster, ceiling; plaster and mortar, interior wall; oak flooring and tatami flooring (first and second floor), vinyl tile flooring and tatami flooring(basement), floor
Site area: 101.1 m²; building area: 48.9 m²; total floor area: 150.6 m²

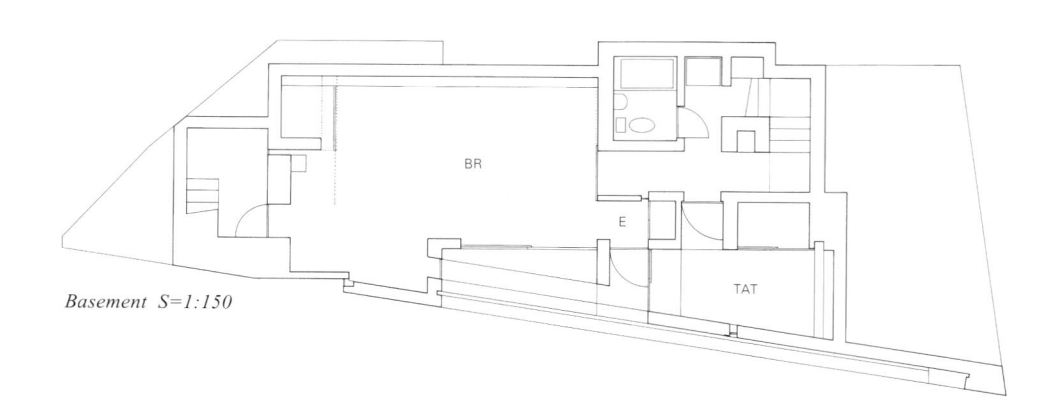

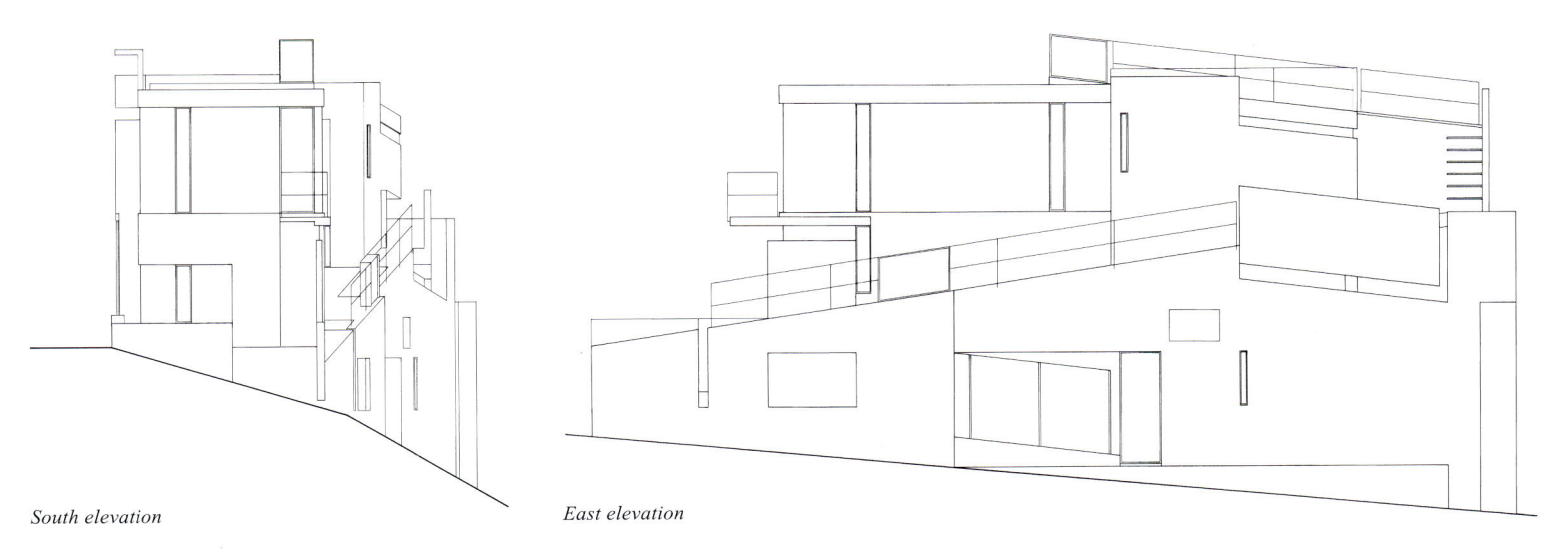

Entrance on west

South elevation *East elevation*

View from south

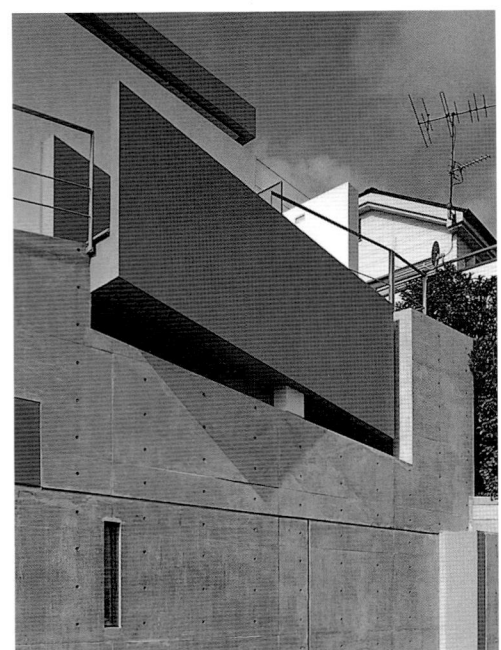

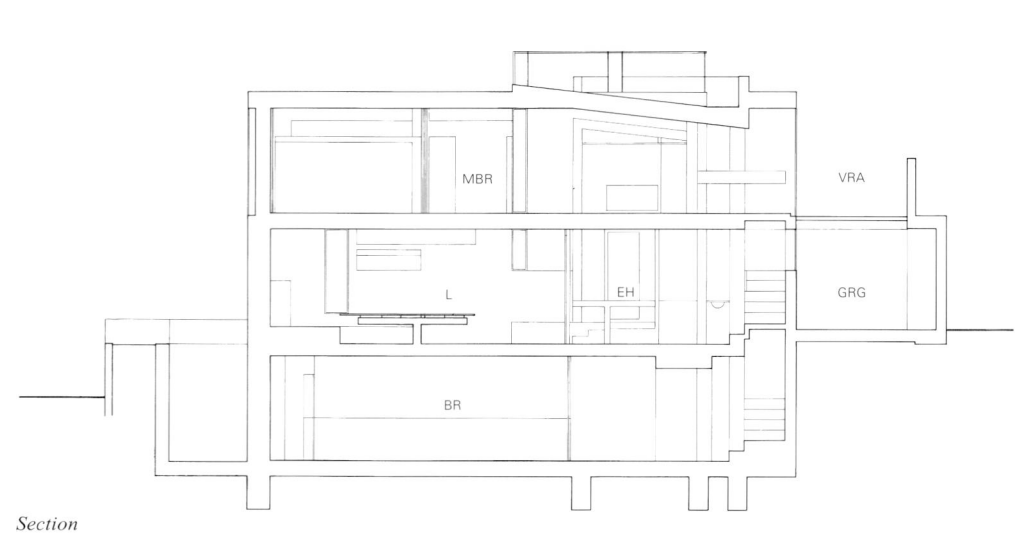

Slope to veranda

Section

Bridge to roof deck

Staircase on north

East elevation

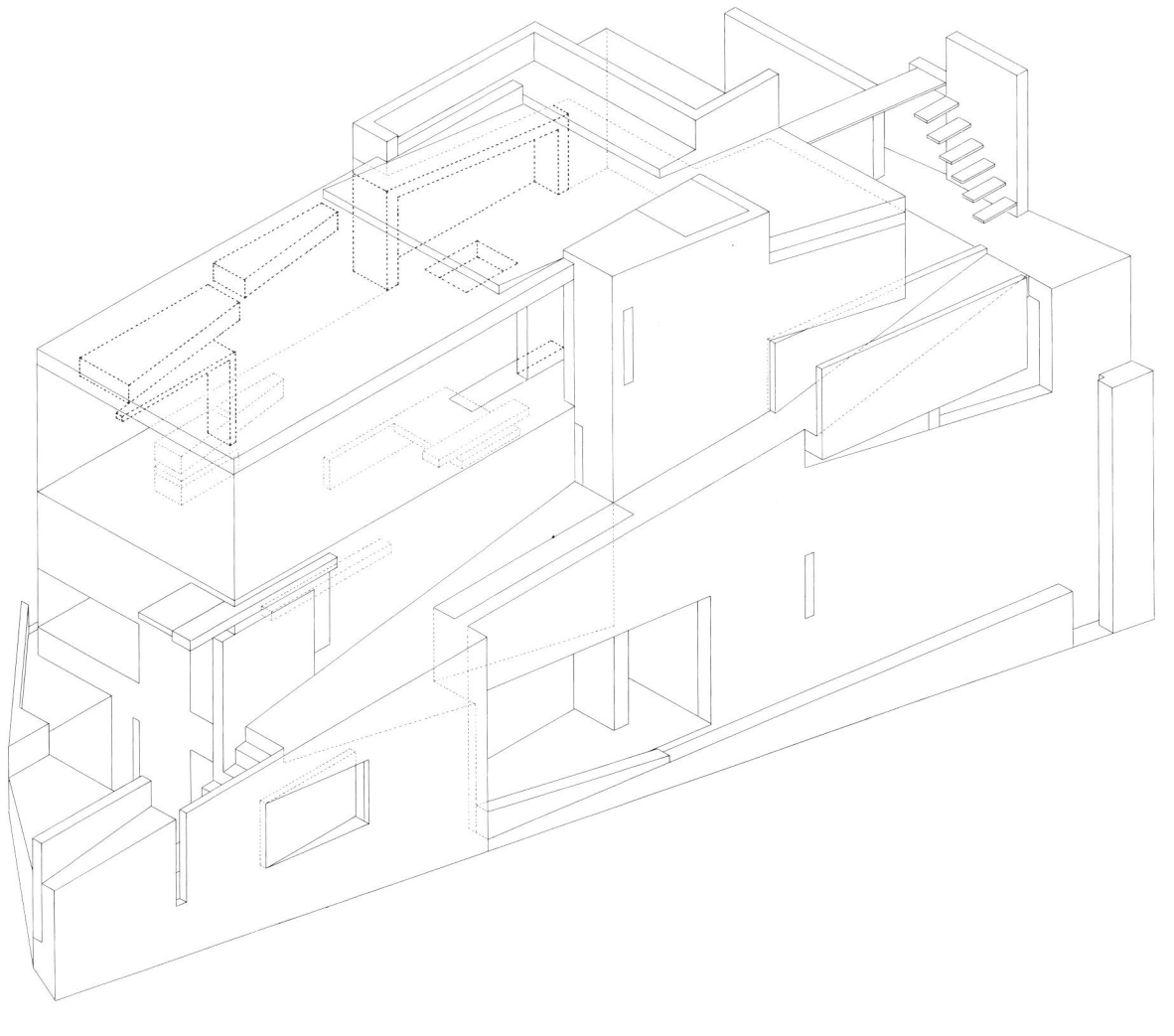

Axonometric

Living room

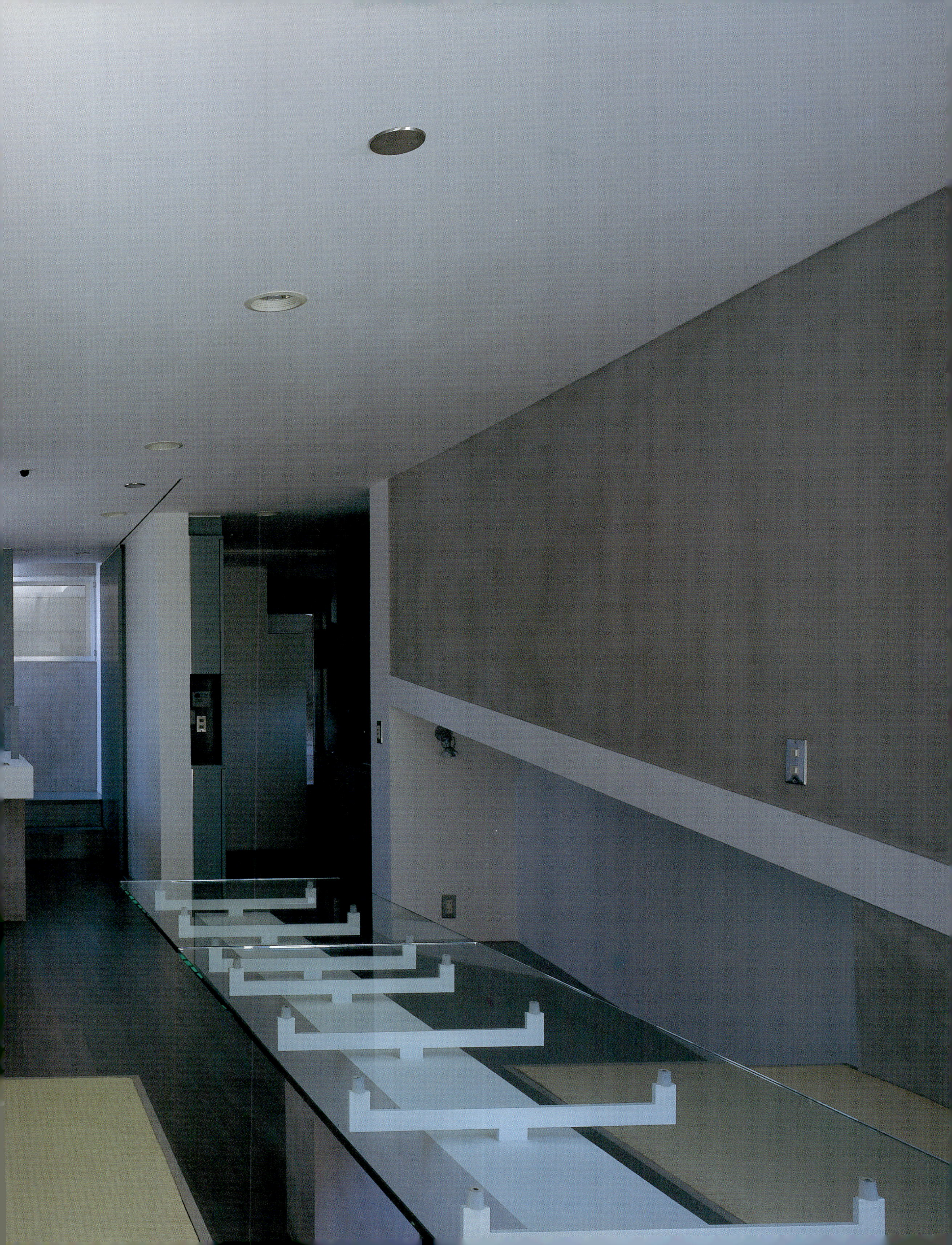

Living room: entrance on right

Entrance on west

Bedroom on second floor

Master bedroom: wall detail

View of staircase from master bedroom

DEAN NOTA

REYNA RESIDENCE
Hermosa Beach, Los Angeles,
California, U.S.A.
Design: 1997–98
Construction: 1998–99

Photos: T. Sakashita

Site
The site is a thirty by eighty foot slice of ocean front sand located in Hermosa Beach, a one mile square, California seaside city, at the western edge of metropolitan Los Angeles. The long axis of the site is bounded by adjacent residential structures on the north and south. A pedestrian path known as The Strand borders the beach to the west and a street provides automobile access from the east. The dominant physical characteristic of the site is the view of the beach and ocean which is framed by the Hermosa Beach Pier to the north and the Palos Verdes Peninsula and Santa Catalina Island to the south. This site resides at an urban edge in transition, where a dense fabric of older, unremarkable structures must coexist with larger more contemporary dwellings.

Program
The Client required a house for one or two people and occasional guests, organized to allow for a public, social interaction with the Strand and the Beach while providing more private domains for entertaining and personal habitation. The program is therefore organized in a vertical sequence of increasing privacy on three levels, with a double entry, guest room, entertainment room and parking on the ground level, living, dining, kitchen and second bedroom on two middle levels, and a master suite at the upper level for the most privacy and best view.

Solution
The experience of the building begins with a double entry that can be approached from two different directions; from the street by car or from the Strand and beach by foot. From these modest, low entries the spatial experience expands in an orchestrated sequence as one moves vertically up the stair. Arrival at each of the upper levels reveals spaces that are progressively more open and ever increasing in light and view. Each of the three levels extends outward on to terraces towards the ocean and the horizon beyond.

The heart of the house is a large volume containing the living areas, which are extended to the view by a gently sloping wall of glass. At the top of the stair, the master suite is contained below a longitudinal vault that defines a visual axis leading to a secluded bathing room at the rear of the dwelling. To the front of the building, a bridge extends to an observation platform that penetrates the window wall and is seemingly suspended above the beach below.

The elevations are a composition of solid, rectilinear elements that are strategically subtracted to reveal a contrasting inner layer with sloping walls and cantilevered deck platforms that suggest the forms of nearby lifeguard towers.

敷地：
ハーモサビーチはロサンジェルス大都市圏の西端に位置するカリフォルニアの海辺の町で，大きさは1マイル平方ほどである。砂浜を前にした30×80フィートの敷地で，長手側は北，南とも住宅が建ち，ザ・ストランドとして知られる遊歩道が西側の海辺沿いに通っている。車は東側の道路から敷地に入る。敷地の特徴は，砂浜と海の景色で，北にはハーモサビーチ埠頭が，南にはパロス・ヴェルデス半島とサンタカタリナ島が望める。また，都市の性格が転換して行く境界域に位置し，密集する平凡な町並みと大きな現代住宅が共存している。

プログラム：
一人または二人の住人，それに時々訪れる客に対応し，遊歩道や浜辺との交流が生まれる一方で，くつろぎや私的な部屋などのよりプライベートな領域も備えた住宅がクライアントの要望である。このため，上に行くに従って私性が高まる3層構成をとることになった。入り口は2つ，客用寝室，娯楽室，パーキングが1階に，居間，食堂，台所，予備の寝室が2つの中間レベルに，最上階には主寝室スイートがあり，最上の眺めとプライバシーを確保している。

解：
異なった方角から入ってくる2つの進入路から——道路から車でまたは遊歩道から徒歩で——この建物の経験が始まる。簡素で低い玄関から，上の階に上がるに従って，一連の場面展開として編成された空間が広がって行く。上に進むにつれて，空間は開放的になり，光も眺望の広がりも増して行く。各レベルとも，海と水平線を望むテラスに面している。

家の中心はリビングエリアを収めた大きなヴォリュームで，その空間は緩やかに傾斜するガラス壁を通して風景のなかへ広がっている。階段を登り詰めると主寝室スイートである。その長手に伸びるヴォールト天井が，背面に隠された浴室に至る視覚的な軸線を構成する。海に向く正面側にはブリッジが伸び展望台へ続いている。展望台はガラス壁を突き抜けて伸び，砂浜に吊り下げられているように見える。

立面は，傾斜壁と対比を描く内部のレイヤーが外に見えるように一部が切り取られた，ソリッドで直線的なエレメントと，近くにある海水浴場の監視塔を連想させる片持ちのデッキによる構成である。

East view

Architects: Dean Nota Architect—Dean A. Nota, Stephen Billings, Joseph Fedorowich, project team
Client: Joe Anthony Reyna
Consultant: Orland Engineering, structural
Builder: Baldwin Construction

West view from beach ▷

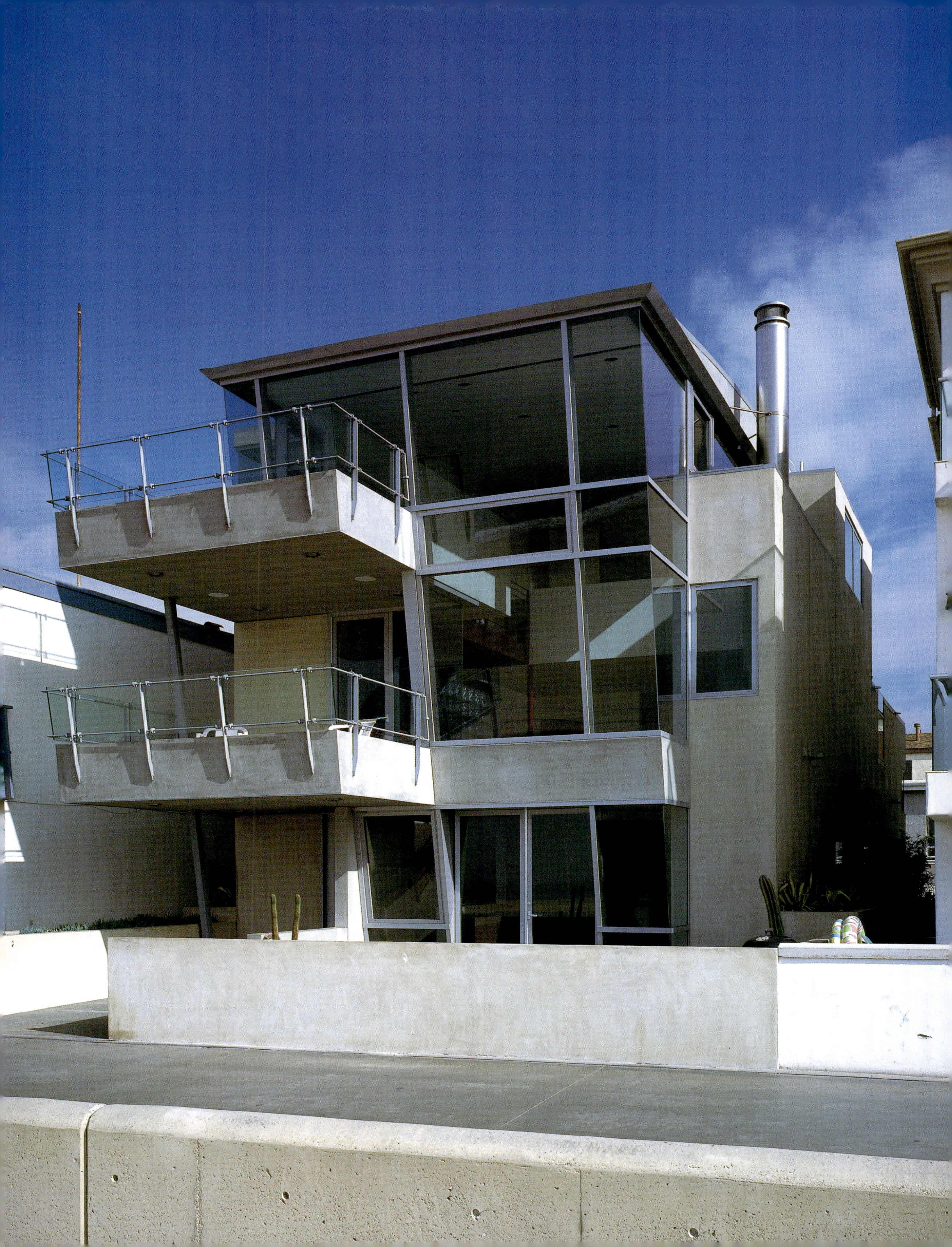

West elevation

East elevation

Roof

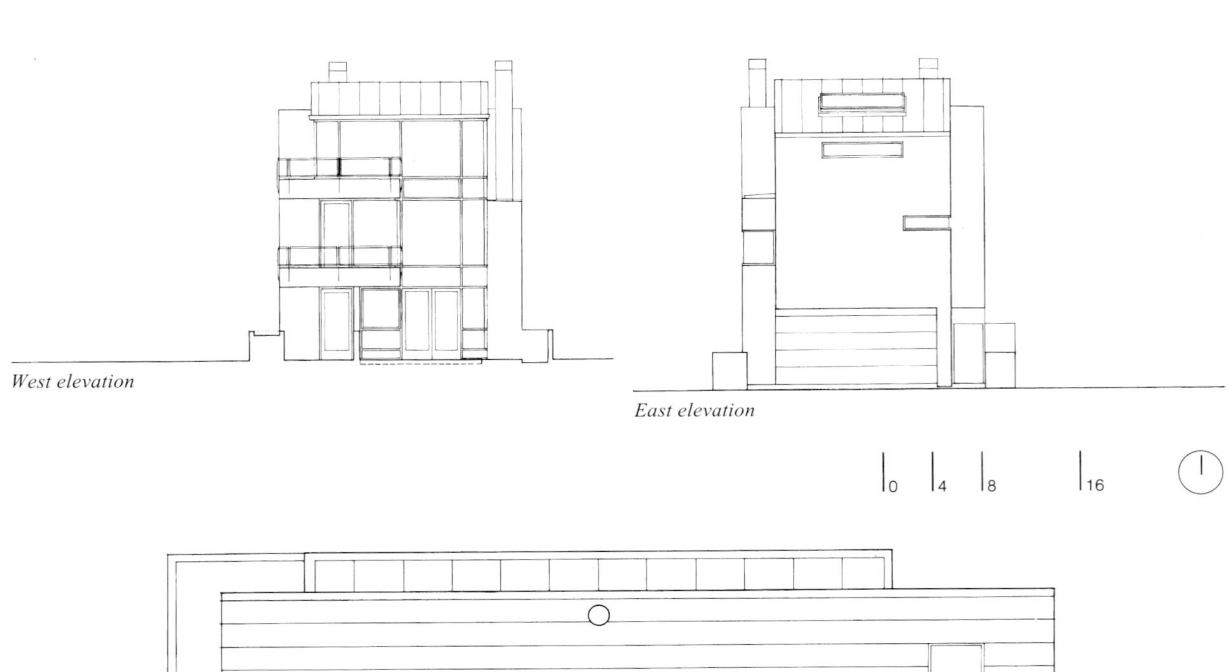

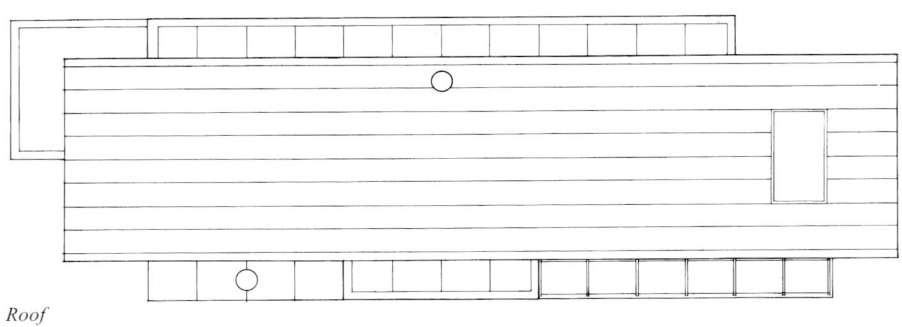

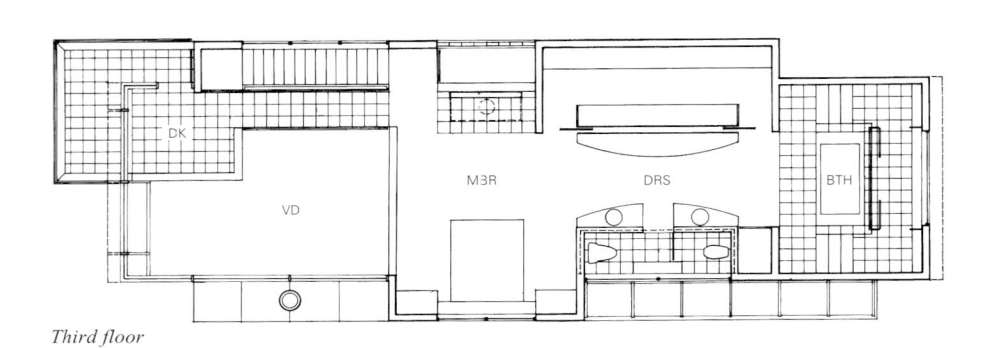

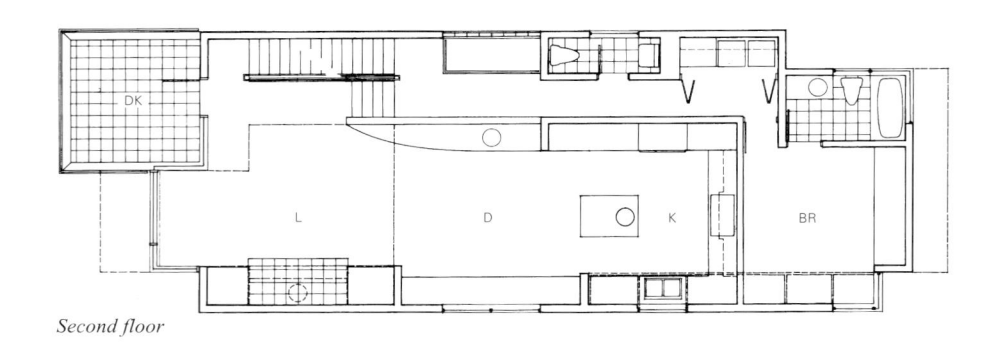

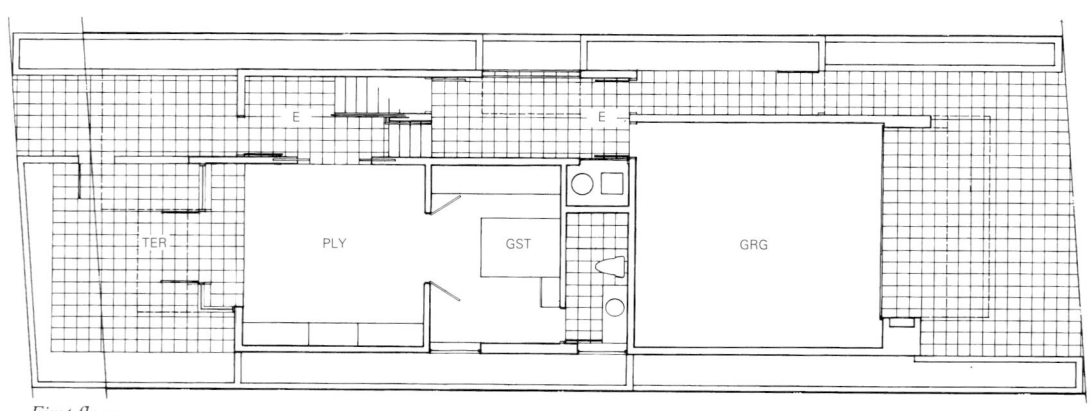

Third floor

Second floor

First floor

92

Section

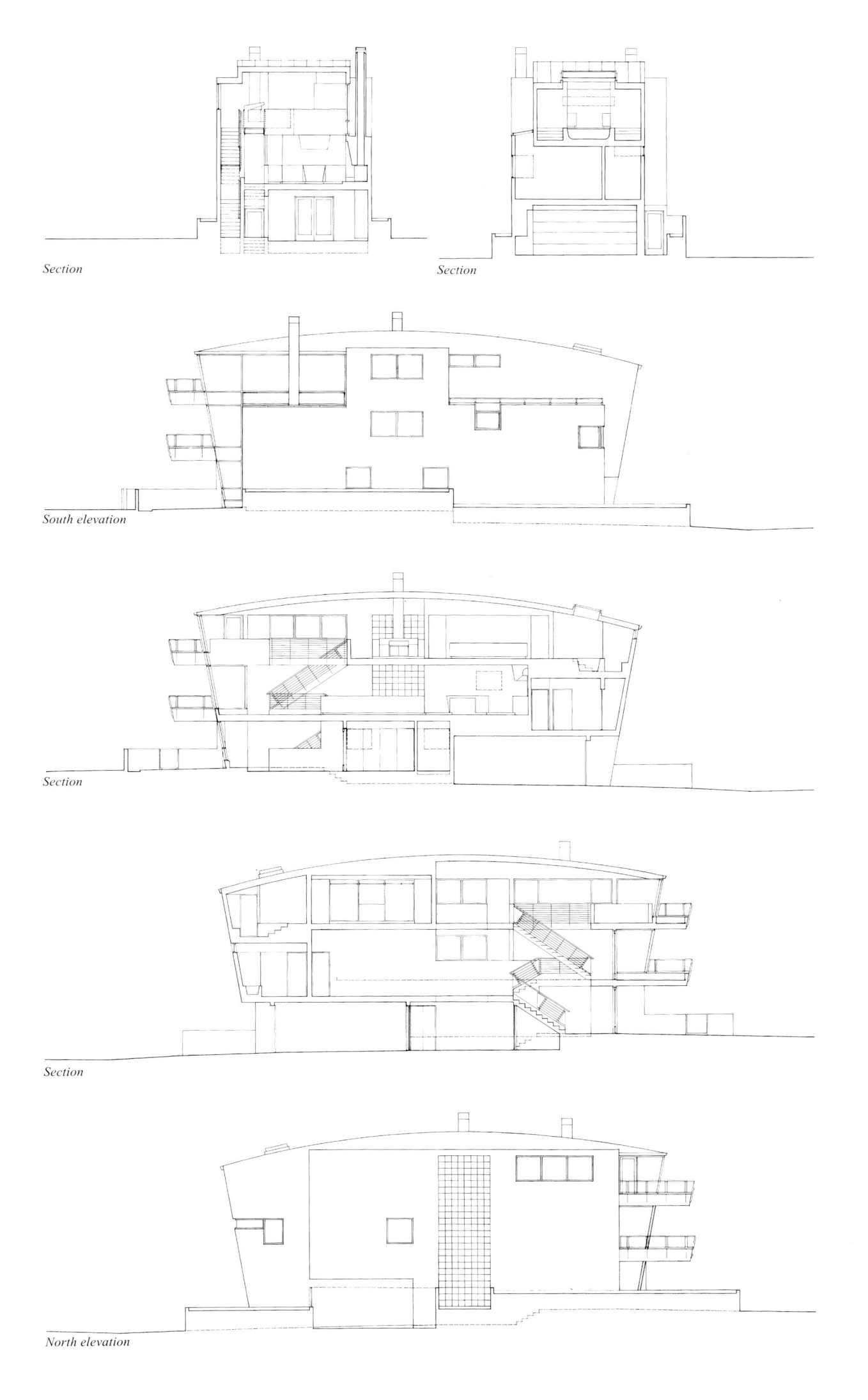

Section

South elevation

Section

Section

North elevation

93

Terrace on west

Staircase on first floor

Playroom

View from living room ▷

94

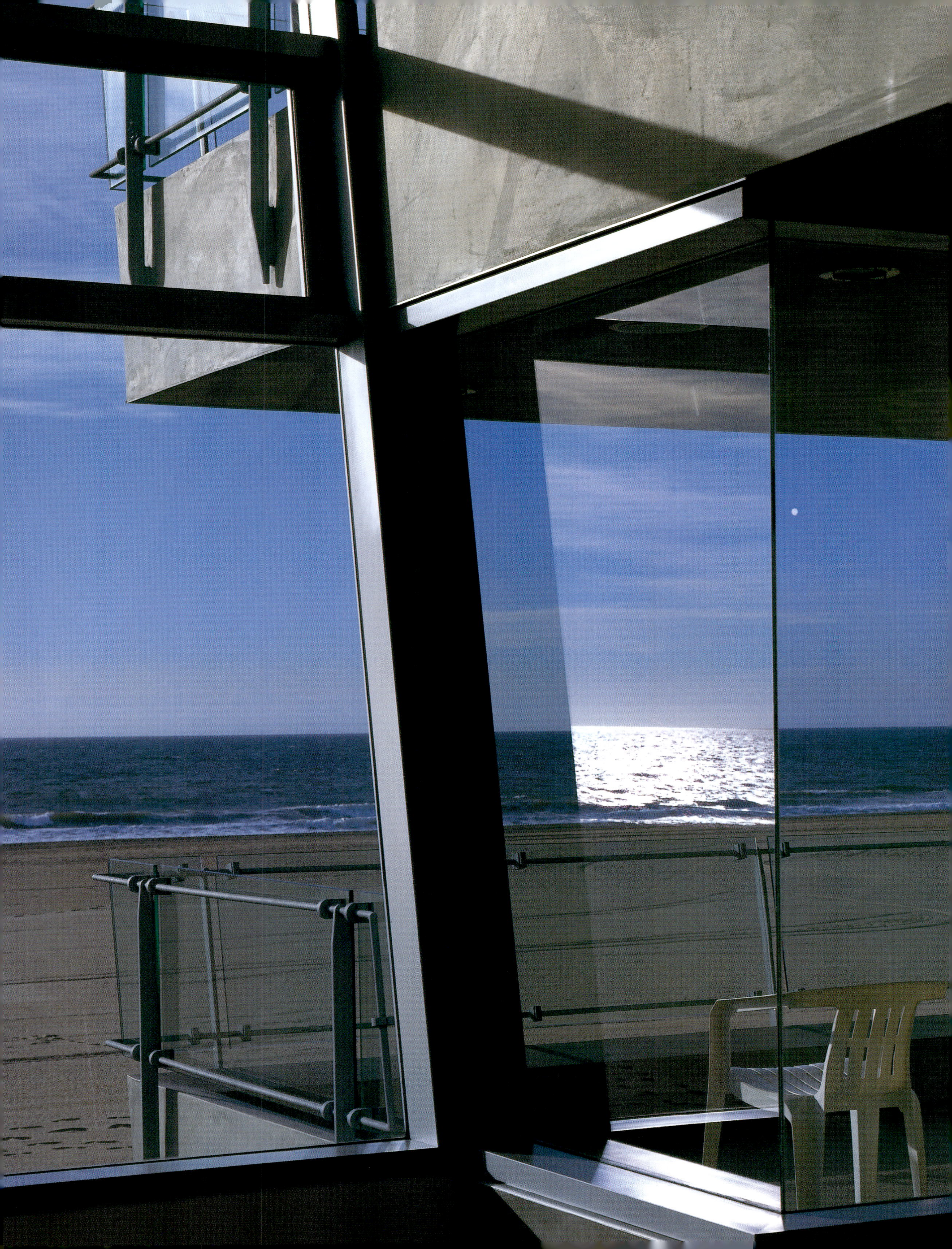

96

Living/dining room

Living room

Fireplace of living room

Kitchen

Living room: view toward west

Bridge to deck on third floor

Fireplace of master bedroom

Double height space: view toward master bedroom

Master bedroom

Bathroom

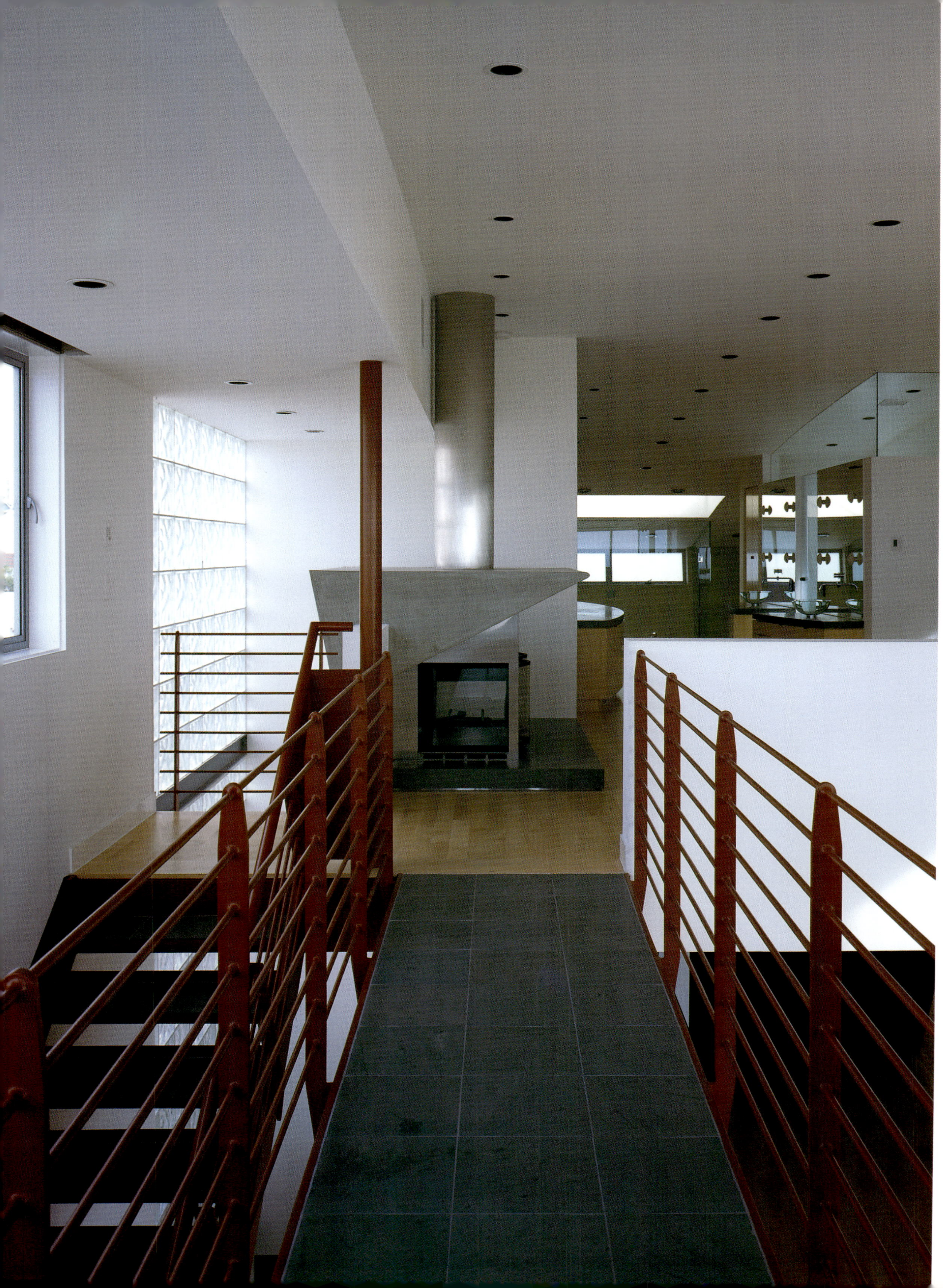

△▽ Bathroom

◁ Bridge

Detail

Detail

SHIGERU FUSE

HOUSE IN MAKUHARI-NISHI
Chiba, Japan
Design: 1998
Construction: 1998–99

Photos: H. Ueda

Architects: Shigeru Fuse
Consultants: Kozosekkeisha, structural
General contractor: Nagano Komuten
Structural system: reinforced concrete, timber
Major materials: exposed concrete, aluminum spandrel, exterior; marble, beech flooring, exposed concrete, plaster board, interior
Site area: 112.77m^2
Built area: 52.75m^2
Total floor area: 109.78m^2
Cost: 25 million yen

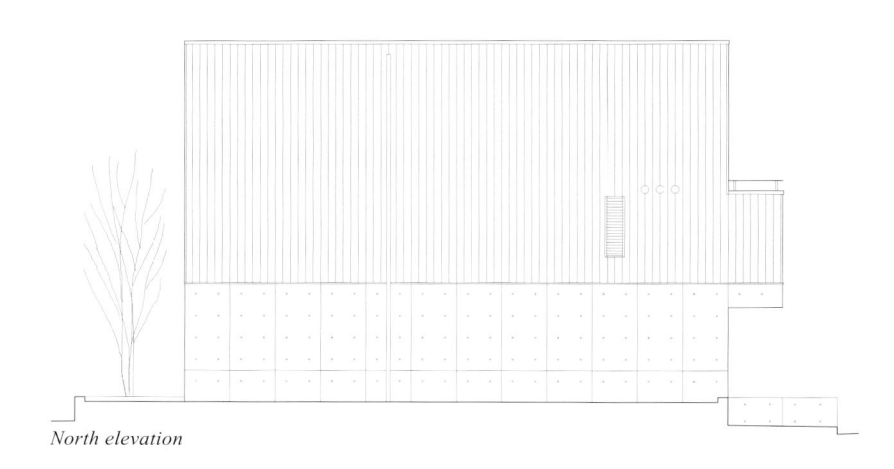

North elevation

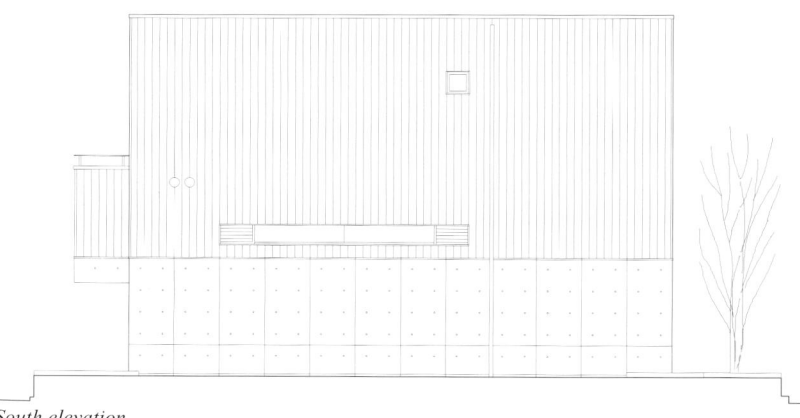

South elevation

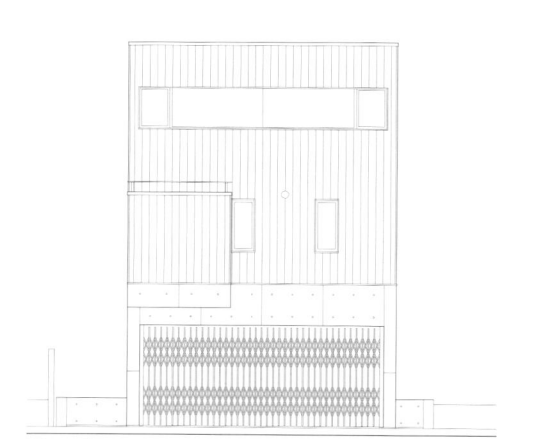

Third floor

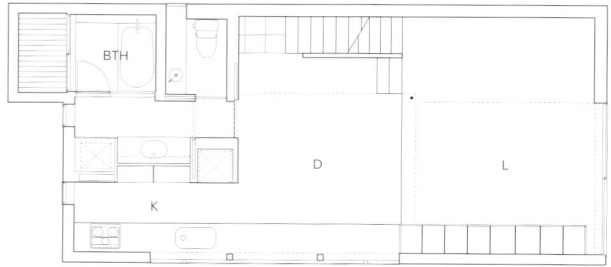

Second floor

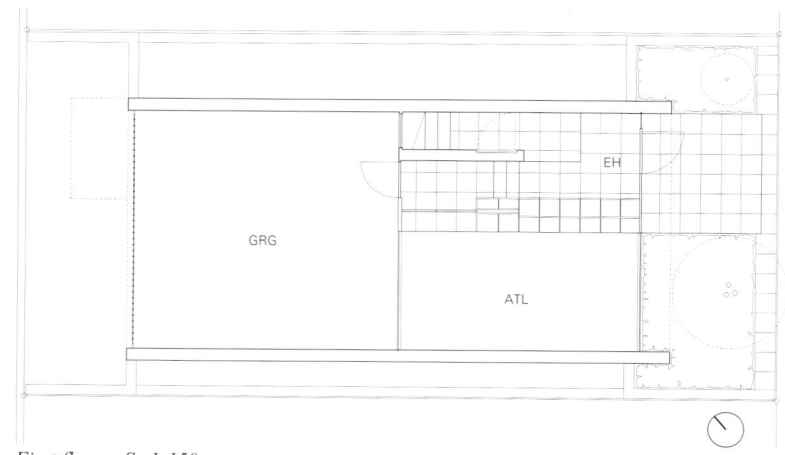

West elevation

First floor   S=1:150

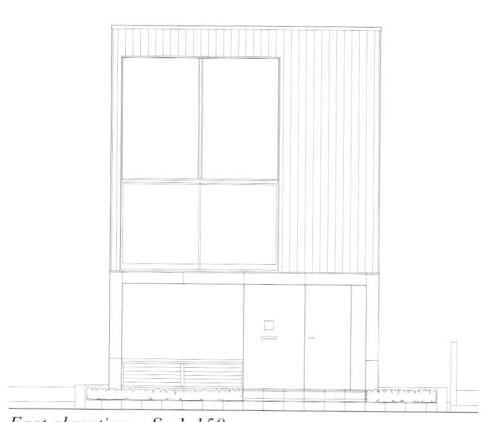

East elevation   S=1:150

Entrance ▷

East elevation

This house stands among a 'seaside new town' situated approximately 2 km from Makuhari New City, mid-way between Tokyo and Narita Airport. Makuhari district is a reclaimed land which came into existance 20 years ago. Subsequently, it has been the object of rapid urban development since the inauguration of 'Makuhari Messe (Nippon Convention Center)' complex. The vicinity of the site is characterized by a number of individual houses built on subdivided lots of land, forming a typical residential district. Measuring 16m on its south-eastern side and 6m on the north-western side, the site is circumscribed on both sides by two roads. The site's spatial direction connects these roads, and offers a view over the cluster of skyscrapers of Makuhari New City to the south-east.

The house is a simple structure consisting of a concrete tube submerged slightly into the ground with the residential section on top of it, positioned to the center of the site. The concrete tube, placed between the adjacent roads, is meant to open toward both sides. Its continuity of space in terms of visibility and indoor human activities emphasizes the site's spatial direction. Compatibility between privacy and openings to provide sufficient lighting/ventilation/view was successfully realized for the residential section.

The shape of the house is a simple box-type whose exterior walls are sharp and flat on the surface, using concrete and aluminium, as a result of a consciousness toward the material's texture. As opposed to the simplicity of the exterior, inner space was divided so that the relationship between each constituent part makes up a whole chain of versatile scenes. These parts create an accentuated spatial integration full of light, through arrangements such as varied floor levels, coloring, materials, and introduction of external factors. Volume, proportion and colors are the main focus of the space, producing a sharp expression using all three dimensions.
Shigeru Fuse

この住宅は，東京と成田空港のほぼ中間にある幕張新都心から約2kmの海浜ニュータウンに位置する。20年前に幕張地区の埋め立てが完了し，その後「幕張メッセ」の完成以来，急速に開発されている地区である。敷地周辺も整備された区画に一戸建が広がる典型的な住宅街を形成している。南東16m，北西6mの両面道路に面する敷地は，両方の道路をつなぐように空間の方向性をもち，南東方向には幕張新都心のビル群が一望できる。

建物は，地盤面からわずかに沈められたコンクリートチューブに居住部分を載せた単純な構成とし，敷地の中央に配置した。両面の道路に開くように置かれたコンクリートチューブは，視覚的・動線的な連続によって，敷地が持つ空間の方向性をより強調した。居住部分は，その上階に載せることによって，プライバシーの確保と同時に十分な採光，通風，眺望の得られる開放性を両立した。

建物外観は，シンプルな箱型で，素材のテクスチャーを意識しながらコンクリートとアルミによって，シャープでフラットな外壁面を構成した。シンプルな外観に対して内部空間は，各スペースの関係を様々な分節によって，多様なシーンの連鎖になるように考えた。空間の分節は，床レベルの変化，色彩，素材，外部の挿入などによって光にあふれた抑揚のある一体空間を創り出している。空間は，ヴォリューム，プロポーション，色彩を意識しながら「面」，「線」，「点」の構成によるシャープな表現とした。
（布施茂）

View of atelier from garage

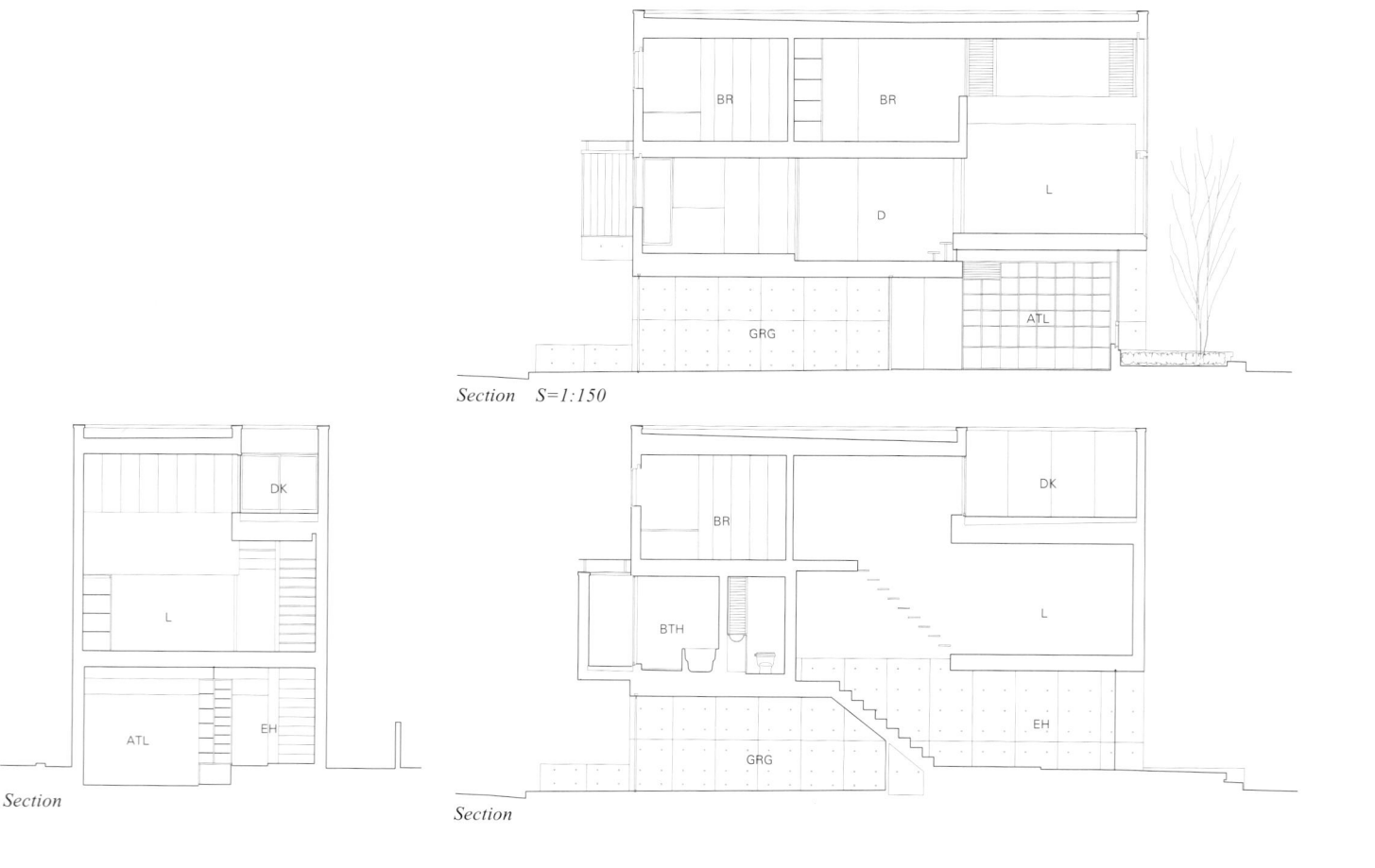

Section   S=1:150

Section

Section

Entrance

Staircase to second floor

Atelier

Living/dining room

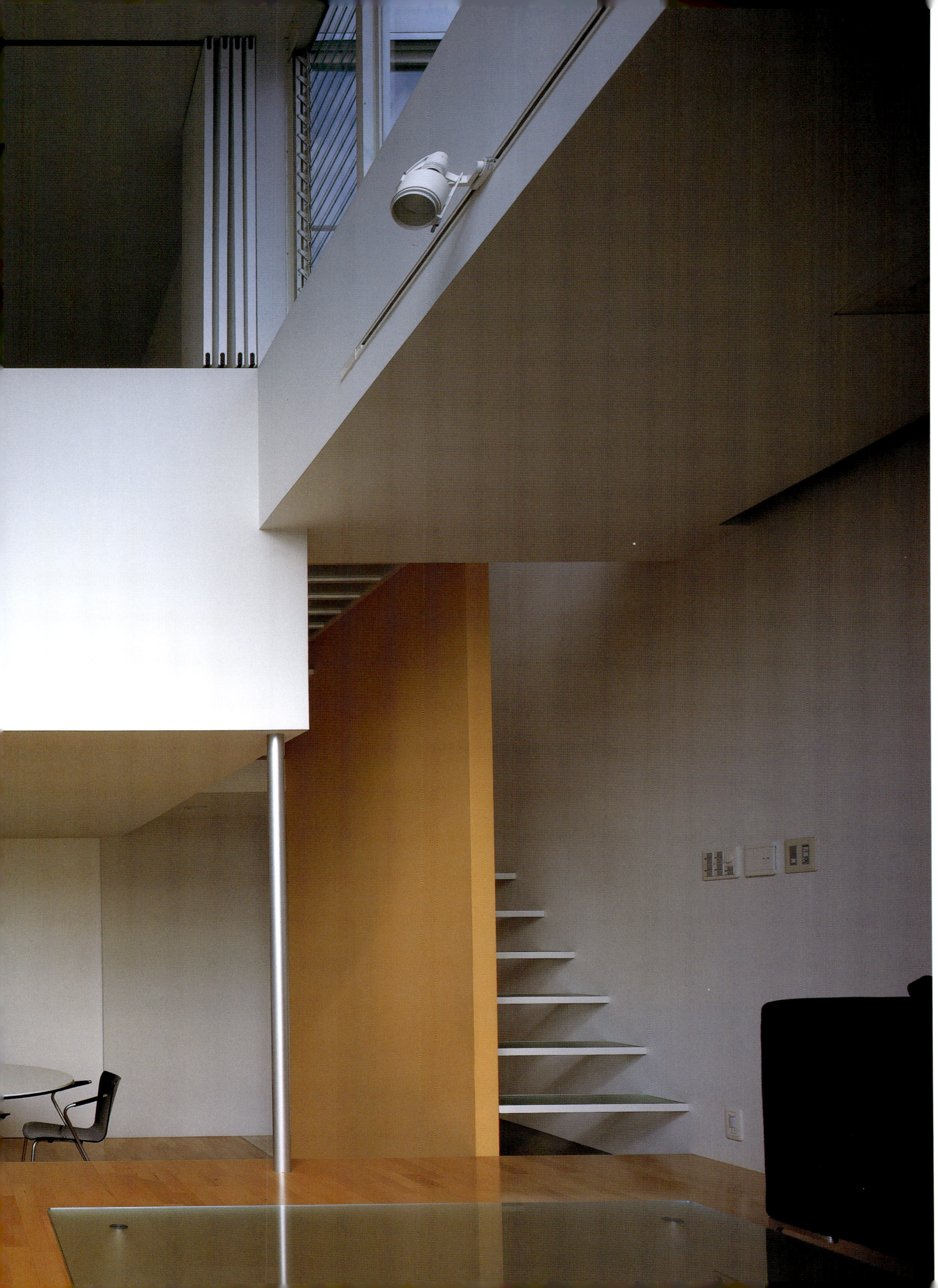

Living area

View of living area from dining area

Staircase

View toward children's bedroom

View toward deck

Kitchen

MARK MACK

THOMAS HOUSE
Las Vegas, Nevada, U.S.A.
Design: 1997–98
Construction: 1998–99

Photos: W. Fujii

Entrance

CG

The Thomas House is located in a gated development and expressed the rigid regulations by withdrawing inward and suppressing the exterior facades. Similar to the traditional Islamic house, which organizes itself from the inside, it addresses the outside only as a collective street element. The traditional courtyard house is modified for the car-dominated society of the 20th century.

Rooms are organized around the inner courtyard, from the formal to the informal and private. One approaches the house by a hidden, Chinese-like entry sequence of walls and cooling water elements. The entry/library serves the formal activities of orientation and entertainment, while the kitchen/family room is the informal room for living. The rest of the house is private and secluded from formal and domestic activities.

The layering of walls provides an intricate relationship between the landscape and the manmade. The solid/neutral colors of the walls provide a backdrop to the more eccentric colors of the landscape. Similarly, the large floating roof serves as a canvas for the changing qualities of light reflected off the water and walls.

Under the burning heat of the desert, this house maintains the scale and appearance of shelter and privacy—a place of refuge and shade away from the hustle and bustle of this mirage-like town.

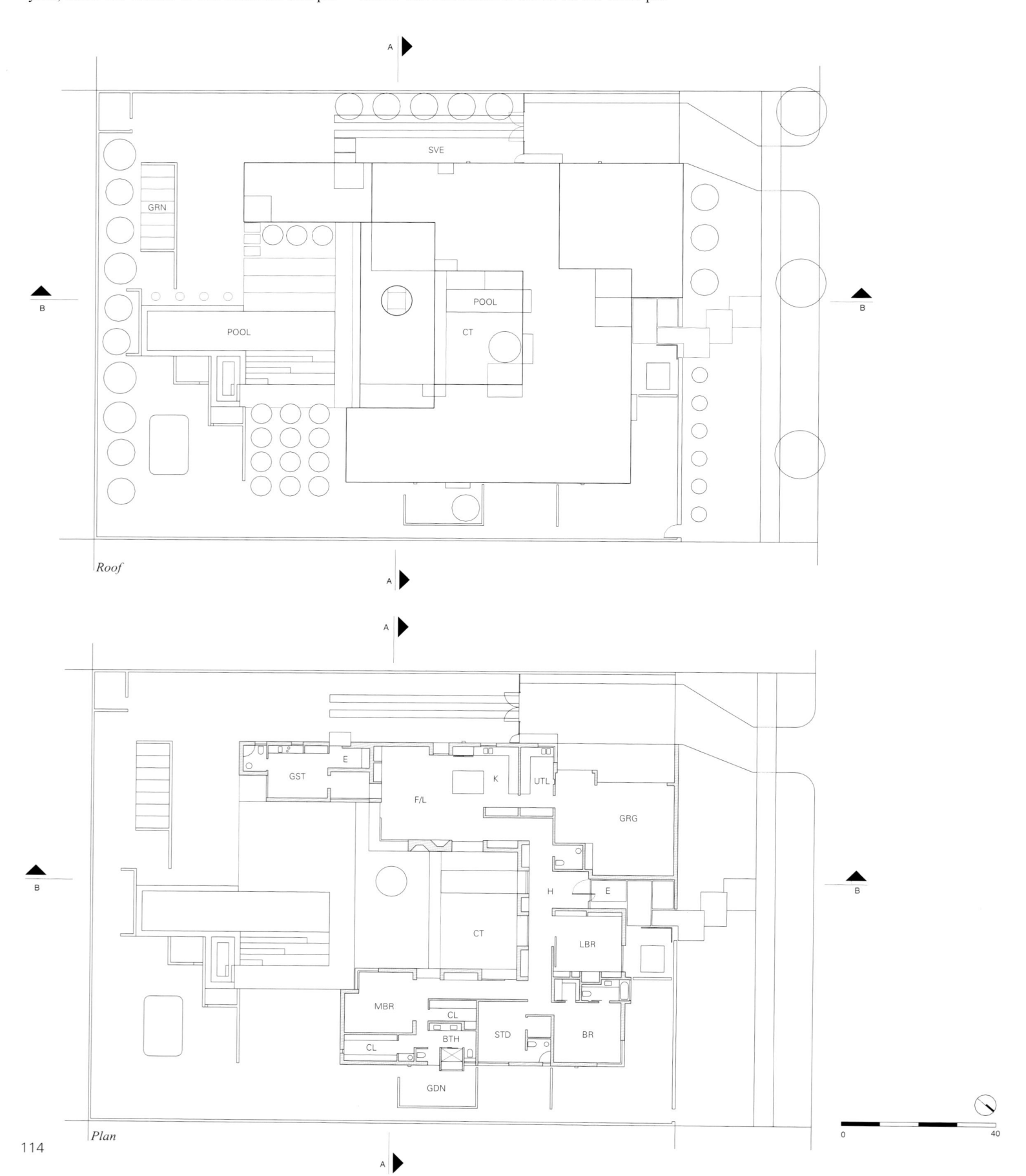

Roof

Plan

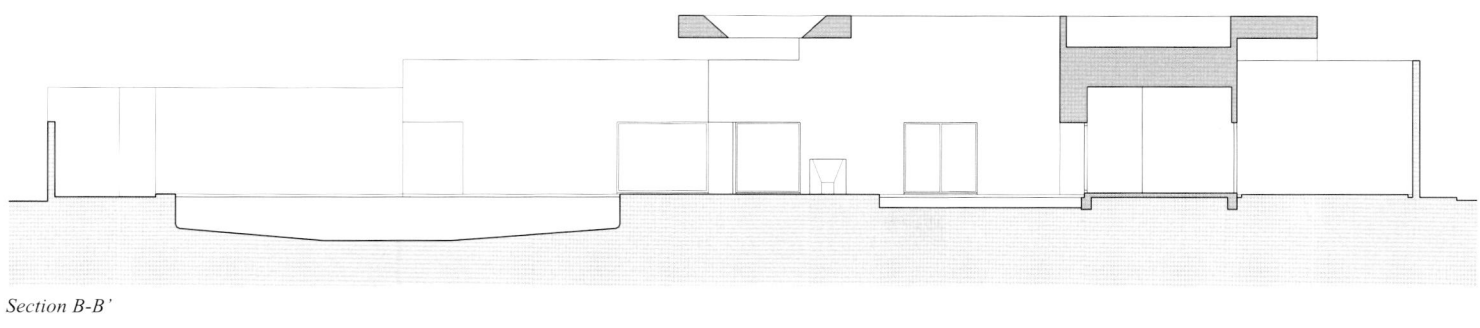

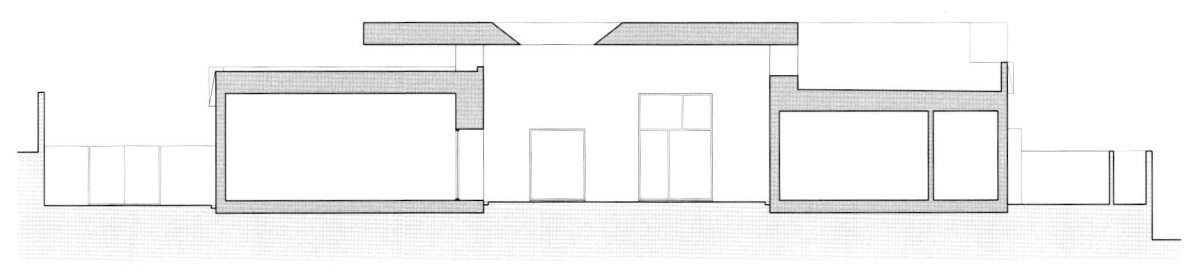

Section B-B'

Section A-A'

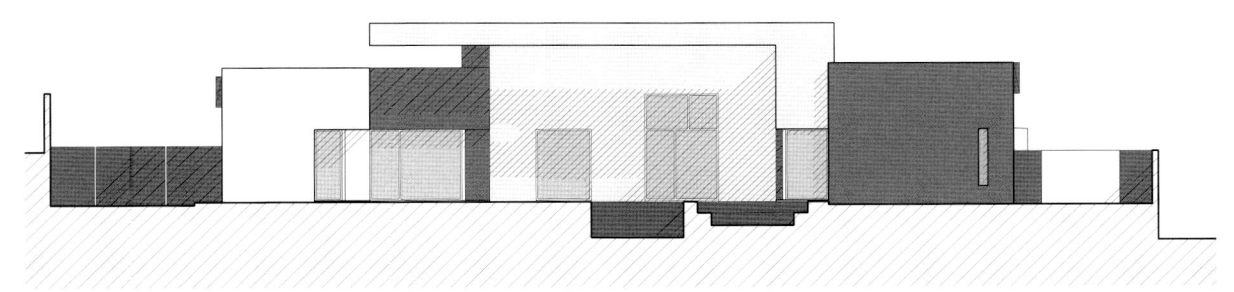

South elevation

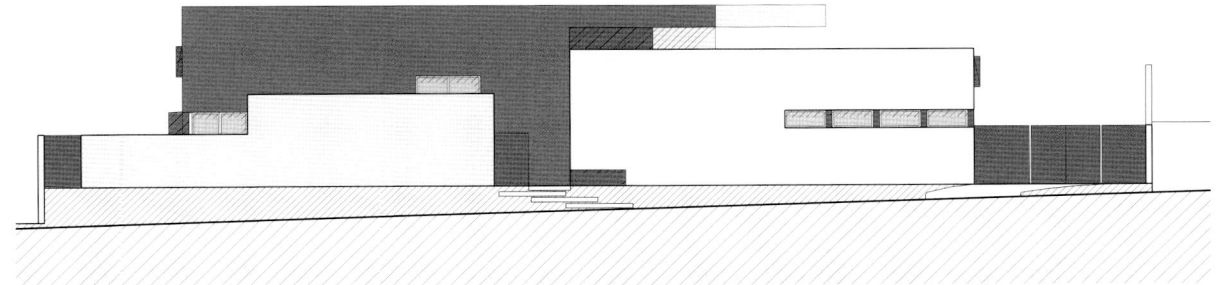

North elevation

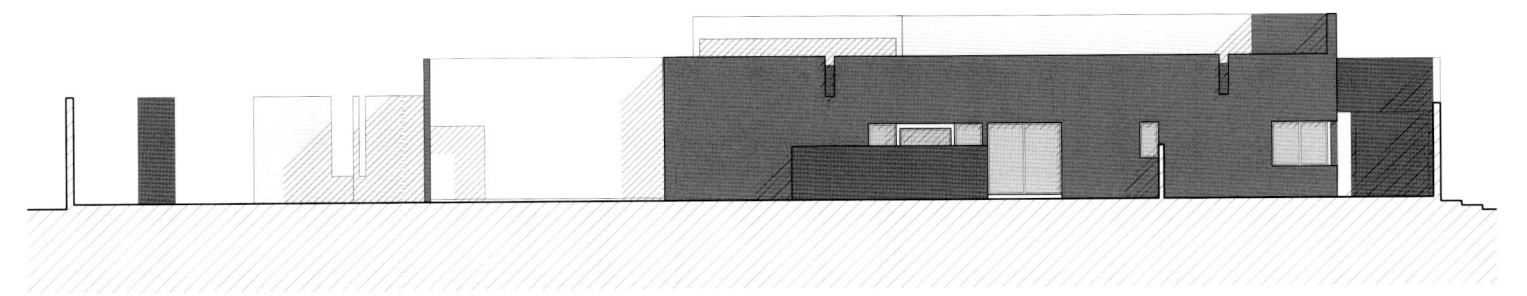

East elevation

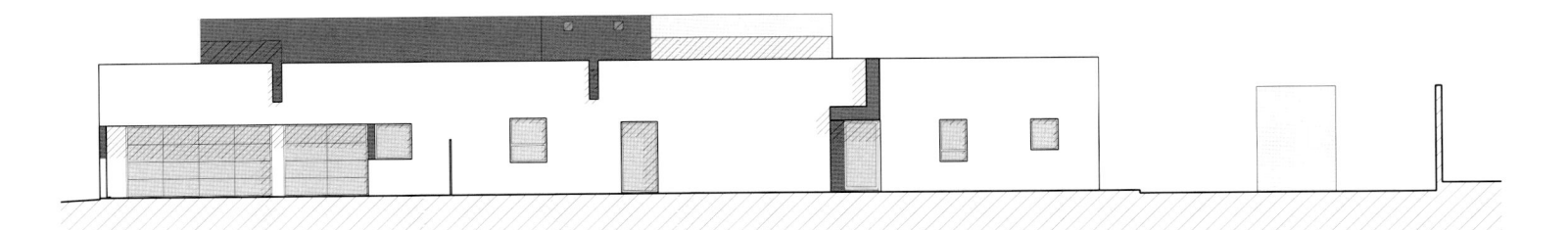

West elevation

115

トーマス邸は門で周辺とは遮断された住宅開発地にあり，内部に後退し，外観を抑制することで開発地内の厳格な建築規制に従っている。内側から構成して行く伝統的なイスラム住宅と同じように，外観は，一つにかたまった道路沿いの一要素というにすぎない。伝統に従ったこのコートヤード・ハウスは，20世紀の車社会に合わせて修正されている。

各部屋は，中庭を囲んで，フォーマルからインフォーマルへ，そしてプライベート空間の順に並んでいる。家に入るには，見え隠れする壁と涼しげな水盤が構成する中国風の進路を経て行く。エントリー／書斎がフォーマルな導入部とエンタテイメント空間の役割を果たす一方，台所／家族用居間はふだんの生活空間となる。その他の部分は，客の接待や家庭生活の場から切り離されたプライベートな場所である。

重層する壁が風景と人工物との入り組んだ関係をつくりだす。壁の持つ硬質でニュートラルな色調は，風景のもつより強烈な色彩の背景となる。同様に，浮かぶような大屋根は，水面や壁に反射し，さまざまに変化する光のためのキャンバスである。

砂漠の燃えるような陽光の下，この住宅は，私的な避難所としてのスケールと外観を保っている——蜃気楼のような街の雑踏から離れ，日射しから守られた退避の場所なのである。

Architects: Mack Architect(s)—Mark Mack, principal-in-charge, Tim Sakamoto, project architect; Ed Diamante, Jeff Allsbrook, project team; Ariel Asken + Roger Kurath, renderings
Eric Strain, architect of record; Assemblage Studio
Client: Roger Thomas
Consultants: Martin & Peltyn, structural; Southwest AC, machanical; Roger Thomas, interior; Anderson Environmental Design, Hadland Landscaping, landscape; Joe Kaplan, lighting; Santor, wood workings; Southpark Fabricators, metal; Arcon, Syndecrete, concrete
General contractor: Merlin Contracting, Bart Jones
Structural system: CMU, steel, non bearing walls, wood
Major materials: stucco covered CMU walls, concrete flooring, mild rusted steel, interior plaster, syndecrete, colored and stained concrete
Area: 4,400 s.f., building area; 1/4 acre, site area
Cost of construction: $ 1,100,000

Courtyard

Pool

Entrance of guest room

Courtyard on west

Entrance court

Entrance

Courtyard

Family/living room

Hall

Family/living room

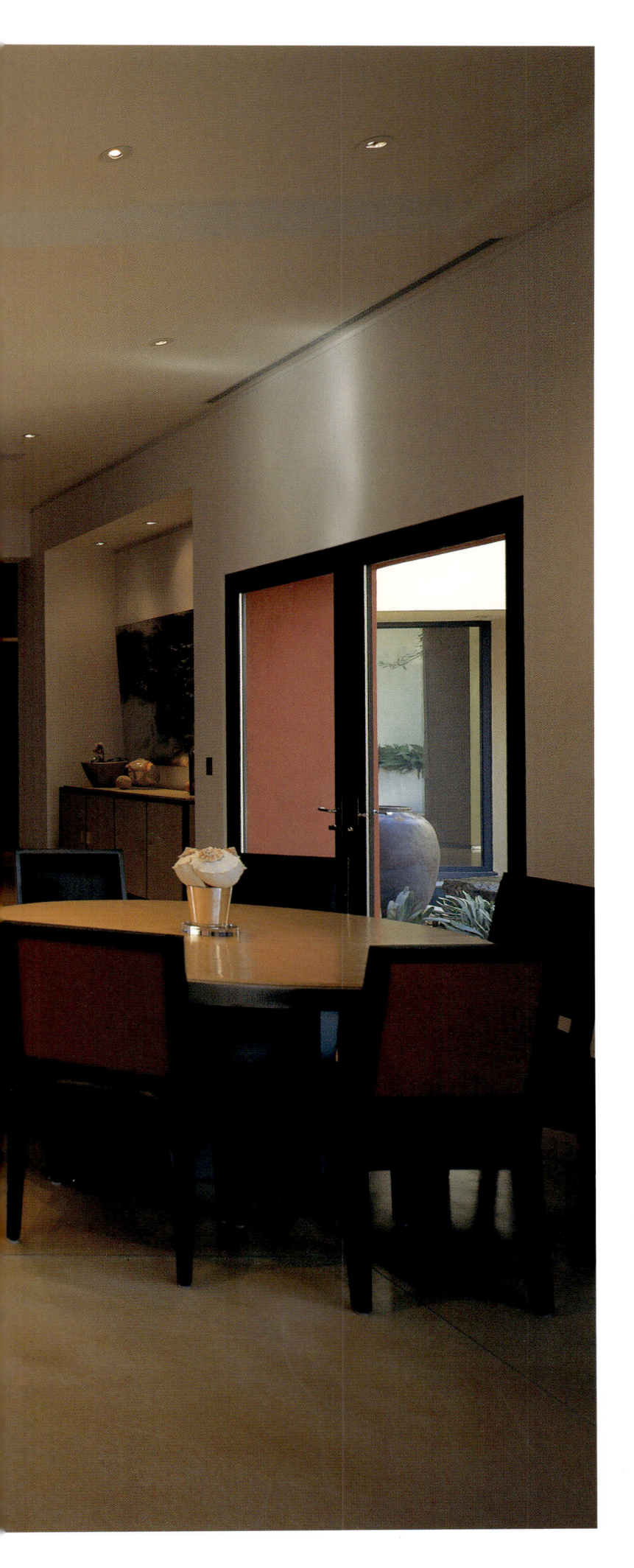

View from library

Hall

121

YOSHINARI SHIODA
INTERDESIGN ASSOCIATES

HOUSE MUR
Tokyo, Japan
Design: 1997–99
Construction: 1999

Photos: H. Ueda

The site is located within a residential district, adjacent to a vast tract of green land to the south. Looking from a bird's-eye view, it is placed at the peak of the gently undulating Musasino Plateau.

The major theme of design was the creation of spatial relationship between this exceptional environment and an inner space whose geometry leaves us no choice than dealing with a tiny, limited amount of space.

The idea here was to create a space where exterior and interior would undergo an infinite topological exchange all the way preserving their originality and difference—just like the "Klein's jar"—to ensure this small house a sense of constant linkage with a larger whole. Boundary planes would always shift and fluctuate, rather than melt away to disappear.

We have worked on various manipulations: slightly digging down so that continuity between the tract of green land in the south and the second level that is the main floor be maintained, and arranging factors to capture the subtle changes of external light; taking the views of the sky and the neighbors' trees into the House; representing some external factors internally; introducing the external finishing material to the interior, so that in turn they come to be wrapped up with internal finishing material; or bringing the landscapes surrounding this residence by reflecting them into a mirror, to find them being surrounded by the internal space. These manipulations, which we have named 'sympathy', 'infiltration', 'metaphor', 'reversal' and 'transmission' respectively, are overlapped with the rhythmical changes of spatial expansion and contraction synchronized with human indoor activity, to compose and develop a continuous whole without interruption.

The roof deck acts as a tool to materialize the whole to be an open-end circuit-something like a moon-observation platform. It offers a view of the abundant greenery of a vast park and the city across the roofs of houses to the north, and looking up, a starry sky stretching as far as the eye can see. This privilege is indeed a gift of this site.

Yoshinari Shioda

敷地は，南にある広い緑地に隣接した住宅街の一角で，より広域的に見るならば，ゆったりと起伏する武蔵野台地の，この辺りでの最頂部に位置するような場所である。

この恵まれた外部環境と，物理的にはとても小さなものにしかなり得ない内部空間との間に，どのような空間関係を創出するかということが設計の主題であった。

ここでは，この小さな住宅がより大きな全体と常に繋がっていることを感じ取れるようにするために，外部と内部が，その独自性と異質性とを保持したままトポロジカルな交換を無限に繰り返していく，ちょうど「クラインの壺」のような空間を創り

たいと考えた。境界面が溶けて無くなってしまうというのではなく，むしろそれが常にズレて揺れ動いている，といった感じである。

南の緑地と主階である2階とを違和感なく連続させるために全体を少し掘り下げた上で，外光の微妙な変化を捕えるように要素を構成したり，隣地の樹木や空の眺めを取り込んだり，外部的な要素を内部にも現したり，この住宅をくるんでいた外部仕上材を内部にも反復させ，それらがいつの間にか内部仕上材にくるまれているようにしたり，あるいはこの住宅を包んでいた風景を鏡に映し込ませて内部に持ち込み，それらがいつの間にか内部空間に包まれているようにしたり（これらをぼくたちはそれぞれ，

感応・浸透・隠喩・反転・転送などと呼んでいた）といった操作を行った。これらの操作を，室内を歩く人の動きに合わせた空間の膨張・収縮のリズミカルな変化と重ね合わせて，全体を切れ目なく連続的に構成・展開させている。

屋上のデッキは，全体をオープンエンドのサーキットとして成立させるための道具立てであり，月見台のようなものなのだが，そこからは，北側住居群の屋根を越えて遠く，広大な公園の豊かな緑と街のたたずまいを眺めることができるし，見上げれば，何物にも遮られることのない全天の星空を獲得することができる。この敷地でしか味わうことのできない特権である。

（塩田能也）

Architects: Yoshinari Shioda/Interdesign Assoc.
Architects—Yoshinari Shioda, Rie Ogawa
Consultants: Inoue structural design office—Motoharu Inoue, structural; BASEMENT—Kouji Asazuma, construction management
General contractor: Yonemura Komuten
Structural system: timber, reinforced concrete
Major materials: galvanized steel, mortal, exterior; maple flooring, plaster board, interior
Site area: 142m^2
Built area: 61.3m^2
Total floor area: 132.8m^2

Night view from south

View from south

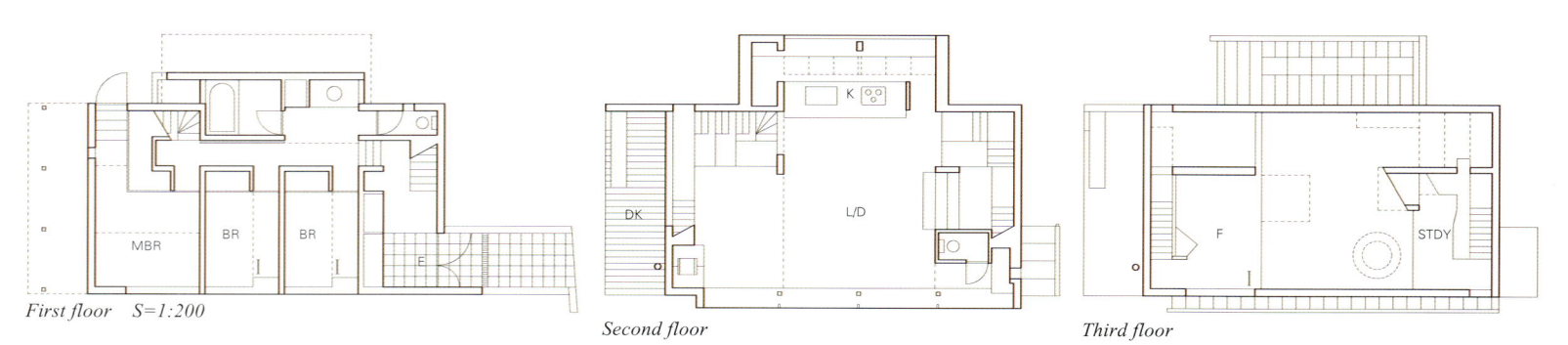

First floor S=1:200

Second floor

Third floor

Site plan   *S=1:800*

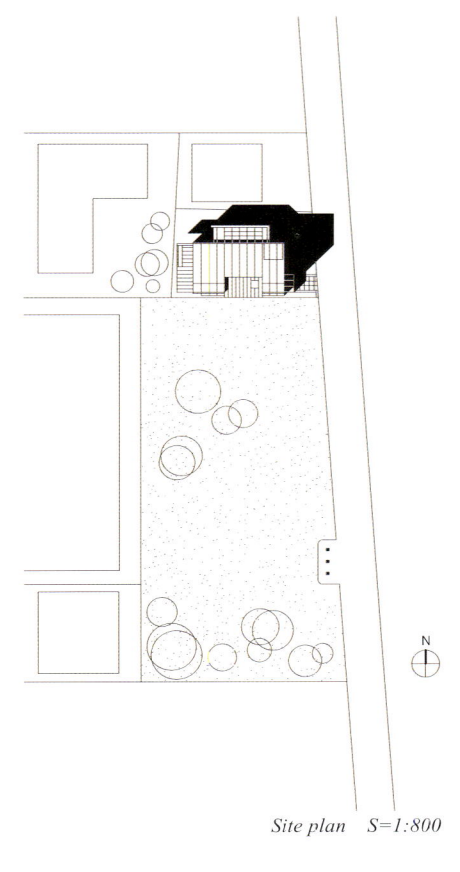

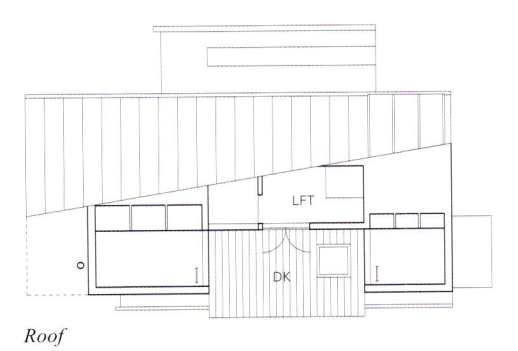

Roof

Entrance

125

Corridor: child's bedrooms on left

Staircase on east

Section   S=1:200

Section

South elevation   S=1:200

Living/dining room between two staircases

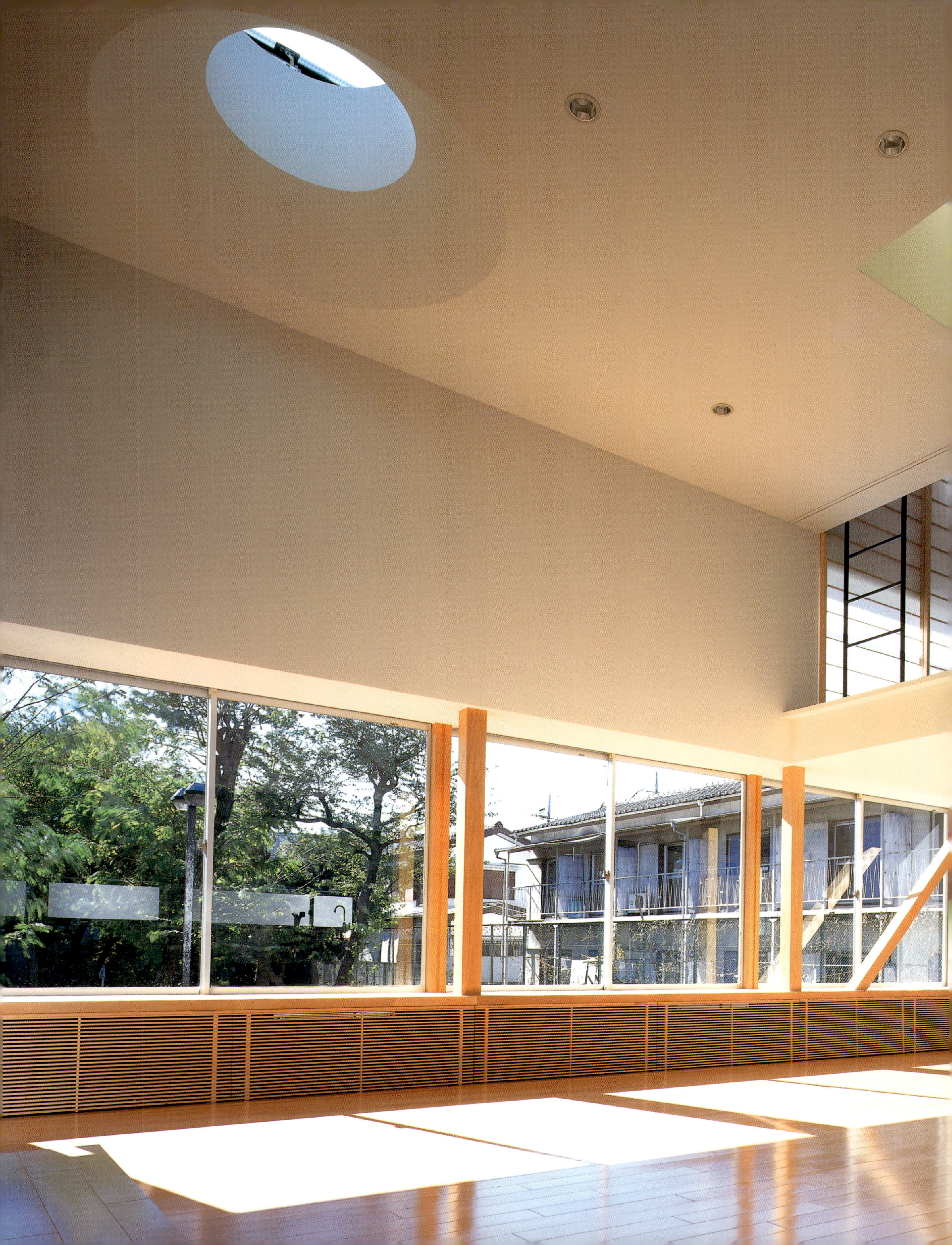

Living/dining room

Living/dining room

Corner of living/dining room: view toward deck

Staircase to study

Downward view of living/dining room from study

Study

Family room△▽

KOICHIRO ISHIGURO

WHITE WOODS
Tokyo, Japan
Design: 1998–99
Construction: 1999

Photos: K. Takada

A private residence for a working couple and their beloved daughter. To satisfy the client's wish to share as much time as possible with the family and to allow space and functions some gradual changes, an integrated space with enough volume was found to be appropriate. The basic space-structuring method consisted of a shelter of thin rigid frame structure ensuring the volume of 900m³, the maximum according to this structure's regulations, into which a floor-space of 200m² (='stage') was inserted as a required function.

The site is located in the midst of Tokyo's typically crowded residential area, flanked by buildings on all of its four sides. Sunlight and view to the sky are secured with an opening on the upper part. In the center, a wellhole topped by a skylight amplifies the natural lighting for this volume of considerable depth. Stages were inserted at positions decided through examination of how these lightings/views and functions might relate with each other. The composition of the house resulted in a loose division into two—bedroom and living/dining—sections, bisected by the huge glass plate set up for the wellhole.

The above-mentioned features call forth the groups of landscapes that involve "individual times", such as a piece of sky, family life, movements of sun and moon, and growth of trees. A multi-layered stage yields a viewpoint looking through these layers, where an act of crossing such space means integration of various landscapes as experiences. Compared to loft apartments in Manhattan that are typical examples of living space with a clear homogeneity, this 'multi-layered loft' is, just like a forest, simple and calm. And yet, it leaves a possibility of a diverse, complex space.
Koichiro Ishiguro

それぞれに仕事を持つ夫婦と愛娘のための住宅である。より多くの時間を家族で共有し，徐々に空間や機能に変化を加えていきたいというクライアントの希望を具現化するには，十分な気積をもつ一体的な空間が適当ではないかと考えた。そこで，薄肉ラーメン構造のシェルターにより，形態規制の上限である900m³の気積を確保し，必要な機能として200m²の床＝ステージを挿入することを基本的な空間構成法とした。

敷地は典型的な東京の住宅密集地にあり，四方を既存建物で囲まれていることから，開口部を上空に開き，日照と空への眺望を確保した。また，中央に天窓を併設した吹き抜けをつくり，奥行きの深いヴォリュームに対して，自然採光を増幅した。挿入された各ステージは，こうした採光・眺望と機能とがどのように連関するかを考察しながら位置決定された。その結果，寝室の領域とリビング・ダイニングの領域とが，吹き抜けに設置された大ガラスによりゆるやかに二分された構成となった。

以上のしつらえは，切り取られた空，家族の営み，太陽と月の運行，樹木の生長，など「固有の時間」を内包する風景群を誘起する。重層したステージはこうしたレイヤーを透視する視点をあたえ，これらの空間を横断することは，様々な風景を体験として積分していくことになる。マンハッタンのロフトアパートメントに代表される明快な均質性をもった住空間に比べると，この「重層化されたロフト」は，例えば森がそうであるように，ひそやかではあるが，多様で複雑性をもつ空間となるかもしれない。

（石黒浩一郎）

Roof floor

Second floor

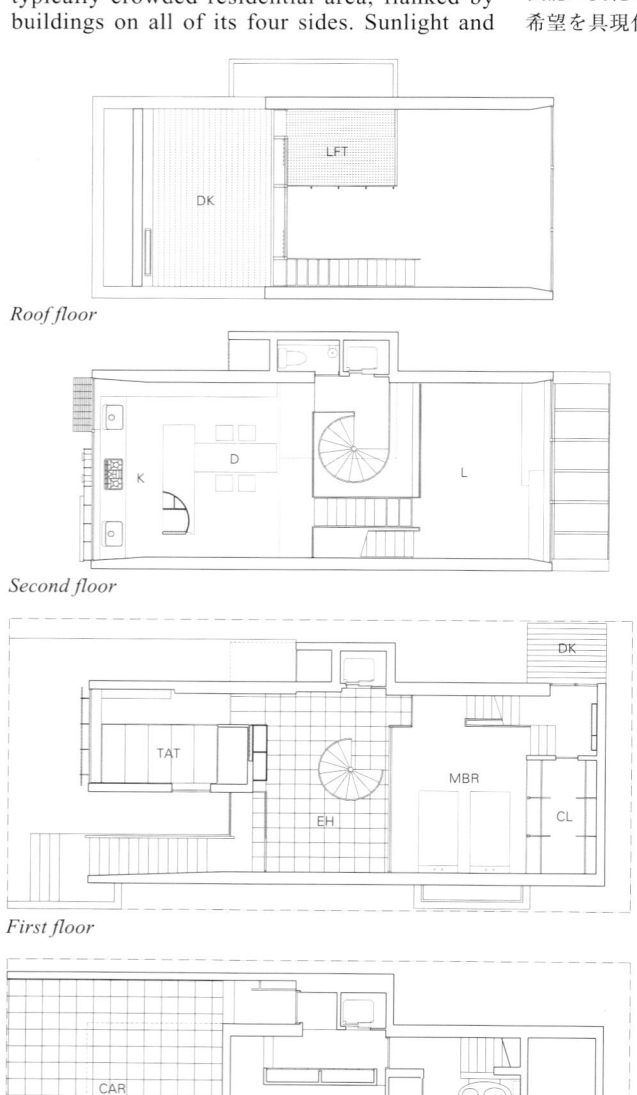

First floor

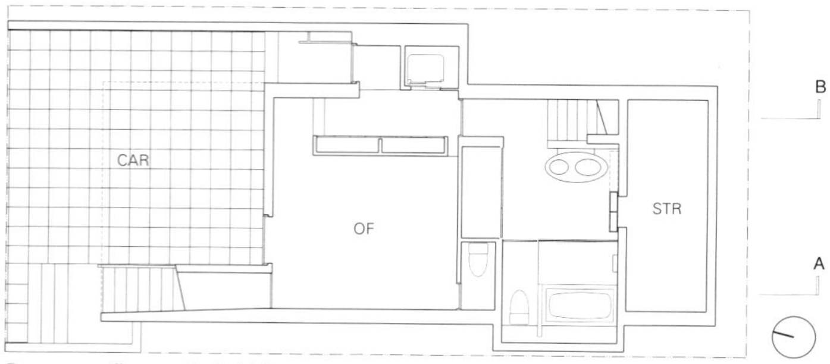

Basement floor S=1:200

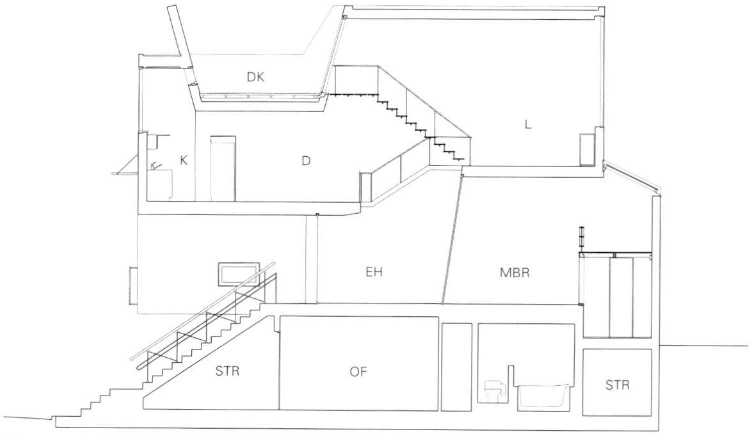

Section A-A

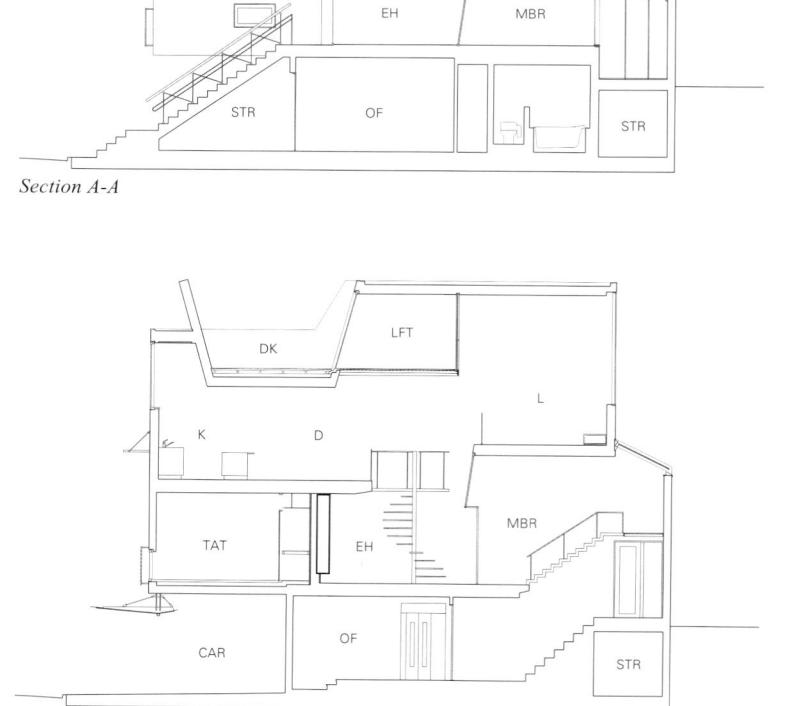

Section B-B

Night view from north

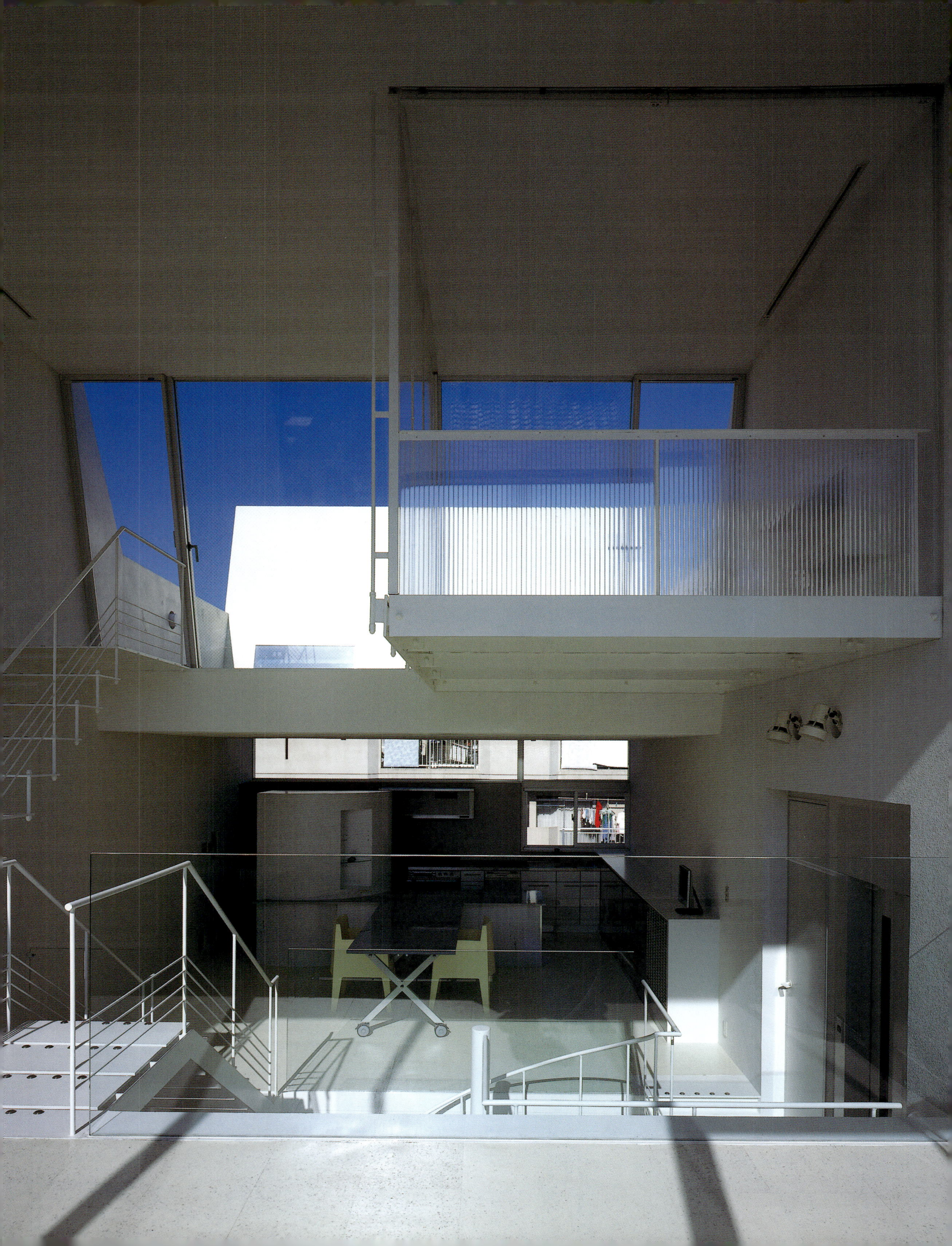

Staircase to deck

Tatami room

View of dining room from living room

Staircase

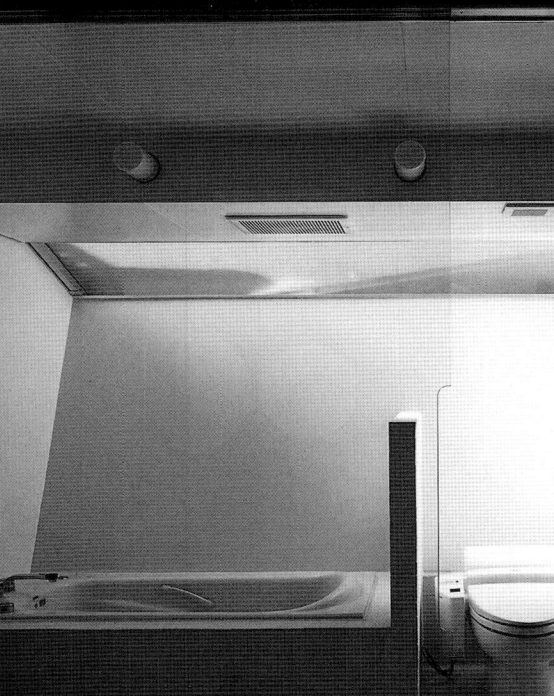

Bathroom

View of entrance hall from master bedroom

Architects: Is Associates Architectural Studio—Koichiro Ishiguro
Consultants: Keishosha—Junichi Igarashi, structural; Is Associates Architectural Studio—Koichiro Ishiguro, furniture; M&C Consulting—Hiroshi Hatanaka, management & finance
General contractor: KY corporation—Hiromichi Miyazawa
Structural system: reinforced concrete
Major materials: ceramic chips paint, glass, exterior; corktile, marble, painted wallpaper, ceramic chips paint, interior
Site area: 132.2m^2
Built area: 75.1m^2
Total floor area: 199.6m^2

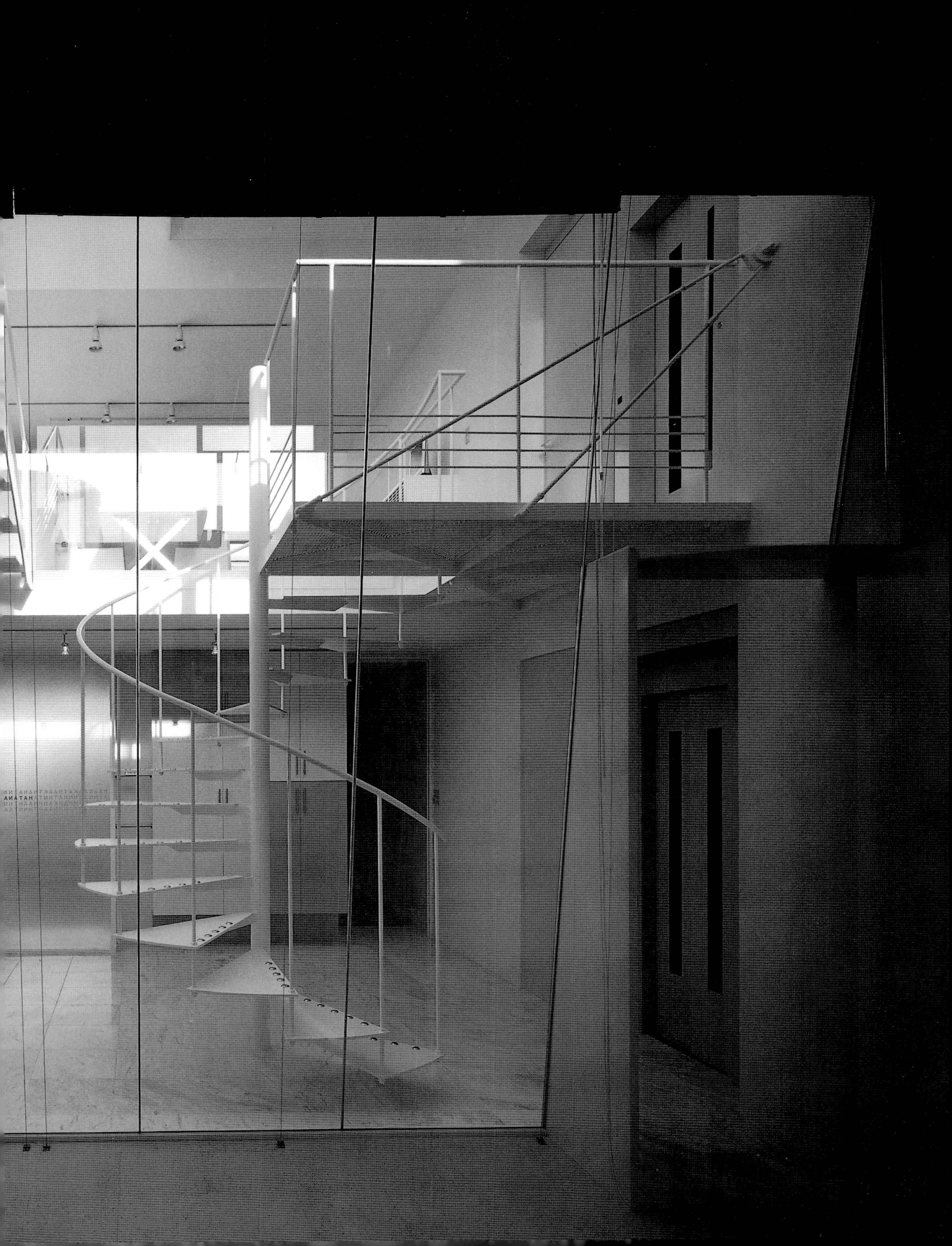

STEVEN EHRLICH

CANYON RESIDENCE
Los Angeles, California, U.S.A.
Design: 1996–97
Construction: 1997–99

Photos: T. Sakashita

The "L" shaped floor plan embraces the grandeur of the sloping site adjacent to a creek. An eighteen foot high entry and living room area separates the two story bedroom wing from the family-kitchen zone. The house strongly connects each indoor space to the verdant landscape beyond replete with large native California trees. An "amphitheater" of stairs and floating decks facilitates this connection.

A series of vertical masses of colored burnished stucco form a structural ordering element that aligns in the north-south direction. These masses house elements that "serve" the adjacent spaces such as fireplaces, stairs, mechanical cores and storage. They cascade through the house responding to need while forming a kinetic rhythm of color and form. Counterpointing these vertical planes are a series of cascading copper clad horizontal canopies. They protect natural wood, glass windows and doors from rain and sun and form a horizontal balance of floating planes that become part of the critical sculptural ordering system.

The ensemble of vertical colored mass in conjunction with the copper horizontal planes, glass, and painted stucco mass dances harmoniously as indoor space fuses with the natural environment.

North view

クリークが脇を流れる，斜面になった敷地の広がりをL型プランの建物が取り囲んでいる。18フィートの高さを持つエントランスとリビングルームが2層の寝室ウイングを家族の居間／台所のある領域と分けている。内部空間はすべて，その彼方に広がる大きなカリフォルニア原産の木々が鬱蒼と茂る青々とした風景に強く結びつけられている。階段のつくる"円形劇場"と，宙に浮かぶデッキがこのつながりをつくりだす手助けをしている。

艶のあるカラー・スタッコ仕上げの垂直に伸びるマッスの連なりが南北方向に整列し，構造的なオーダリングの要素を構成する。これらのマッスには，暖炉，階段，機械室，収納といった，隣接する空間に"仕える"要素が置かれている。そして，必要に応じて建物の数箇所を帯のように巻いて行く一方で，色彩と形態のリズムをつくりだす。これらの垂直面に対抗するのは，幾段にもわたって，水平に広がる銅張りのキャノピーである。キャノピーは木やガラスで構成されている窓や扉を雨や日差しから守るとともに，主要な彫刻的オーダリング・システムの一部である躯体から浮いた面に対し，水平方向の均衡をとる役割を果たしている。

彩られた垂直のマッスと銅の水平面，ガラス，塗装されたスタッコ仕上げのマッスが結合して，内部空間を自然環境と融合させながら，音楽的なリズムをつくりだす。

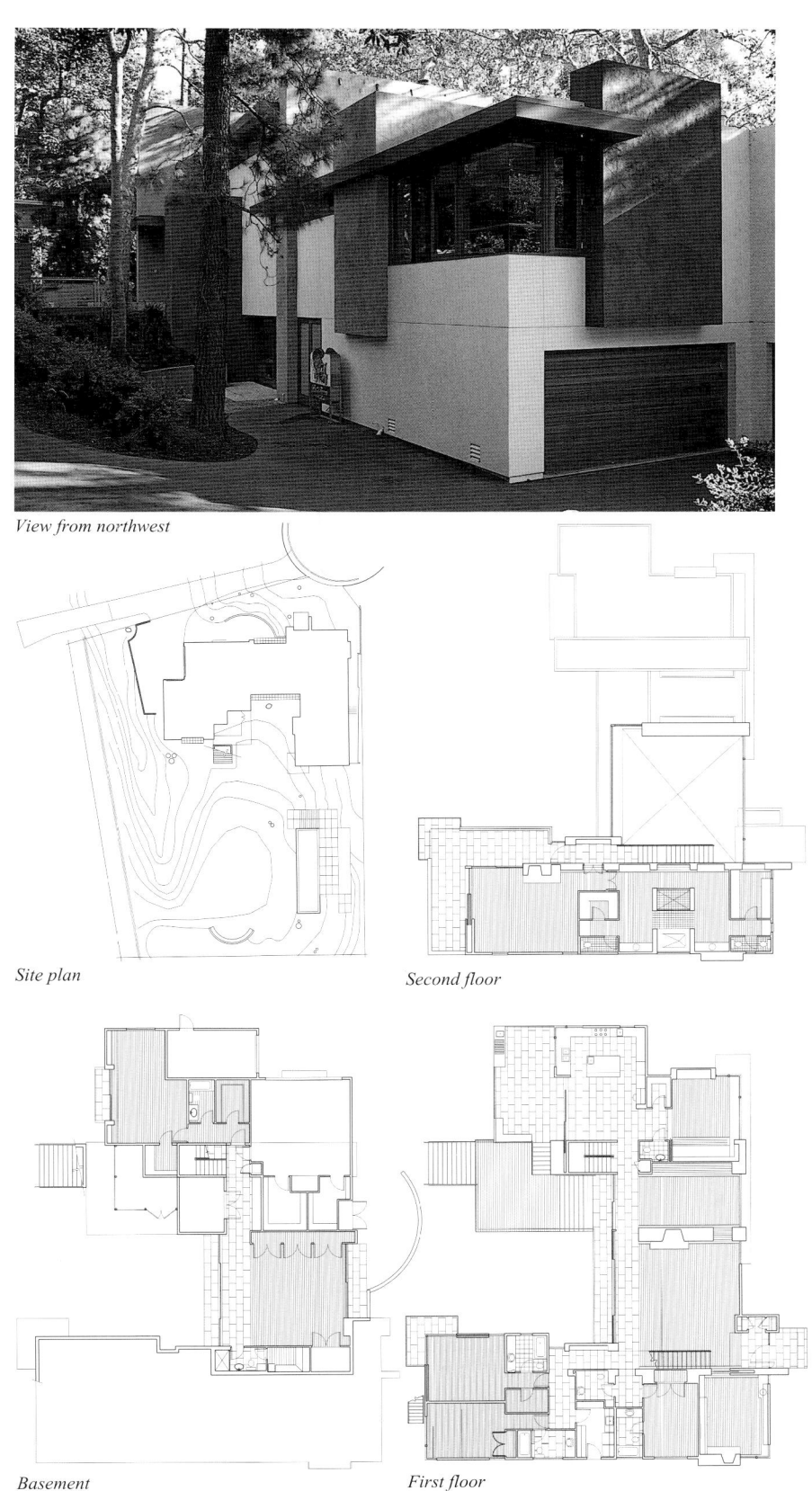

View from northwest

Site plan

Second floor

Basement

First floor

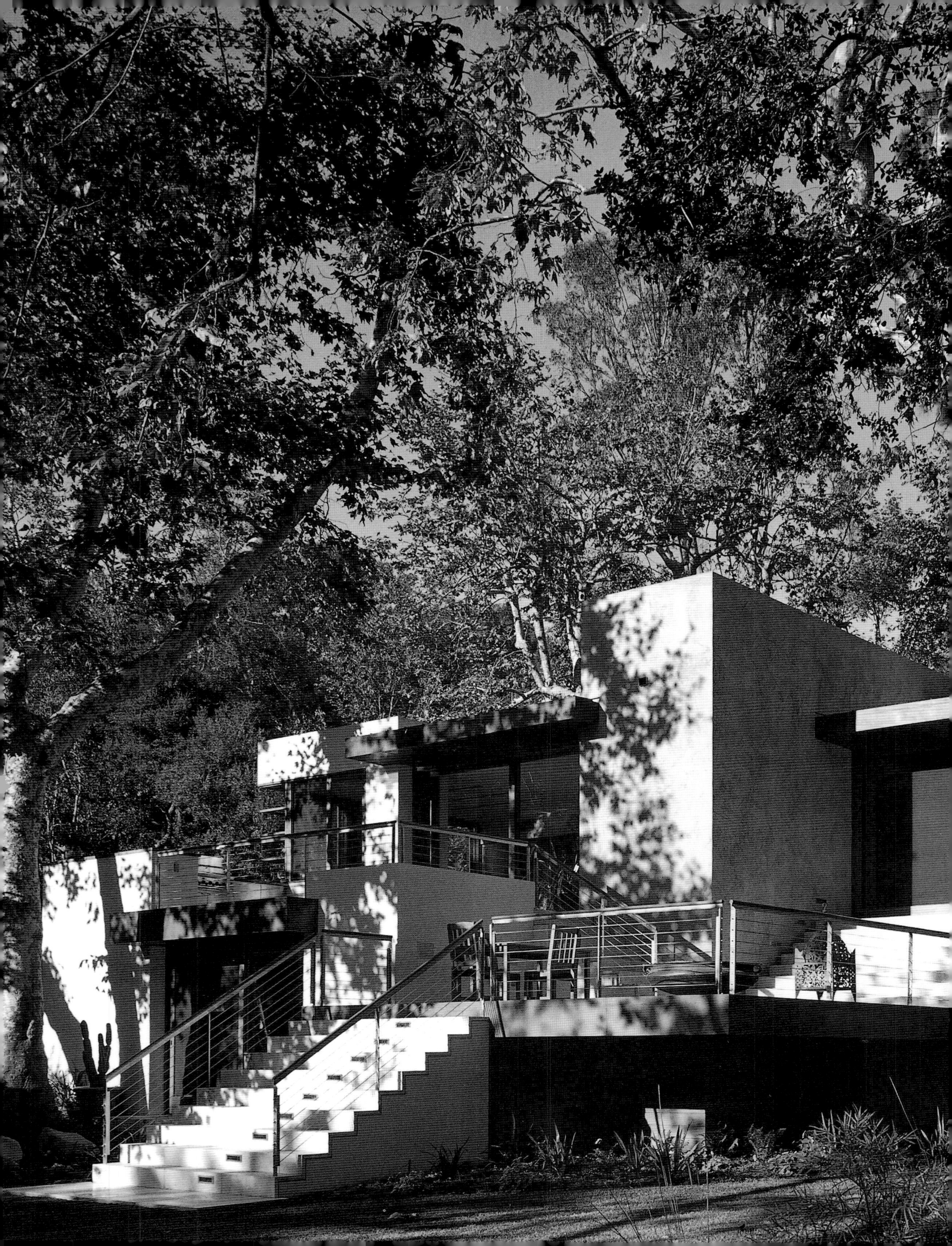

North elevation

South elevation

West elevation

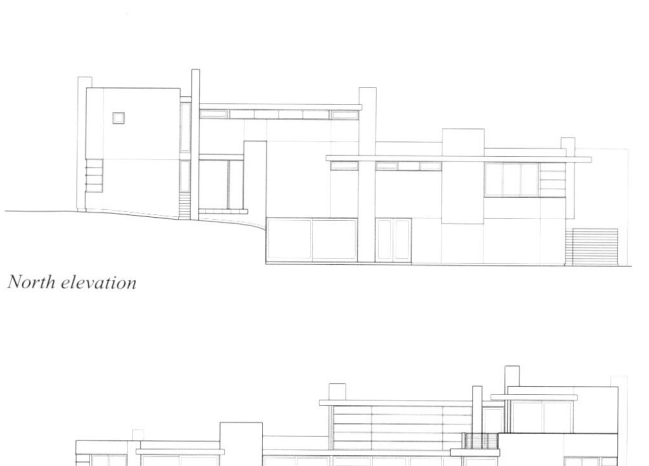

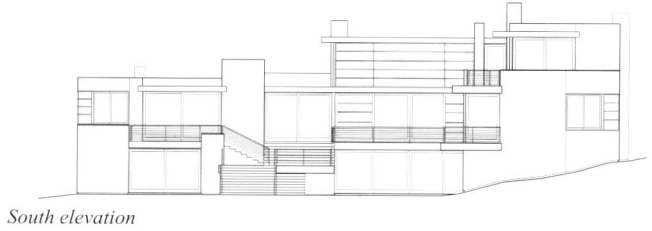

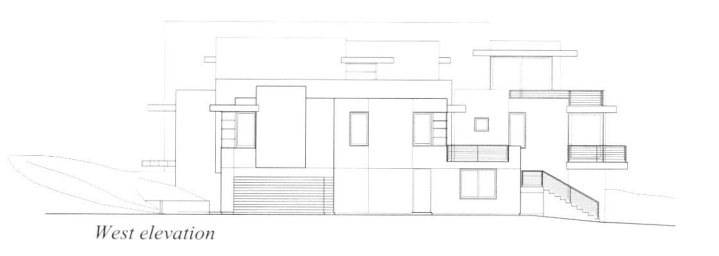

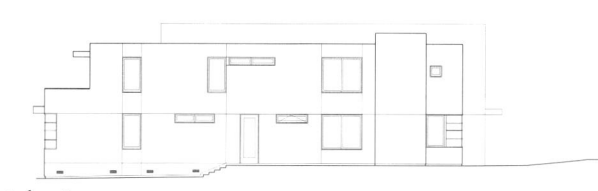

East elevation

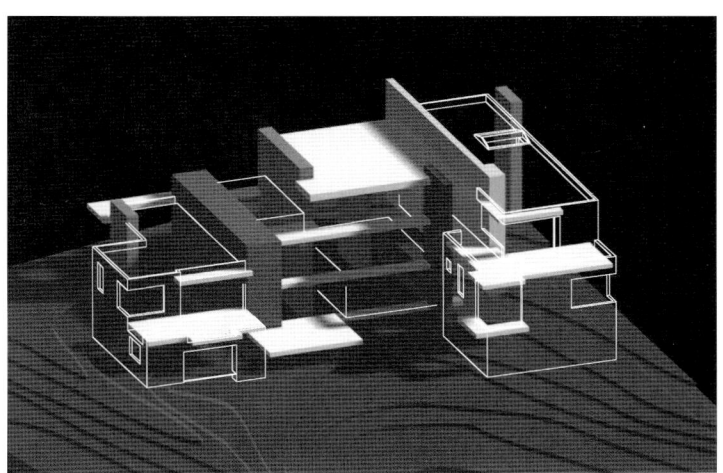

◁ *South view*　　　　　　　　　　　　*Model/diagram*

Terrace

Entrance

Entrance

Living room ▷

144

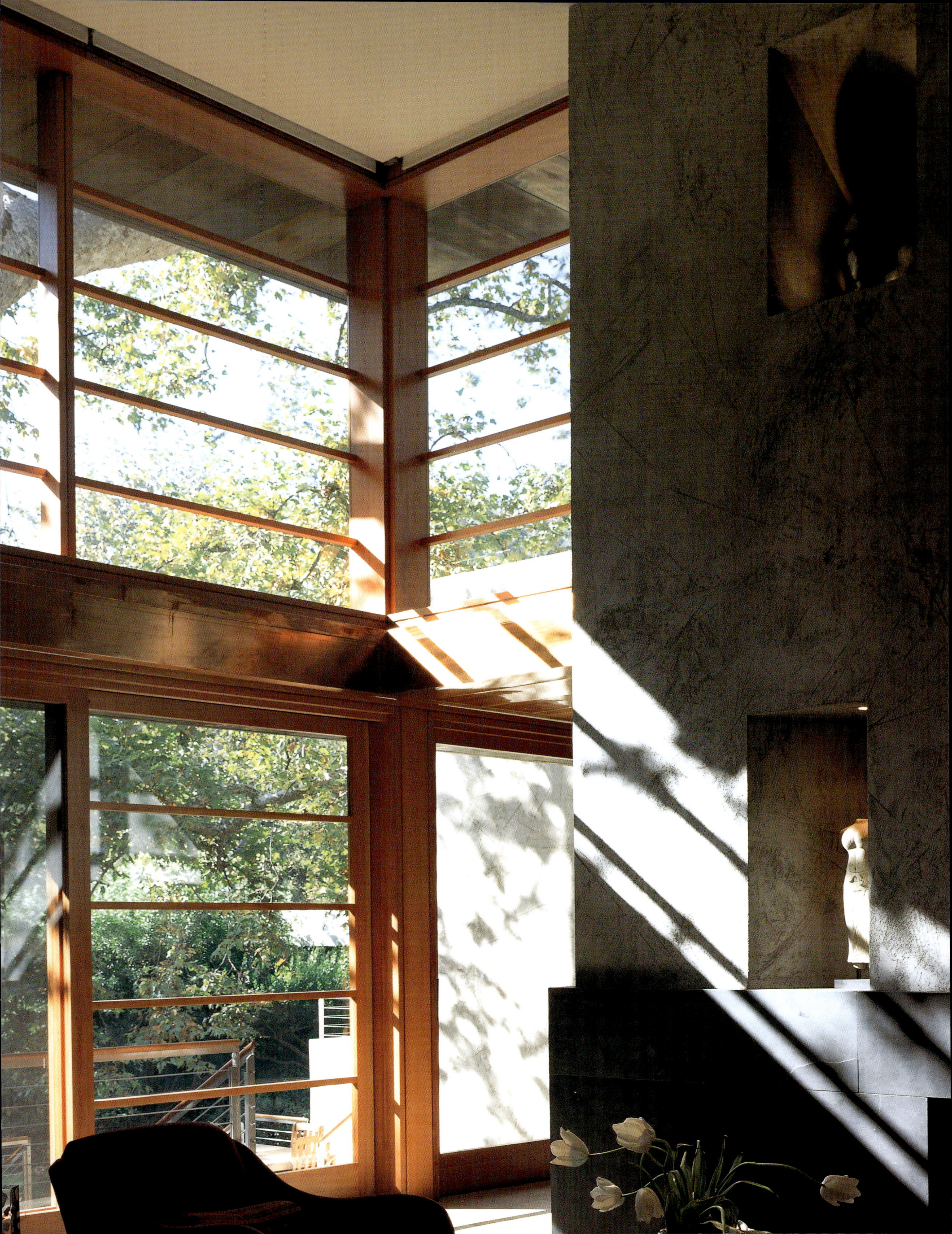

△▽*Living room*

Detail

Kitchen/breakfast room

Architects: Steven Ehrlich Architects—Steven Ehrlich, principal-in-charge; James Schmidt, project architect; Nick Seierup, Brent Eckerman, Eric Hammerlund, Supachai Kiatkwankul, Thomas Zahlten, Scott Hunter, Alec Whitten, project team
Consultants: Parker Resnick, structural; Moshe Susser, mechanical; Philippa Seth-Smith, interior; Griffith & Steiner, landscape; Brown+Trowbridge, steel furniture
General contractor: C.E.R. Development
Structural system: Wood frame & steel beams
Major materials: Custom colored & textured stucco, copper horizontal canopies, douglas fir windows & doors, Brazilian cherry floors, Tivoli stone flooring
Site area: 1 Acre
Total floor area: 7,400 s.f.

Staircase

Kitchen

147

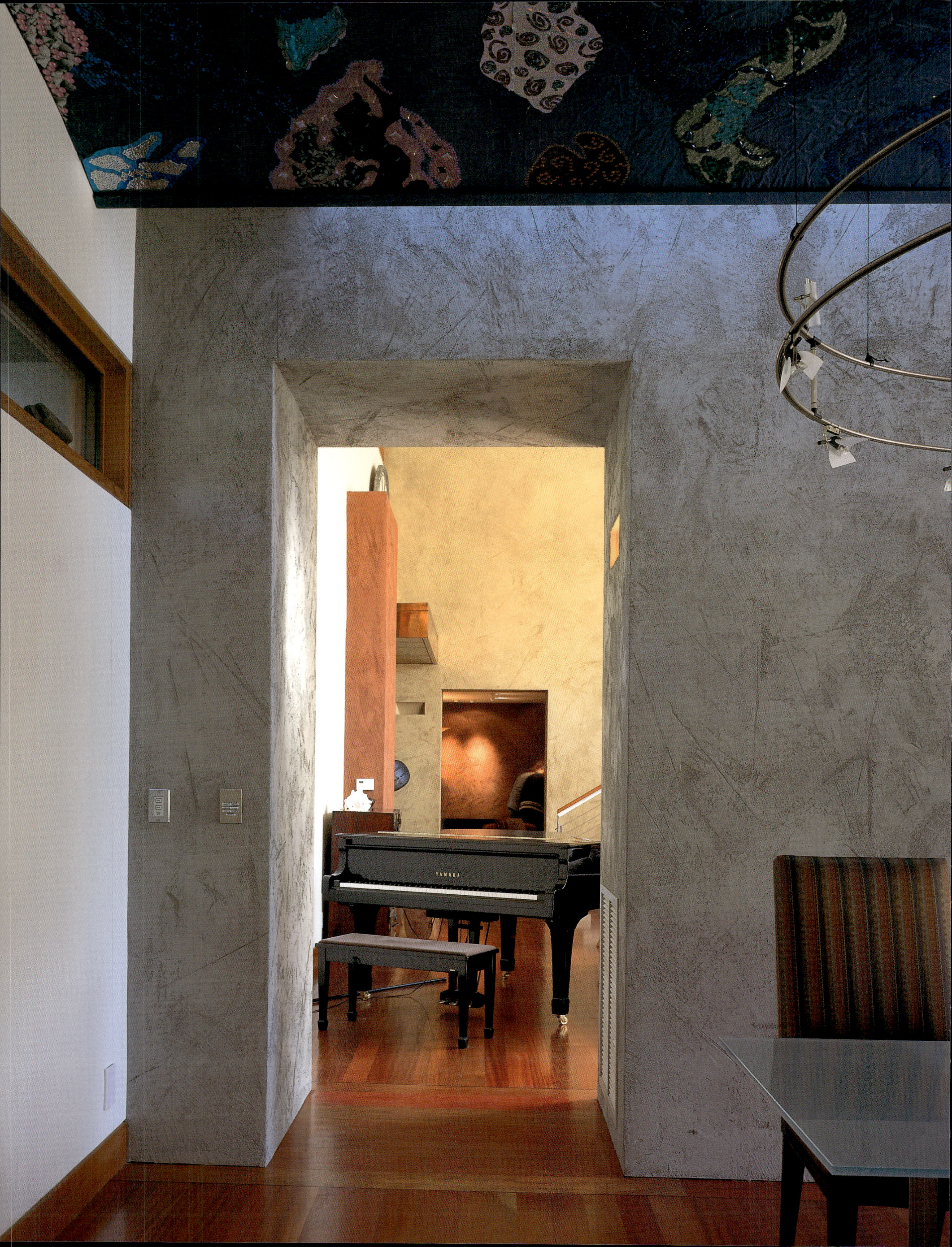

◁ View of living room from dining room

Dining room △

149

FERNAU & HARTMAN

ANDERSON/AYERS RESIDENCE
Nicasio, California, U.S.A.
Design: 1994–96
Construction: 1996–1999

Photos: T. Sakashita

Our work is as concerned with informal strategies of composition as it is with formal ones. The formal strategies we employ address the world idealized: the informal strategies address the world as we find it. The vernacular is our source of inspiration for adaptive informal strategies. It is the street language of architecture. It re-writes formal intentions to adapt to immediate circumstances. Circumstantial architecture alternatively accepts and manipulates the chance conditions that define an architectural situation. We begin each design with a formal strategy that we in turn "remodel," conceptually, to adapt to the givens of site and client. Our aesthetic is circumstantial and our method improvisational.

Site: The vernacular, agricultural buildings of Marin County in Northern California, with its barrel vaulted barns and improvisational poultry sheds, inspire this House. The site is located in the hills of west Marin. The land slopes steeply toward the west and overlooks a reservoir with farmlands and the Pacific Ocean beyond. Although often quite sunny, the local "coastal" microclimate is subject to intense breezes and fogs that can become very uncomfortable in fall and winter. Periodically the rain is very heavy.

Program: The program was simple but the expectations were not. The house is a second home for a dramatist, a writer and their young child. With the exception of two studios and a pool, their program could be typical for a family of this size. However, their desire was for a "barn / theater" —introverted on the exterior and extroverted in the interior. The house is not only a retreat from the wind and fog, but also a venue for travelling players.

Solution: Because the site is exposed and potentially visible from a distance, we adapted two primary siting strategies: 1) to straddle a wind-blown, tree-covered rock outcropping, and 2) to dig the house into the hill. This initial position was modified by an underground spring that stretched the "parti" out and away from the outcropping. In the final design, we divided the house into two wings - one comprised of the writing studio, future pool and poolhouse and the other of the main living space.

The main living space is a barrel vaulted "bar" that is situated across the slope and oriented more or less east-west, with its narrow face turned to the wind. At one end the house disappears into the grade, and at the other it gestures out, affording a view over the wind-dwarfed oaks to the reservoir below. The bar is stepped along its length, naturally creating the slope of a theater, establishing the central common space as the stage, with the kitchen and master bedroom occupying stage left and stage right. The barrel roof piece is the structure, or the "chart" as it is called in jazz, around which the other elements improvise. Like riffs, these secondary pieces modify and re-interpret the whole. Architecturally, they create contrasting "sets" on the interior and sheltered rooms on the exterior.

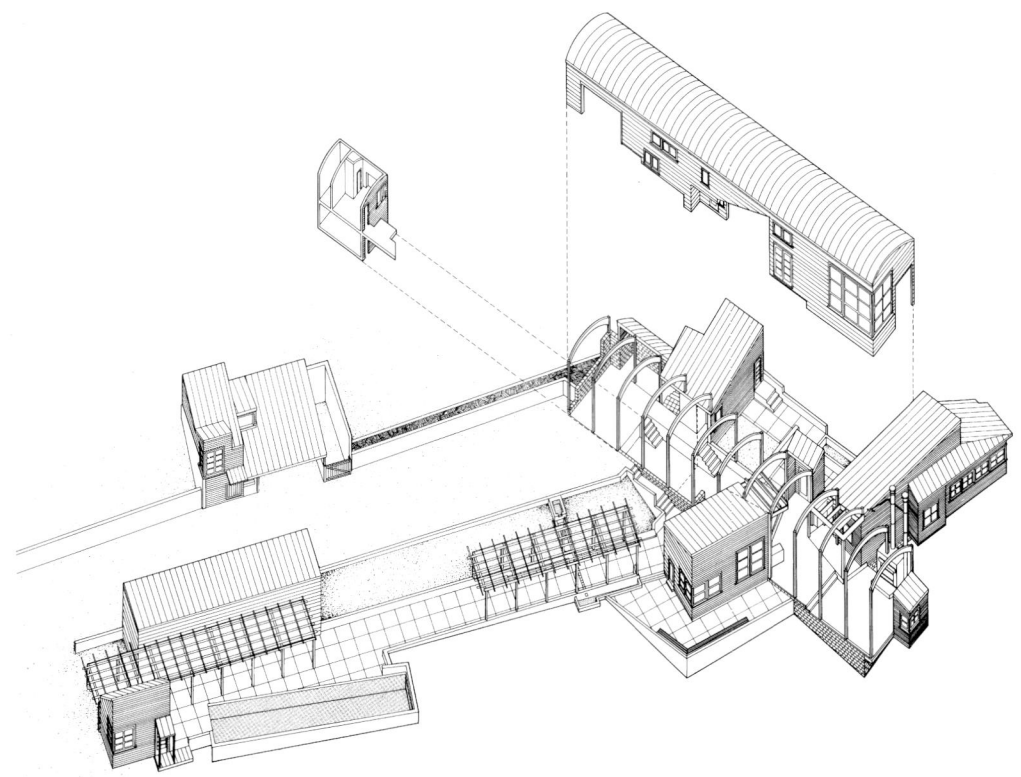

Exploded axonometric

Elevation

Section

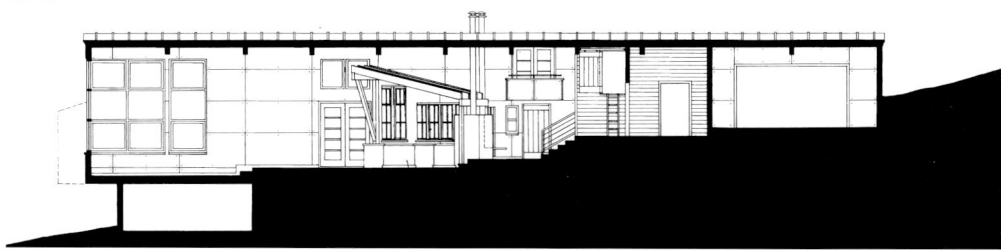

Plan

われわれの作品は、フォーマルな戦略同様に、インフォーマルな構成戦略とも関わっている。フォーマルな戦略は理想化された世界を表現し、インフォーマルな戦略は発見された世界を表現する。ヴァナキュラーは適応力を備えたインフォーマルな戦略のための発想源である。それは普段着の建築言語であり、身近な環境に適応させるためにフォーマルな意図をリライトする。状況に対応した建築は、建築的なポジションを決定する偶発的な条件を受容しあるいは操作する。フォーマルな戦略から設計を始め、次に、敷地とクライアントの条件に適合させるために、コンセプチュアルな"再編"を行う。われわれの美意識は状況に対応したものであり、方法は即興的なものである。

敷地：北カリフォルニアのマリン郡によく見られるヴァナキュラーな農家やかまぼこ屋根の納屋、即興的につくられた家畜小屋がこの住宅デザインの発想源である。敷地は西マリン郡の丘にある。西に急傾斜し、農場と貯水池、太平洋が望める。晴れ渡った日が多いのだが、この地方の"海岸線"に特有の気候は、毎日風が吹き、晩秋や冬には居心地の悪いものとなる。定期的に激しい降雨がある。

プログラム：プログラムは単純であるが建主の期待するものは単純ではない。劇作家と作家、そして夫妻の小さな子供達のための住宅である。2つのスタジオとプールを除けば、プログラムはこの人数の家族には典型的なものだろう。しかし、彼らの望みは、外部に面しては内向的、内部に面しては外向的な"納屋であり劇場である"ような場所であった。この住宅は風や霧からの待避所であるばかりでなく、いわば旅芸人の興業の場でもある。

解：敷地はむきだしで、遠くからも見えるので、2つの主要方針を配置に際して用いた。1）風に吹きさらしになった岩の露頭をまたがせること。2）家を丘のなかに掘り込むことである。最初の位置は地下水のために修正されている。"設計概念"を拡張して、露頭から遠く引き離すことにした。最終設計では、住宅は2つのウイングに分割された。一つには著作のためのスタジオ、プールそして未来のプールハウスが、もう一方には主要なリビング・スペースが置かれる。

この家の主要躯体はかまぼこ屋根をもつリニアーな建物である。それは斜面を横断し、ほぼ東西を向き、その狭い面を風に向けている。その一端は地表に消えて行き、もう一端は外に伸びて、風のため背丈の低いカシの梢越しに、下の貯水池まで広がる景色をとらえる。断面はその全長に沿ってステップを刻み、自然に劇場の傾斜面をつくりだし、舞台となる中央の共有空間を構成する。舞台の左右を台所と主寝室が占める。かまぼこ屋根は構造体または、ジャズで言う"コードネーム"で、その回りに他の要素が即興的につくられる。リフ（ジャズ。独奏者のための伴奏。または伴奏の一部として即興的に演奏される短い楽節）のように、これらの二次的な断片は全体を修正し再解釈する。そして建築的には、内部に面しては"一群"の対比的なものを、また外部に面しては覆われた部屋をつくりだす。

Architects: Fernau & Hartman Architects—Laura Hartman and Richard Fernau, partners-in-charge; Susan Stoltz, Scott Donohue, project architects; Anni Tilt, Keith Dubinsky, Alice Lin, Tom Powers, Jeff L. Day, Chat Chuenrudeemol, Ramon Ramirez, Alexis Masnik, project team; Aaron Thornton, Hyejin Cho, Jason Bell, Aleksander Baharlo, presentation team
Clients: Jane Anderson & Tess Ayers
Consultants: MKM & Associates (phase 1), Richard Hartwell (phase 2), structural; Lefler Engineering, Inc., mechanical; Lutsko Associates, landscaping
General contractor: Kerr Construction (phase 1)—Jeff Kerr, G.C., Greg Forsberg, foreman; Roger Peacock, G.C. (phase 2)—Jim McCracken, foreman
Structural system: wood framing with steel moment frames
Mechanical system: radiant slab floor heating with high efficiency boiler
Major materials: stained cedar siding, painted metal roofing, painted aluminum windows, ground faced and split faced concrete block, bluestone pavers, board formed concrete, sealed cedar and redwood
Total floor area: 3,000 sq. feet

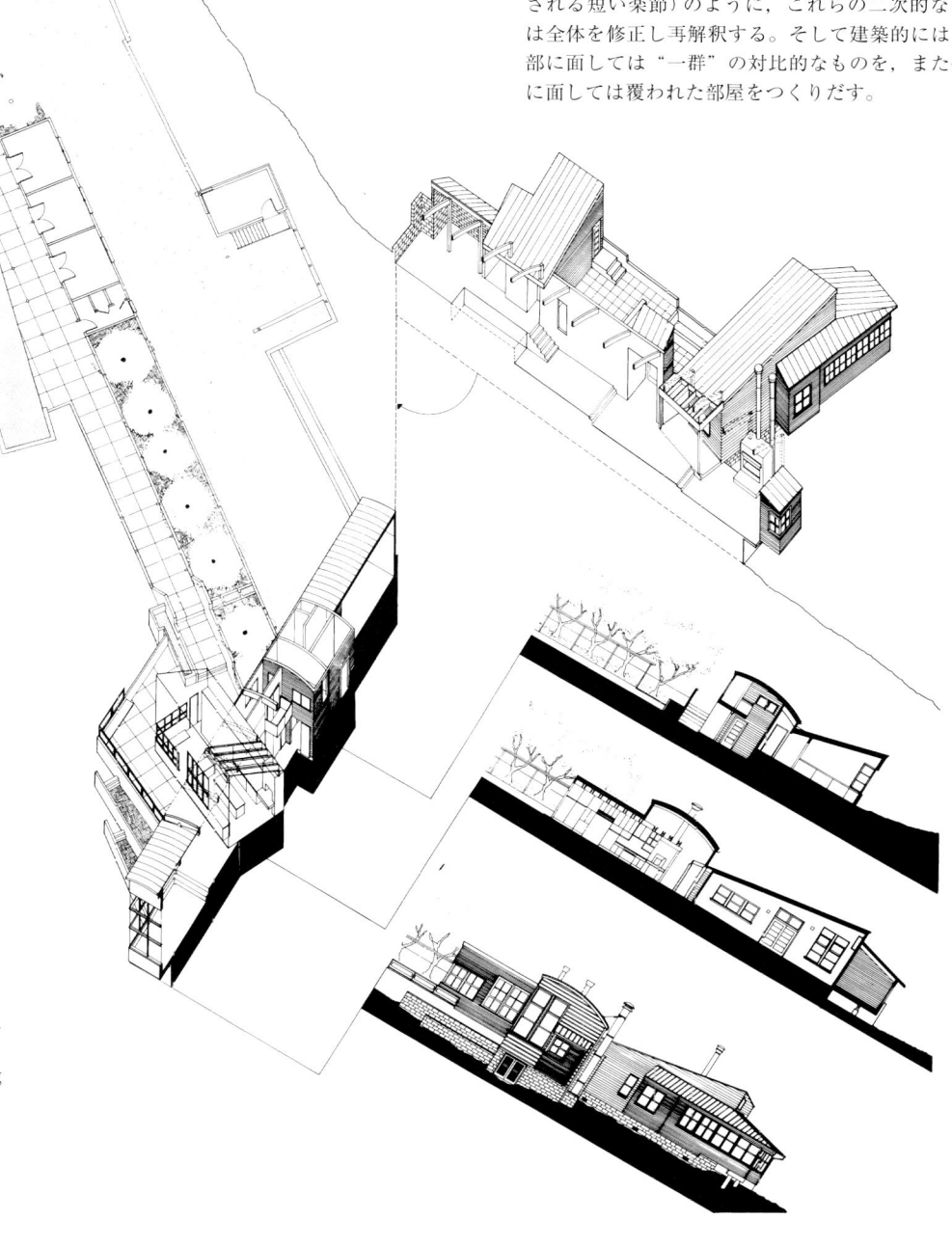

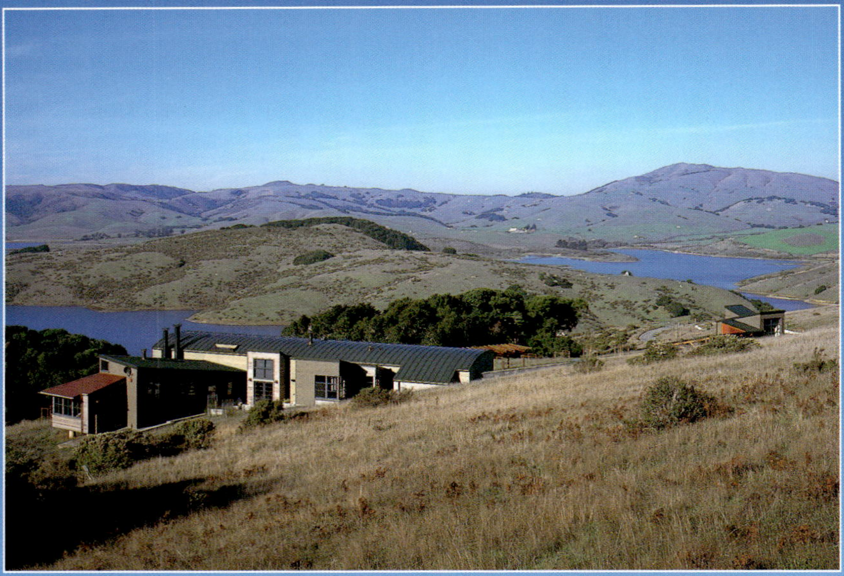
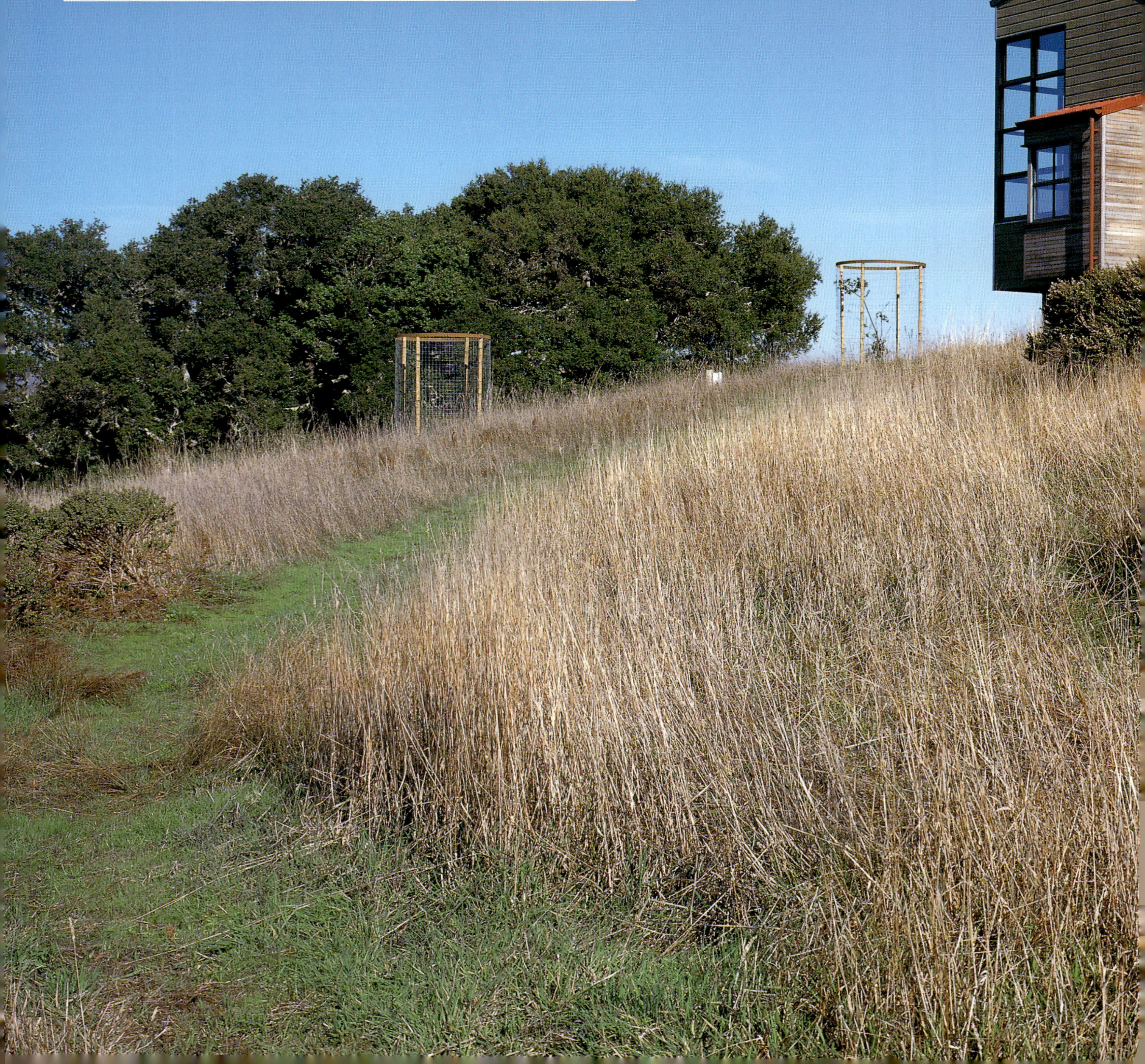

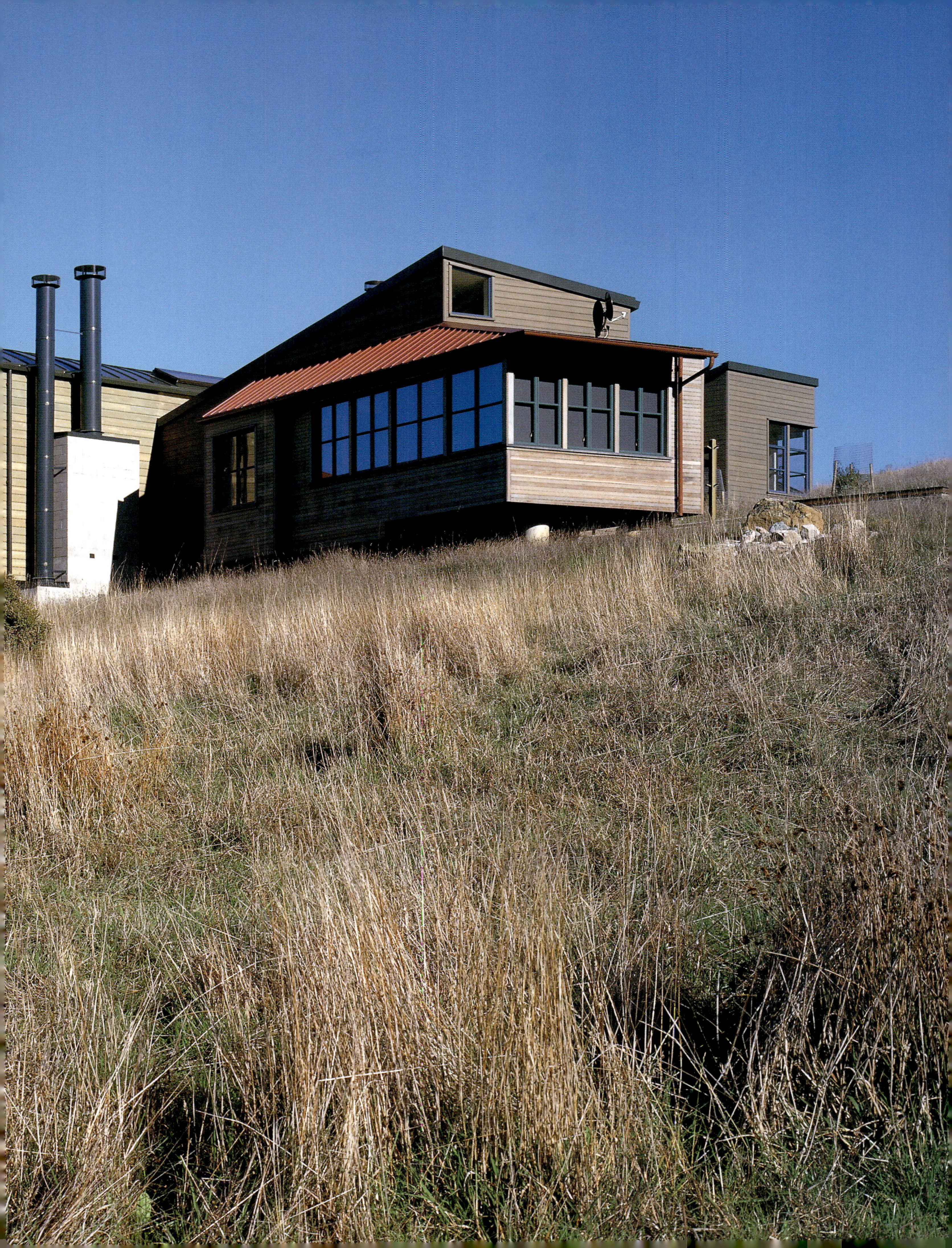

South view

Study/garage

Master bedroom wing

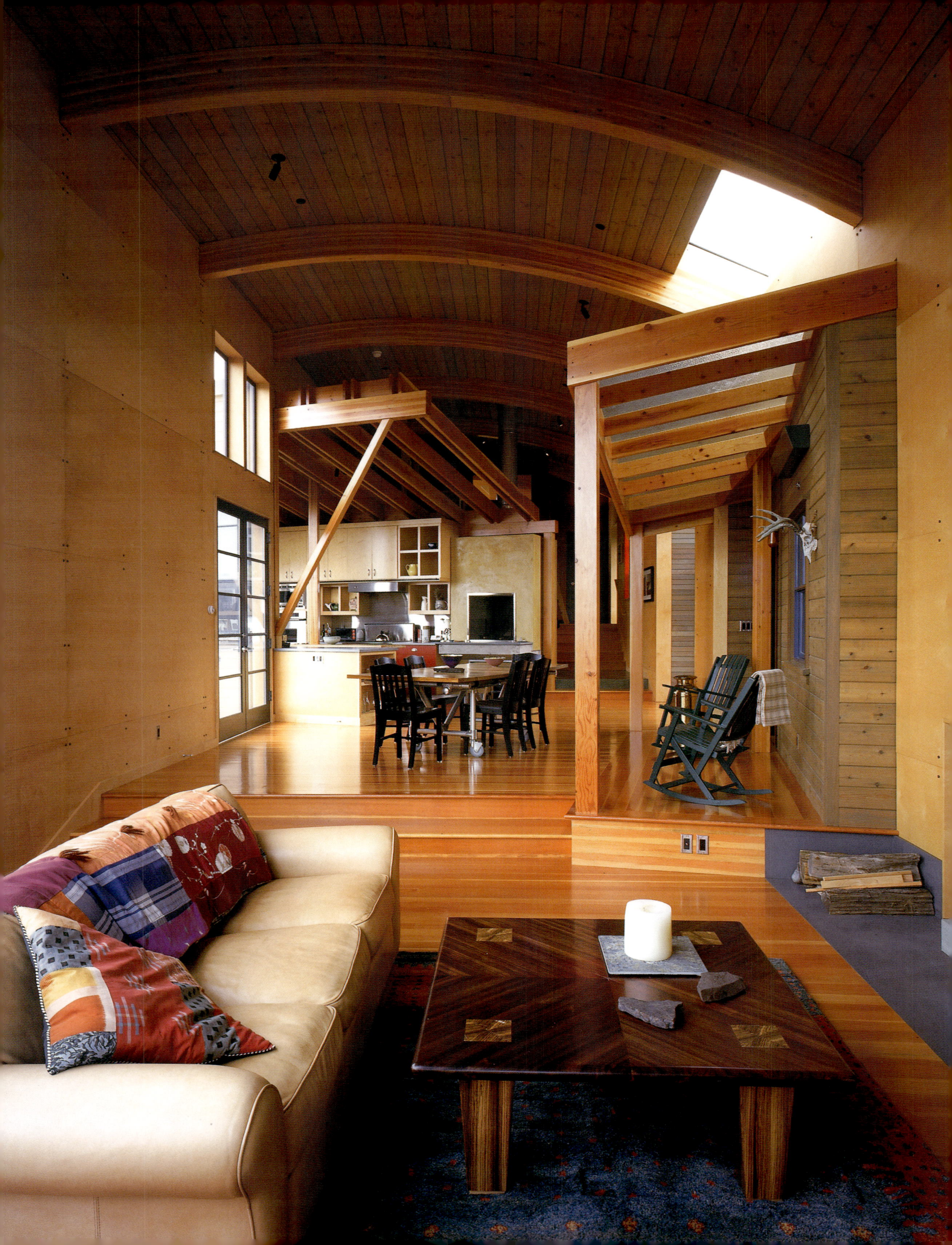

△▽ Kitchen

◁ Living/dining room

Living/dining room: view toward west

157

View from balcony on mezzanine level

View from north

Terrace on south

Bay window of living room

Study

△▽ *Master bedroom*

Bathroom *Master bedroom* ▷

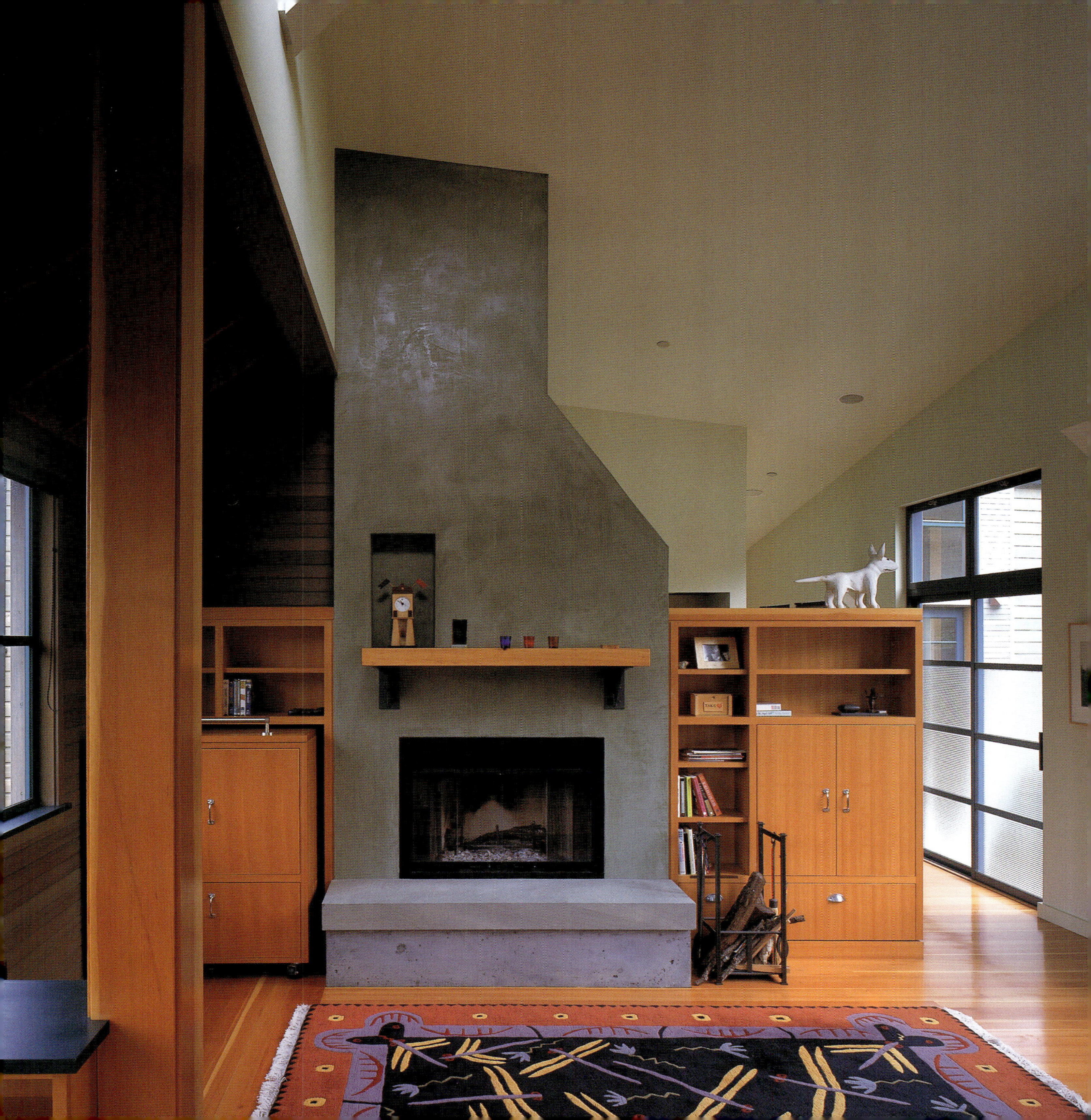

F.L. WRIGHT SELECTED HOUSES 8 vols.
フランク・ロイド・ライトの住宅 全8巻

Edited and Photographed by Yukio Futagawa　Text by Bruce Brooks Pfeiffer
企画・編集・撮影：二川幸夫　文：ブルース・ブルックス・ファイファー　翻訳：玉井一匡

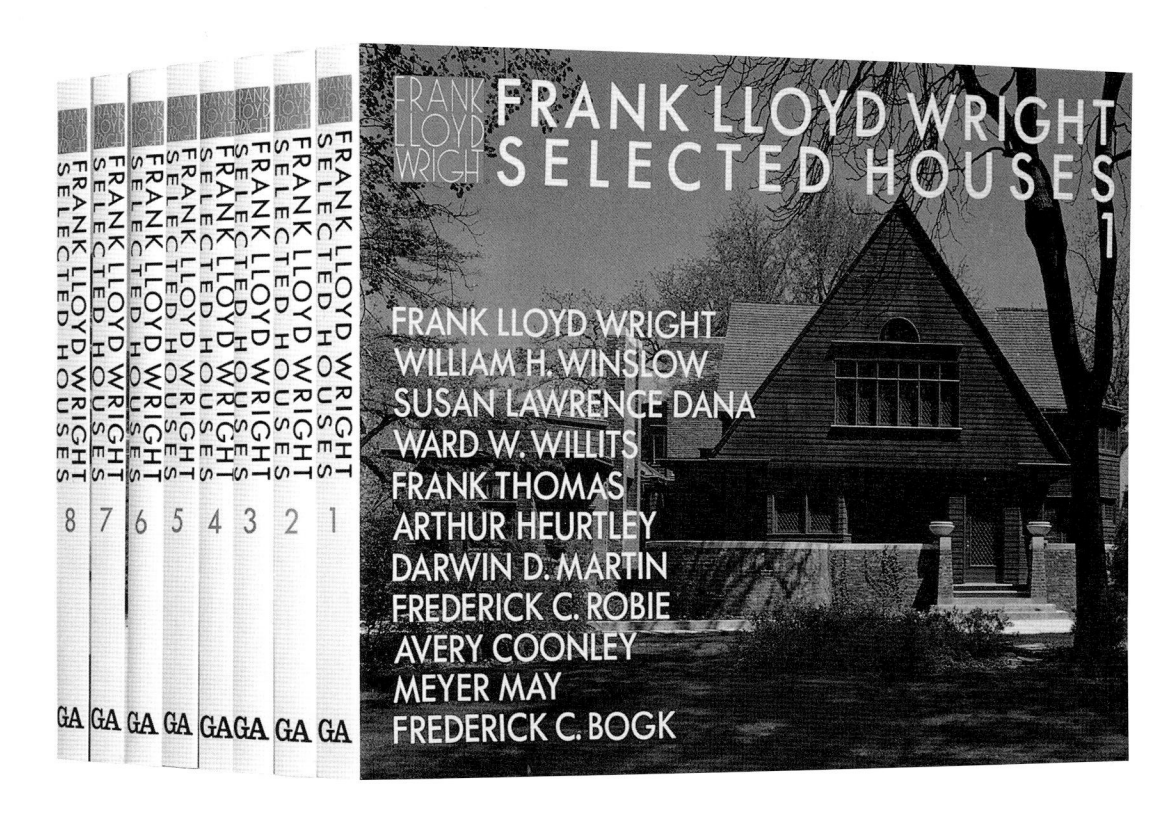

This series focuses on the finest houses of Frank Lloyd Wright, selecting 52 representative works from the over 300 that were realized during his career. Five volumes focus on specific styles such as his famed Prairie Houses, Usonian Houses, or his concrete block houses. Three volumes focus on single buildings—Taliesin, Taliesin West, and Fallingwater—presenting each with a totality that was heretofore unknown. Combining new photographs, period photos and original drawings, this series embodies the essense of Wright's residential design.

『フランク・ロイド・ライトの住宅』シリーズは，ライトの最大の遺産である住宅に焦点をあて，300軒にも及ぶ実施作品の中から特に優れた52軒を選び，プレイリー・ハウス，ユーソニアン・ハウス，コンクリート・ブロックの住宅等，カテゴリー別に分類して構成。全8巻のうち，タリアセン，タリアセン・ウェスト，落水荘については各1巻を費やし，これまで知ることのできなかった全体像を初めて明らかにした。新たに撮影したディテールにいたるまでの写真とオリジナル・ドローイングを通して，真の住まいのあり方，ライトの空間の本質が明らかとなろう。

Size: 227×300mm／160〜208 total pages(48〜64 in color)／¥4,806

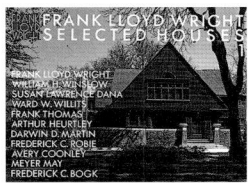

vol.1 PRAIRIE HOUSES
Wright House and Studio, Illinois, 1889-95
Winslow House and Stables, Illinois, 1893
Dana House, Illinois, 1900
Willits House, Illinois, 1901
Thomas House, Illinois, 1901
Heurtley House, New York, 1904
Robie House, Illinois, 1906
Coonley House, Illinois, 1907
May House, Michigan, 1909
Bogk House, Wisconsin, 1916

208 pages, 48 in color

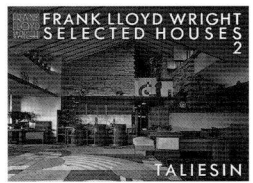

vol.2 TALIESIN
Taliesin, Wisconsin, 1911-

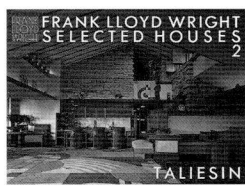

176 pages, 48 in color

vol.3 TALIESIN WEST
Taliesin West, Arizona, 1937-

176 pages, 64 in color

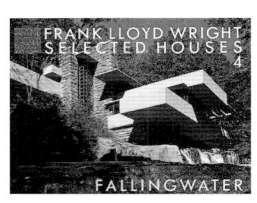

vol.4 FALLINGWATER
"Fallingwater," Kaufmann House, Pennsylvania, 1935

160 pages, 48 in color

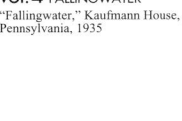

vol.5 MASTERPIECES: 1930S & 40S
Hanna House, California, 1917-21
Johnson House, Wisconsin, 1937
Stevens House, South Carolina, 1939
Affleck House, Michigan, 1940
Walter House, Iowa, 1945
Mossberg House, Indiana, 1946

192 pages, 48 in color

vol.6 USONIAN HOUSES I
Jacobs House, Wisconsin, 1938
Pew House, Wisconsin, 1938
Winckler/Goetsch House, Michigan, 1939
Lewis House, Illinois, 1939
Pope House, Virginia, 1939
Rosenbaum House, Alabama, 1939
Schwartz House, Wisconsin, 1939
Sturges House, California, 1939
Baird House, Massachusetts, 1940
Wall House, Michigan, 1941
Smith House, Michigan, 1946

176 pages, 40 in color

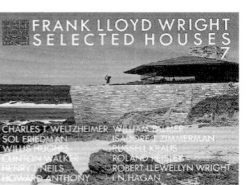

vol.7 USONIAN HOUSES II
Weltzheimer House, Ohio, 1948
Friedman House, New York, 1948
Laurent House, Illinois, 1949
Walker House, California, 1949
Palmer House, Michigan, 1950
Zimmerman House, New Hampshire, 1950
Kraus House, Missouri, 1951
Reisley House, New York, 1951
Llewellyn Wright House, Maryland, 1953
Hagan House, Pennsylvania, 1954

176 pages, 64 in color

vol.8 CONCRETE HOUSES
Barnsdall House, California, 1917-21
Yamamura House, Japan, 1918
Millard House, California, 1923
Storer House, California, 1923
Ennis House, California, 1923
Jones House, Oklahoma, 1929
David Wright House, Arizona, 1950
Price House, Arizona, 1954
Tonkens House, Ohio, 1954
Kalil House, New Hampshire, 1955

184 pages, 40 in color

Vol. 2, 4, 6, 8 is out of print　2, 4, 6, 8号は絶版

表記価格には消費税は含まれておりません。

LIGHT & SPACE 光の空間
MODERN ARCHITECTURE

企画・撮影＝二川幸夫
序文＝パオロ・ポルトゲージ
文＝三宅理一

Edited and Photographed by Yukio Futagawa
Introduction by Paolo Portoghesi Text by Riichi Miyake

空間を構成する根源的な要素である光。
あふれる自然の光をとらえ，
絞り込み，屈折させ，形を与えて内部に導き入れる。
近代建築の黎明期から現代にいたる，光と影を主役
として織りなされてきた建築空間の集大成。

Light is a fundamental element of architecture.
Through the finest examples
from the beginning of Modernism to the present,
this compendium examines
the way natural light is captured, altered,
and shaped in architectural space.

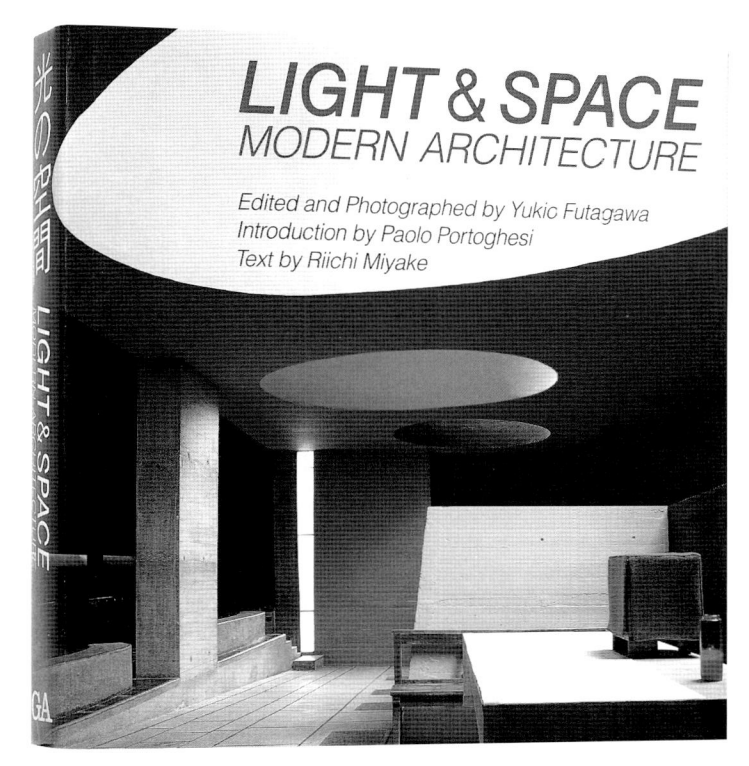

Vol. 1
Size: 300×297mm／216 pages, 30 in color／¥5,806

光と近代建築―パオロ・ポルトゲージ
Light and Modern Architecture by Paolo Portoghesi
鉄とガラスの神話　The Myth of Iron and Glass
空の簒奪　Usurpation of the Sky
樹木のアレゴリー　Allegory of Trees
世紀末の光と影　Light and Shadow in the Fin-de-Siècle
胎内への窓　Window to the Womb
透明な質感　The Texture of Transparency
形而上学的な光　Metaphysical Light

Vol. 2
Size: 300×297mm／216 pages, 24 in color／¥5,806

輝く額　The Shining Brow
建築の快楽　The Pleasure of Architecture
東方への旅　Travel to the Orient
ガラス箱の神話　The Myth of the Glazed Box
透視できる建築　See-Through Architecture
影のない光　Light without Shadow
始原の光　Primitive Light
ねばっこい空間　Sticky Space
メカニカルな空　The Mechanical Sky
被膜の建築　Architecture of Membrane

COMBINED ISSUE 合本 （HARD COVER 上製）
Size: 300×297mm／426 pages, 54 in color／¥14,369

表記価格に消費税は含まれておりません。

GA

Global Architecture

An Encyclopedia of Modern Architecture

企画・撮影：二川幸夫
Edited and Photographed by Yukio Futagawa

現代建築の名作をじっくり見ていただくために企画された大型サイズのシリーズ。現代建築の巨匠たちの古典的名作から，今日最も新しい傾向を示す作品に至るまで1軒ないし2軒の建築を総48頁で構成し，現代建築の持つ空間の広がり，ディテール，テクスチュアなどを確実に，明確に，見事に表現。加えて，原稿執筆にあたっては世界の建築界の最高峰の協力を得た文字どおりグローバルな規模の企画であり，回を重ねるごとに現代の名建築の百科事典となろう。

Having now published more than 70 volumes, GLOBAL ARCHITECTURE has become a classic among architectural publication. GA is meant for those who would like to "experience" masterpieces of modern architecture. Apart from those seminal works of architecture which imply new directions, those columns also introduce some of the classic work by such masters of modern architecture. Each volume thoroughly documents one or two works illustrated by the stunning photography of Yukio Futagawa in a large format (364 × 257mm), accompanied by a critique written by a prominent architectural critic or historian. As the columns accumulate in your library, they will gradually become an encyclopedia of modern architecture.

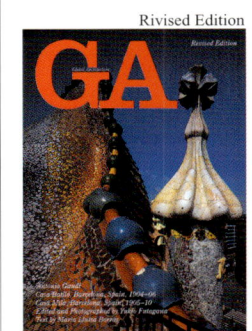

GA 17 ¥2,800円
ANTONIO GAUDÍ
Casa Batlló, Casa Milá

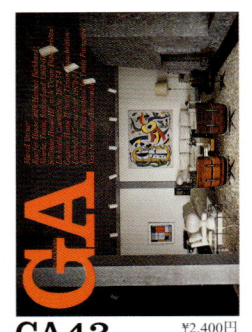

GA 43 ¥2,400円
MARCEL BREUER
Koerfer House, Stillman House III and Gagarin House II

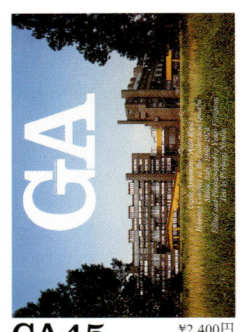

GA 45 ¥2,400円
CARLO AYMONINO/ ALDO ROSSI
Housing Complex at the Gallaratese Quarter

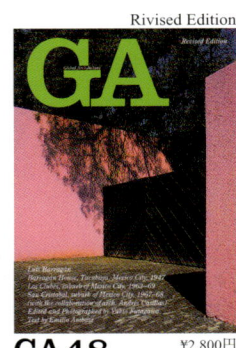

GA 48 ¥2,800円
LUIS BARRAGÁN
Barragán House, Los Clubes, San Cristobal

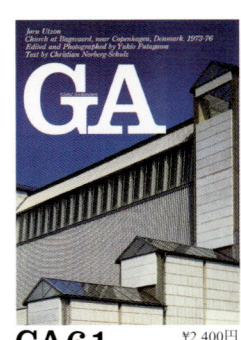

GA 61 ¥2,400円
JØRN UTZON
Church at Bagsvaerd

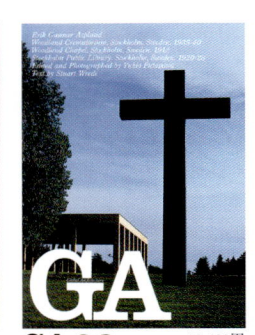

GA 62 ¥2,400円
ERIK GUNNAR ASPLUND
Woodland Crematorium & Chapel, Stockholm Public Library

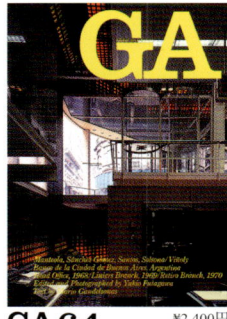

GA 64 ¥2,400円
MANTEOLA, SANCHEZ GOMEZ, SANTOS, SOLSONA/VINOLY
Banco de la Ciudad de Buenos Aires

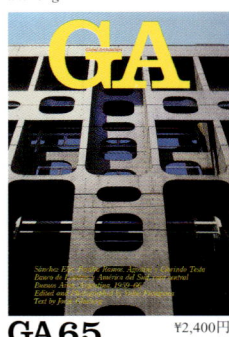

GA 65 ¥2,400円
SEPRA Y CLORINDO TESTA
Banco de Londres y América del Sur

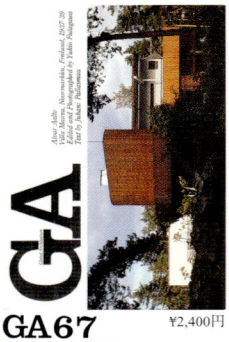

GA 67 ¥2,400円
ALVAR AALTO
Villa Mairea

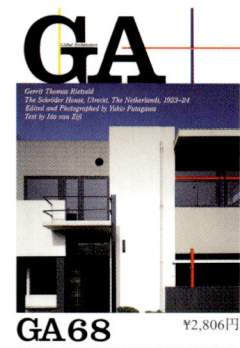

GA 68 ¥2,806円
GERRIT THOMAS RIETVELD
The Schröder House

GA 69 ¥2,806円
ARATA ISOZAKI
Tsukuba Center Building

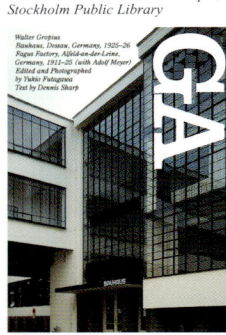

GA 70 ¥2,806円
WALTER GROPIUS
Bauhaus & Fagus Factory

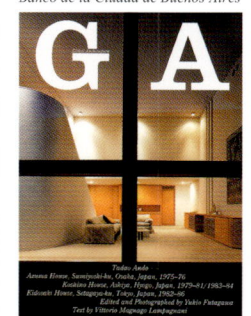

GA 71 ¥2,806円
TADAO ANDO
Azuma House, Koshino House & Kidosaki House

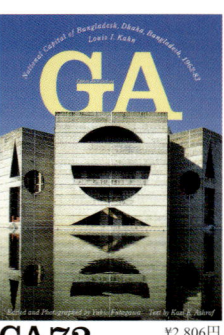

GA 72 ¥2,806円
LOUIS I. KAHN
National Capital of Bangladesh

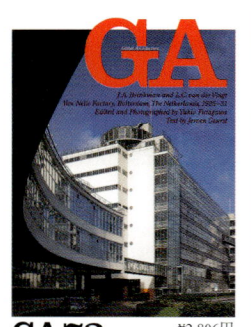

GA 73 ¥2,806円
J. A. BRINKMAN AND L.C. VAN DER VLUGT
Van Nelle Factory

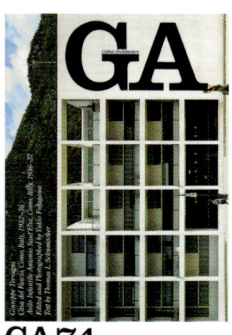

GA 74 ¥2,806円
GIUSEPPE TERRAGNI
Casa del Fascio, Asilo Infantile, Antonio Sant'Elia

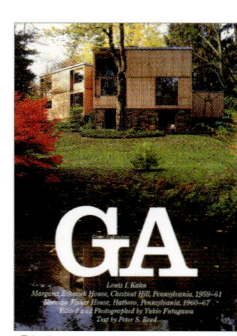

GA 76 ¥2,806円
LOUIS I. KAHN
Margaret Esherick House & Norman Fisher House

表記価格に消費税は含まれておりません。

GA77 *Rudolph M. Schindler*
R.M.Schindler House / J.E.How House

Edited and Photographed by Yukio Futagawa   Text by Lionel March

Rudolph M. Schindler
R.M. Schindler House, Hollywood, California, 1921-22
James E. How House, Los Angeles, California, 1925
Edited and Photographed by Yukio Futagawa
Text by Lionel March

Size 364 × 257mm
48 total pages, 12 in color / ¥2,800

ルドルフ・M・シンドラー：シンドラー自邸／ハウ邸

企画・撮影：二川幸夫　文：ライオネル・マーチ

These two houses built in early twenties, and later became masterpieces of Californian modern living, were designed by R.M.Schindler who studied at Wagner's and Loos' office in Vienna then Wright's in U.S.A. Both of two houses, the architect's own house-the R.M.S. house and the Dr. How house on steep hillside, are applied Schindler's unique vocabulary, such as simple combinations of material and operations of various spatial changes, to realize a rich space for living. The works could be still a reference for residential design now.

1920年代前半，南カリフォルニアに相次いで建てられた2つの住宅は，ウィーンでワグナー，ロースに学び，ライトのもとで修行を重ねたシンドラーの多面的な才能が花開いた，カリフォルニア・モダンリビングの名作である。自邸であるキンググス・ロードの家も急斜面に建つハウ邸も，コンクリートと木とガラスによる単純な材料構成や，微妙に変化する空間構成などシンドラー独特のデザイン言語がつくりだす魅力的な生活空間を持ち，現代の住宅デザインへのヒントに溢れている。

Planning Issues　新版刊行予定

- **GA2**　*Frank Lloyd Wright: Kaufmann House, "Fallingwater"*
- **GA3**　*Le Corbusier: Villa Savoye*
- **GA15**　*Frank Lloyd Wright: Taliesin East & West*
- **GA27**　*Mies van der Rohe: Farnsworth House*

To be continued　以下続刊

表記価格に消費税は含まれておりません。

TADAO ANDO DETAILS
安藤忠雄ディテール集

Overlayered plans, sections and perspectives, with various details in different scales, Ando's drawing has unique three dimensional character. The drawings represent not only the literal information of details, but also his philosophy of architecture.
From "Row house in Sumiyoshi" to recent projects, these two volumes contain Ando's architectural details of major projects and embody the spirits of Ando, who is the evangelist of the essence of architecture.

平面や断面，パースが重ね合わされ，スケールの異なるディテールが挿入された三次元性を持つ独自の図法。その図面には，あらゆる事象を捉えながら結晶化させた建築理念が投影され，建築を創造することの意志が凝縮される。
住吉の長屋から現在まで，主要作品を網羅するこのディテール集の中に，時代に流されず，建築の本質を求めて止まないもう一つの安藤空間が展開する。

1
EDITED BY YUKIO FUTAGAWA
CRITICISM BY PETER EISENMAN
企画・編集：二川幸夫
論文：ピーター・アイゼンマン
翻訳：渡辺洋（英訳），丸山洋志（和訳）
Size: 300×307mm／168 total pages／￥4,806

2
EDITED BY YUKIO FUTAGAWA
CRITICISM BY FRANCESCO DAL CO
企画・編集：二川幸夫／論文：フランチェスコ・ダル・コ
Size: 300×307mm／148 total pages／￥4,714

表記価格には消費税は含まれておりません。

La Maison de Verre

Pierre Chareau
EDITED & PHOTOGRAPHED by **Yukio Futagawa**
TEXT & DRAWINGS by **Bernard Bauchet**
TEXT by **Marc Vellay**

ガラスの家：ダルザス邸

企画・撮影＝二川幸夫

文・図面＝ベルナール・ボシェ／翻訳：三宅理一

Built in the center of Paris, La Maison de Verre is neither a work which can be overlooked for it avant-garde qualities, nor as a landmark in the history of Modern Architecture. This volume attempts to give an overall picture of this major work with photographs and survey drawings.

1932年，パリのサンジェルマン大通りに近い，古いアパートの1，2階に嵌め込まれた〈ガラスの家〉は，スチールとガラスブロックの大胆な構成で，近代建築史上，その前衛性からも注目すべき建築である。光の浸透というテーマがどのような構成の原理と空間構成のテクニックのうえに成立しているのか。特別撮影の写真と実測図面により解明する。

Size: 300×307mm／180 total pages, 42 in color／¥5,806

表記価格に消費税は含まれておりません。

GA DOCUMENT
Global Architecture

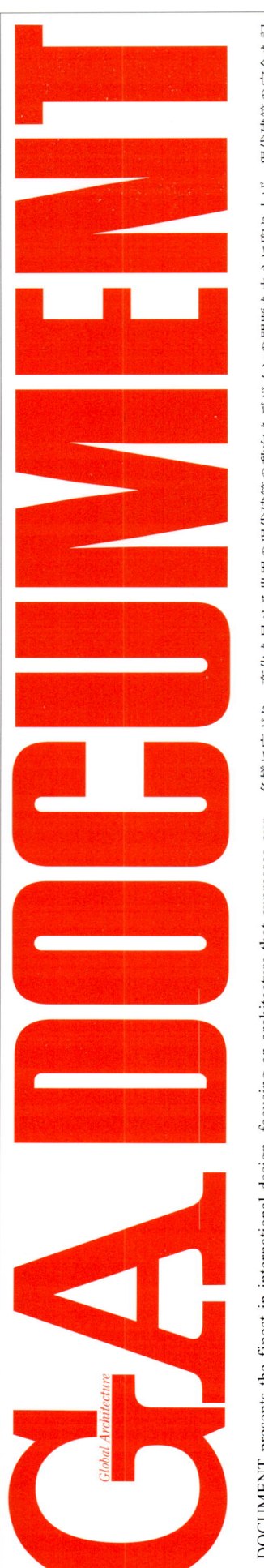

GA DOCUMENT presents the finest in international design, focusing on architecture that expresses our times and striving to record the history of contemporary architecture. Striking black-and-white and vibrant color photographs presented in a generous format make for a dynamic re-presentation of spaces, materials and textures. International scholars and critics provide insightful texts to further inform the reader of the most up-to-date ideas and events in the profession.

Vols. 1, 16, 18, 20, 23, 25, 29, 36, 47 are out of print.
Size: 300 × 297 mm

多様に広がり、変化を見せる世界の現代建築の動向をデザインの問題を中心に取り上げ、現代建築の完全な記録をめざしつつ、時代の流れに柔軟に対応した独自の視点から作品をセレクションし、新鮮な情報を世界に向けて発信する唯一のグローバルな建築専門誌。掲載する作品をすべて現地取材し、撮影することで大型版面にダイナミックに表現し、その空間、ディテールやテクスチャーを的確に再現する。

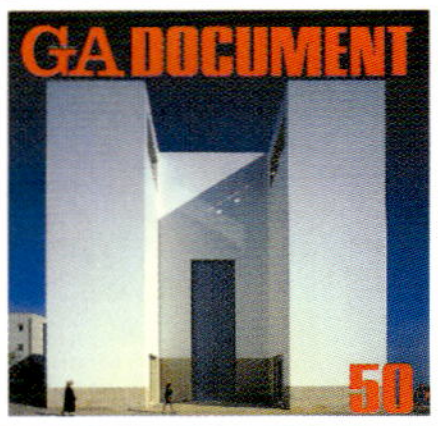

50
インタヴュー・作品・プロジェクト：トッド・ウィリアムズ&ビリー・ツィン 作品：アルヴァロ・シザ，マルコ・ドゥ・カナヴェーゼスの教会，アダルベルト・ディアス，アヴェイロ大学機械工学科棟／J・マヌエル・ガリェゴ，コルーニャの美術館／磯崎新，岡山西警察署／エンリケ・ノルテン，テレビ局の複合施設／リカルド・レゴレッタ，メキシコシティ芸術都市／他
Interview, Works & Projects: T. Williams & B. Tsien *The NSI, Phoenix Art Museum, Cranbrook Athletic Complex*; and others Works: A. Siza *Church of Marco De Canavezes*; A. Dias *University of Aveiro, Department of Mechanical Engineering*; J. M. Gallego *Museum of Fine Art, La Coruña*; A. Isozaki *Okayama-Nishi Police Station*; E. Norten *Televisa Mixed Use Building*; R. Legorreta *The City of the Arts*; and others
120 pages, 48 in color ¥2,848

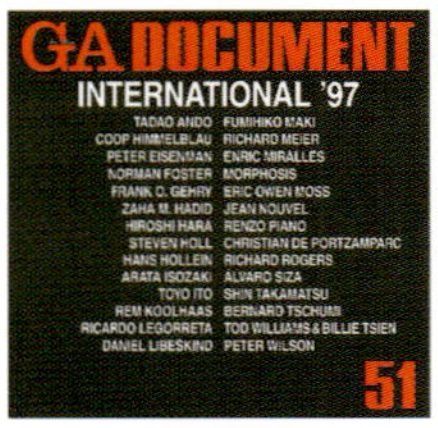

51
特集：GA INTERNATIONAL '97 第6回＜現代世界の建築家＞展
Special Feature: "GA INTERNATIONAL '97" Exhibition at GA Gallery
Tadao Ando, Coop Himmelblau, Peter Eisenman, Norman Foster, Frank O. Gehry, Zaha M. Hadid, Hiroshi Hara, Steven Holl, Hans Hollein, Arata Isozaki, Toyo Ito, Rem Koolhaas, Daniel Libeskind, Ricardo Legorretta, Fumihiko Maki, Richard Meier, Enric Miralles, Morphosis, Jean Nouvel, Eric Owen Moss, Renzo Piano, Christian de Portzamparc, Richard Rogers, Ávaro Siza, Shin Takamatsu, Bernard Tschumi, Peter Wilson, Tod Williams & Billie Tsien
120 pages, 24 in color ¥2,848

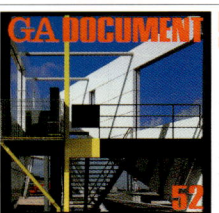

52
作品：E・O・モス，オフィス・コンプレックス／A・プレドック，アリゾナ・サイエンス・センター／槇文彦，風の丘葬祭場／ボレス+ウィルソン，ロッテルダムの埠頭広場，他／H・ホライン，ロワー・オーストリア展示場，他／原広司+アトリエ・ファイ，京都駅ビル／N・フォスター，ビルバオ市地下鉄駅／P・シメトフ，エヴルーの図書館／R・ボフィル，オリンピック・プール
Works: E.O. Moss *Pittard Sullivan*; A. Predock *Arizona Science Center*; F. Maki *Kaze-no-Oka Crematorium*; Bolles + Wilson *Quay Building, Light Forum, Albeda College*; H. Hollein *Lower Austrian Exhibition Hall, Light Forum*; Hiroshi Hara+Atelier Φ *Kyoto Station Building*; N. Foster *Bilbao Metro*; P. Chemetov & B. Huidobro *Library in Evreux*; R. Bofill *Olympic Swimming Pool*
120 pages, 48 in color ¥2,848

53
作品：OMA，ユトレヒト大学・エデュカトリアム／S・ホール，シアトル大学・聖イグナティウス礼拝堂／N・フォスター，コメルツバンク本社屋，他／R・ロジャース，テームズ・ヴァレー大学・LRC／W・P・ブルーダー，リッデル・アドヴァタイジング&デザイン／B・チュミ，ル・フレノワ国立現代芸術スタジオ／C・ド・ポルザンパルク，ナシオナル通りのハウジング／他
Works: OMA *Educatorium, Utrecht University*; S. Holl *Chapel of St. Ignatius*; N. Foster *Commerzbank Headquarters, American Air Museum in Britain*; R. Rogers *L.R.C. Thames Valley University*; C. de Portzamparc *Paris, Rue Nationale*; F. Soler *Suite Sans Fin, Rue Emile Durkheim*; Studios Architecture *North Charleston Campus, Silicon Graphics Computer System*
120 pages, 54 in color ¥2,848

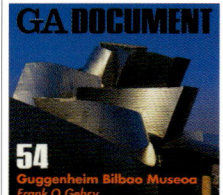

54
フランク・O・ゲーリー　ビルバオ・グッゲンハイム美術館
Frank O. Gehry Guggenheim Bilbao Museoa
96 pages, 42 in color ¥2,848

55
作品：R・マイヤー，ゲッティ・センター／R・ピアノ，バイエラー財団美術館／磯崎新，群馬県立近代美術館現代美術棟／安藤忠雄，綾部工業団地交流プラザ／安藤忠雄，TOTOセミナーハウス／MZRC，フランス・スタジアム／メカノ，デルフト工科大学図書館／原広司，宮城県図書館／R・レゴレッタ，サン・アントニオ中央図書館
Works: R. Meier *Getty Center*; R. Piano *Beyeler Foundation Museum*; A. Isozaki *Museum of Modern Art, Gunma—Contemporary Art Wing*; T. Ando *Ayabe Community Center*; T. Ando *TOTO Seminar House*; MZRC *Stade de France*; Mecanoo *Library of the Delft University of Technology*; H. Hara *Miyagi Prefectural Library*; and others
132 pages, 54 in color ¥2,848

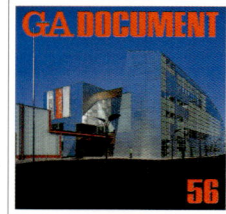

56
作品：S・ホール，ヘルシンキ現代美術館／S・フェーン，氷河博物館／S・フェーン，アウクルト・センター／コープ・ヒンメルブラウ，UFAシネマ・センター／P・アンドルー，シャルル・ドゴール空港2・ホールF／S・カラトラヴァ，アラメダ橋と地下鉄駅／S・カラトラヴァ，貿易センター／S・カラトラヴァ，カンポ・ボランティン歩道橋
Works: S. Holl *Kiasma, Museum of Contemporary Art*; S. Fehn *Glacier Museum*; S. Fehn *The Aukrust Centre*; Coop Himmelblau *UFA Cinema Center*; P. Andreu *CDG 2—Hall F*; S. Calatrava *Alameda Bridge and Underground Station*; S. Calatrava *Alameda Bridge and Underground Station*; and others
120 pages, 42 in color ¥2,848

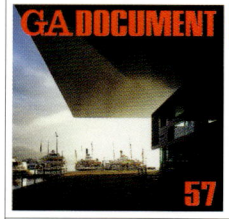

57
作品：ジャン・ヌヴェル，ルツェルン・コンサートホール／アルヴァロ・シザ，アリカンテ大学管理・教室棟／アーキテクチュア・スタジオ，ヨーロッパ連合議事堂／磯崎新，秋吉台国際芸術村　静岡県コンベンションアーツセンター「グランシップ」　なら100年会館
論文：磯崎新「パノプティコンからアーキペラゴへ」
Works: J. Nouvel *Lucerne Culture and Convention Centr*; Á. Siza *Rectory of The University of Alicante*; Architecture Studio *European Parliament*; A. Isozaki *Akiyoshidai International Art Village, Shizuoka Convention & Arts Center "Granship", Nara Centennial Hall*
Essay: A. Isozaki *"From Panopticon to Archipelago"*
132 pages, 54 in color ¥2,848

58
特集：GA INTERNATIONAL '99 第7回＜現代世界の建築家＞展
Special Feature: "GA INTERNATIONAL '99" Exhibition at GA Gallery
Tadao Ando, Coop Himmelblau, Peter Eisenman, Norman Foster, Frank O. Gehry, Zaha M. Hadid, Hiroshi Hara, Steven Holl, Hans Hollein, Arata Isozaki, Toyo Ito, Ricardo Legorretta, Fumihiko Maki, Mecanoo, Richard Meier, Enric Miralles, Rafael Moneo, Morphosis, Eric Owen Moss, Dominique Perrault, Renzo Piano, Christian de Portzamparc, Richard Rogers, Ávaro Siza, Bernard Tschumi, Tod Williams & Billie Tsien
108 pages, 42 in color ¥2,848